WAS THE FIRST GIFT REALLY GOLD?

How Much Do You Really Know About Christmas?

WAS THE FIRST GIFT REALLY GOLD?

How Much Do You Really Know About Christmas?

Dr. William D. Crump

Pleasant W rd

A Division of WINEPRESS PUBLISHING

Printed in the United States of America

Packaged by Pleasant Word, a division of WinePress Publishing, PO Box 428, Enumclaw, WA 98022. The views expressed or implied in this work do not necessarily reflect those of Pleasant Word, a division of WinePress Publishing. Ultimate design, content, and editorial accuracy of this work are the responsibilities of the author.

All Scripture quotations are taken from the Authorized (King James) Version of the Bible.

ISBN 1-57921-668-4
Library of Congress Catalog Card Number: 2003104849

Endorsement

This book has something for anyone who's interested in Christmas: from the purely biblical account to traditions around the world; from sacred music to secular; from literature to movies to television specials, *Was the First Gift Really Gold* is jam-packed with facts and fun quizzes which will challenge your knowledge surrounding the season. Did Mary really ride a donkey? And *was* the first gift really gold? An excellent resource.

Kimberly Smith, author of *Oh, Be Careful Little Ears* (WinePress Publishing, 1997) and *Let Those Who Have Ears to Hear* (WinePress Publishing, 2001).

Table of Contents

Preface

Christmas: For nearly 1,700 years since the fourth century A. D., Christians have celebrated this blessed anniversary of the birth of Jesus Christ, God Incarnate, born to the Virgin Mary more than two millennia ago for the sole purpose of redeeming mankind from the sins of the world. It is a season filled with holiness and reverence, thanksgiving and rejoicing, tradition and magical fantasy.

This book was conceived in part as the result of a surprising experience I had at a Christmas gathering with friends a few years ago. There I hosted a little Bible quiz, in which the participants, most of whom were members of various churches, all received a sheet of twenty fairly simple questions about the Nativity of Christ. I reasoned that, because we as Christians either read the account of the Nativity in the New Testament at Christmastime or hear it read in Christmas services, the quiz would just be a light exercise. In fact, I really feared that everyone would regard it as rather elementary. Much to my dismay, however, the highest score was only eleven correct answers or 55%. While hardly a scientific experiment, these figures suggest that many of us are not as familiar with the Nativity as we should be. If this is the case, it follows that we are probably even less familiar with the origins and significance of those classic, beloved Christmas traditions, customs, and symbols that have evolved over the centuries. In short, we often follow the same routine at Christmastime year after year without knowing why and, in some instances, not even caring why we do so.

Utilizing an interrogative approach that presents more than 800 thought-provoking questions, *Was the First Gift Really Gold* begins with the Nativity itself and thoroughly reviews the whole Christmas season from sacred as well as secular viewpoints. In essence, the book is a Christmas tutorial. Included are principal historical events and the role of ancient, pagan symbols and customs that have impacted on and influenced Christmas observances since the Nativity; personages who bring the Christmas gifts; myths, legends, and inspirational and heart-warming selections from literary masterpieces; beloved carols and contemporary songs; memorable movies and television specials; and selected international customs.

Readers may use this book either as a means of testing their knowledge, in which they first attempt to answer each question before reviewing the answer; or they may use the questions as attention-grabbers, then seek enlightenment in the answers.

Because questions are often derived from information presented on prior pages, I recommend that readers begin with chapter one. For the sake of variety, I have included a large assortment of question formats to challenge and amuse the reader, including multiple choice varieties with one or more correct answers, matching, true-false, fill-in-the-blanks, complete-the-tables, short-answer, selective comparisons, and "odd man out." Directions accompany each question format as necessary; all answers and any appropriate comments immediately follow each question or block of questions as indicated; and, unless otherwise specified, the multiple choice questions have only <u>one</u> correct answer.

While I have striven to provide detailed answers and comments as much as possible, a full encyclopedic treatment is beyond the scope of the present book.

A prerequisite before proceeding to chapter one is familiarity with the term "winter solstice," meaning "winter sun standing still." An astronomical event that now occurs around December 21, the winter solstice is that time when the sun is at its greatest declination south of the celestial equator and appears to remain in one place for a few days. To the ancient pagans in the northern hemisphere, the progressively shorter days leading up to the solstice evoked the annual fear that if the sun did not eventually "return," the world would plunge into a frozen chaos of darkness. Following the solstice, however, came the gradual lengthening of days, the promise of Spring, and the "rebirth of the sun," hence a time for rejoicing and revelry. With the establishment of Christmas as a Church festival, many of the rituals and superstitions that had surrounded the winter solstice were Christianized, and these subsequently evolved into, or significantly impacted upon, our present-day Christmas practices.

Many unfortunately dismiss the Christmas season as a holiday intended only for children, yet it is much more than that. Neither does Christmas consist solely of Santa Claus and gifts, nor is it merely a "time for toys and time for cheer," according to a line from a popular holiday song. It is my sincere wish that, through this book, Christian and non-Christian readers alike will come to understand and appreciate the very essence of *all* that is Christmas today and the principals that have made it so over 1,700 years.

All Scripture quotations are taken from the Authorized (King James) Version of the Holy Bible.

May the Spirit of Christmas that is Jesus Christ always dwell within you.

Bill Crump

Acknowledgment

I am most grateful to Kimberly Smith, who reviewed the manuscript and provided many valuable suggestions and comments. Many thanks, Kim, for your sincere support and enthusiasm for this project.

CHAPTER ONE

The Nativity

Open your Bible and get ready to explore that Story of stories, the coming of Christ—with Mary and Joseph, the angels, shepherds, Wise Men, and the little town of Bethlehem. But the story of Christ's coming lies not only in the New Testament, but in the Old Testament as well, in the writings of the ancient prophets. It's a simple story, really, and all too brief. But from that story arose the Spirit of Christmas with all its warmth and beauty that has come to us through two millennia.

Answers and comments for questions 1–9 follow this group.

1. "Therefore the Lord himself shall give you a sign; Behold, a virgin shall conceive, and bear a son, and shall call his name Immanuel." This prophecy regarding the expected Messiah is found in which of these Old Testament books?

   A. Ezekiel
   B. Daniel

    C. Isaiah
    D. Joel

2. Continuing with the same Old Testament prophecy from the previous question, another name for the Messiah is "Immanuel." What is the literal meaning of this name?

    A. "God is with us"
    B. "The Lord is mighty"
    C. "Praise ye the Lord"
    D. "Given of the Lord"

3. Which Old Testament book contains a prophecy which has been interpreted to mean that the Messiah would be born in Bethlehem of Judea?

    A. Isaiah
    B. Micah
    C. Amos
    D. Zephaniah

4. As the Star in the East led the Wise Men to the Christ Child, which Old Testament book mentions a Star and contains the prophecy that the Messiah would be someone spiritually great from the seed of Jacob?

    A. Daniel
    B. Numbers
    C. Exodus
    D. Genesis

5. "For unto us a child is born, unto us a son is given: and the government shall be upon his shoulder: and his name shall be called ___." The remainder of this verse from Isaiah contains all of the following labels about the expected Messiah, except:

    A. "Wonderful, Counselor"
    B. "The mighty God"
    C. "The everlasting Father"
    D. "The Holy One of Israel"

6. Which of the four New Testament Gospels presents an account of the Nativity?

    A. Matthew and Mark only
    B. Luke and John only
    C. Matthew and Luke only
    D. All of them, of course

7. According to the biblical accounts of the Nativity, which one of the following statements is correct?

    A. Mary rode a donkey to Bethlehem because she was "great with child."
    B. Christ was born at midnight.
    C. Augustus Caesar, Cyrenius, and Herod the Great were rulers when Christ was born.
    D. Herod ordered the murder of Bethlehem children who were one year old and under.

8. By the third century, the Wise Men mentioned in the Nativity story were considered to be kings and were thought to be the fulfillment of this prophecy: ". . . the kings of Sheba and Seba shall offer gifts. Yea, all kings shall fall down before him: all nations shall serve him." Which Old Testament book contains this prophecy?

    A. Hosea
    B. Jeremiah
    C. Zechariah
    D. The Psalms

9. According to the angel delivering the "good tidings of great joy," by what sign(s) would the shepherds recognize the Child in Bethlehem?

    A. He would be wrapped in swaddling clothes and attended by three kings.
    B. The Star of Bethlehem overhead would identify His abode.
    C. He would be lying on a cushion of hay.
    D. He would be wrapped in swaddling clothes and lying in a manger.

Answers to 1–9: 1-C (Is. 7:14); 2-A (Mt. 1:23); 3-B (Mi. 5:2); 4-B (Num. 24:17); 5-D (Is. 9:6); 6-C; 7-C (Mt. 2:1–23, Lk. 2:1–20); 8-D (Ps. 72:10–11); 9-D (Lk. 2:12).

Comments: "Immanuel" is the Hebrew word for "God is with us." Matthew 1:23 quotes this passage from Isaiah but uses the spelling of "Emmanuel" in the King James Bible. This latter spelling reflects the translation from the New Testament Greek.

The correct ending to Isaiah 9:6 is "... The Prince of Peace," not "... The Holy One of Israel." Other translations may omit the comma between Wonderful and Counselor, thus combining the two separate designations into one.

Augustus was Roman Emperor, Cyrenius was governor of Syria, and Herod was king of Judea when Christ was born. Stories of Mary riding a donkey to Bethlehem and Jesus being born at midnight are popular traditions, but neither of them are substantiated in the Gospels. The latter tradition serves as a basis for the Christmas Eve Midnight Mass or Service. Whereas tradition as well as most modern Bible translations state that Herod sought to destroy only the *boys* in Bethlehem who were *two* years old and under, the Authorized Version states that he slew "all the children" in that age group. Using the generic word "children" is based on the fact that "παιδας" (from παις) of Matt. 2:16 in the original Greek New Testament (Received Text or *Textus Receptus*) does not specify the gender of those slain. Strong's Concordance rather widely defines "παις" as "child, maid(-en), (man) servant, son, young man." Furthermore, "children" implies that baby girls could have been victims. This translation is more realistic in that Herod's soldiers, very likely murdering in haste, would probably have taken little time to confirm each child's gender, especially newborns. This crime is known as the Slaughter of the Innocents.

Matthew's account relates that when the Wise Men visited the Christ Child, they fell down and worshipped Him.

But it does not specify whether these Wise Men were actually kings, nor does it specify how many were present. Any assumptions along those lines are only a matter of tradition, for they are not biblically substantiated. Matthew's phrase "wise men from the east" (2:1) implies the various scientists, astrologers, and other practitioners of the occult arts of that time. That they came from Persia (now Iran) is a good possibility, for the priests of Zoroaster, also known as magi (hence our word "magic") dwelt there as masters of the occult. The ancient cities of Sheba and Seba, mentioned in the prophecy from the Psalms, were also located in "the east," in what is now the Republic of Yemen.

Swaddling clothes were narrow strips of cloth wrapped around an infant to ensure that its limbs would grow straight.

Questions 10–23 present certain key events in the Nativity story and compare the accounts of those events as described in the Gospels of Matthew and Luke. For each one of the following events, determine whether it is found in A-Matthew, B-Luke, C-both Gospels, or D-neither Gospel. Answers and comments follow this group.

10. Jesus is born in Bethlehem of Judea.

11. Shepherds visit the manger.

12. The Christ Child receives gifts of gold, frankincense, and myrrh.

13. Mary and Joseph journey to Bethlehem to pay taxes to Caesar.

14. King Herod orders the slaying of Bethlehem children.

15. Joseph learns in a dream that Mary will bear Jesus.

16. The Star in the East guides the Wise Men to Jesus.

17. Joseph, Mary, and the shepherds all marvel at the Star in the East.

18. Angels relay a nocturnal message to shepherds about the birth of a Savior.

19. The angel Gabriel reveals to Mary that she will bear Jesus.

20. Mary and Joseph find shelter in a stable.

21. Three Wise Men visit the manger.

22. Mary wraps Jesus in swaddling clothes.

23. Caspar, Melchior, and Balthazar pay homage to the Christ Child.

Answers to 10–23: 10-C (Mt. 2:1 and Lk. 2:4); 11-B (2:15–17); 12-A (Mt. 2:11); 13-B (Lk. 2:1–5); 14-A (Mt. 2:16); 15-A (Mt. 1:18–21); 16-A (Mt. 2:9); 17-D; 18-B (Lk. 2:8–12); 19-B (Lk. 1:26–35); 20-D; 21-D; 22-A (Lk. 2:7); 23-D.

Comments: With a bright star lighting up all the heavens to guide the Wise Men, it must indeed have been a breathtaking sight. But Matthew's account is concerned only with that Star's appearance to the Wise Men and excludes everyone else. It is only assumed that, because of the manger, Jesus was born in a stable. But a stable is not mentioned at all in the Gospels, which only tell us that the Nativity took place somewhere in Bethlehem and not at an inn. At that time in that part of the world, establishments, commercial and private, often housed their livestock close by in regions of the same building, for stables as we know them were unknown at that time. There were a number of caves near Bethlehem, and Jesus could have been born in one of them. In fact, Justin Martyr, a Christian writer in the second century, spoke of Jesus' birth in one such cave. Origen (A.D. 185–254), a theologian from Alexandria, Egypt, also reported that even the pagans had known the cave where Jesus was born. Origen numbered the Wise Men to three, primarily because of their three gifts, and that number has since remained traditional. However, none of the Gospels specifies the exact number of Wise Men. Other speculations on their number have ranged from two to twelve. Melchior, Caspar (also Gaspar or

Kaspar) and Balthazar are names of the traditional three Wise Men or kings, yet the Gospels do not give their specific identities at all.

Questions 24–33. For each of the following biblical quotations, identify the character(s) who either said it or to whom it applies.

24. ". . . fear not to take unto thee Mary thy wife: for that which is conceived in her is of the Holy Ghost."

> Matthew 1:20b. The angel of the Lord assures Joseph in a dream that Mary's pregnancy is divine, for Joseph had assumed that Mary had committed adultery, a crime punishable by death, according to the Mosaic Law.

25. ". . . Where is he that is born King of the Jews?"

> Matthew 2:2a. The Wise Men make inquiry in Jerusalem about where they can find Jesus.

26. ". . . Go and search diligently for the young child; and when ye have found *him*, bring me word again, that I may come and worship him also."

> Matthew 2:8. Herod frankly lies to the Wise Men.

27. ". . . Hail, *thou that art* highly favored, the Lord is with thee: blessed *art* thou among women."

> Luke 1:28b. Thus begins the angel Gabriel's annunciation to Mary, that she would conceive Christ.

28. ". . . Behold the handmaid of the Lord; be it unto me according to thy word."

> Luke 1:38. Mary submits to the Will of God.

29. ". . . Fear not: for, behold, I bring you good tidings of great joy, which shall be to all people. For unto you is born this day in the city of David a Savior, which is Christ the Lord."

> Luke 2:10–11. The angel of the Lord brings the annunciation of Jesus' birth to the shepherds.

30. "Glory to God in the highest, and on earth peace, good will toward men."

> Luke 2:14. This is the magnificent angel chorus which follows their annunciation to the shepherds.

31. "And they came with haste, and found Mary, and Joseph, and the babe lying in a manger. And when they had seen *it*, they made known abroad the saying which was told them concerning this child."

> Luke 2:16–17. After receiving the "good tidings of great joy" from the angelic host, the shepherds rush to Bethlehem to see Jesus. Then they publish the news to everyone else.

32. "And she shall bring forth a son, and thou shalt call his name JESUS: for he shall save his people from their sins."

> Matthew 1:21. The angel Gabriel announces to Joseph that Mary will bear Jesus.

33. "And, lo, the angel of the Lord came upon them, and the glory of the Lord shone round about them: and they were sore afraid."

> Luke 2:9. This introduces the angel's appearance to the shepherds.

Questions 34 and 35 respectively pertain to portrayals of the Annunciation and the Nativity in classic art.

34. The following three items or themes often appear in depictions of the Annunciation to the Virgin Mary. What is the symbolic significance of each?

    A. Dove

    _____

    B. Spray of lilies

    _____

    C. Mary reading the Scriptures

    _____

    The dove is symbolic of the conception from the Holy Spirit (Mt. 1:18). The lilies symbolize absolute purity. Either the angel Gabriel holds them, or they are nearby in a vase. Reading Scriptures symbolizes piety.

35. Traditional art depicting the Holy Family (Baby Jesus, Mary, and Joseph) at the Nativity often does not conform to Scripture because of the inclusion of what three items or concepts?

    In addition to the concepts of a conventional stable and three Wise Men discussed previously, Nativity art often shows a number of angels hovering over the stable and the manger. While the scene is comforting, it is not biblically accurate. According to Luke 2:15, the angels returned to Heaven after visiting the shepherds.

CHAPTER TWO

Time Forges a Holiday

W hen Jesus was born, no one decked the halls, decorated a tree, or drank any wassail. There were a few gifts, though, and one angelic carol. Centuries would pass before the Spirit of Christmas would begin to take the world by storm. And from that early time, on up through the Middle Ages and beyond, key events came to pass which would sit at the very heart of numerous Christmas customs and traditions on this planet. This chapter explores some of those important events.

1. A church calendar dating back to the year A.D. 336 provides the earliest written evidence for celebrating Christmas on December 25. This calendar has been traced to which civilization?

    A. Greek
    B. Roman
    C. Babylonian
    D. Philistine

This was more specifically the Philocalian Calendar, compiled by Furius Dionisius Philocalus of Rome. Before the declaration of December 25 as Christmas Day, the calendar implied that early Christians were already observing the day, possibly to offset a series of pagan celebrations such as the Roman Saturnalia, which had long been observed on that date (see below).

2. Lacking concrete evidence that Jesus Christ was born on December 25, why did the early Christian Church single out this particular date?

   A. Dead Sea scrolls implied that Christ was born on December 25.
   B. The Church adopted this date to Christianize certain pagan festivals which occurred around the same time.
   C. The Church determined the date from biblical prophecies.
   D. The Magi foretold that Christ's birth would occur on December 25.

Many ancient civilizations throughout the world have celebrated winter solstice festivals which hailed the victory of life and light over death and darkness by honoring pagan gods and the sun. For example, in Roman times the Saturnalia, a riotous, year-end festival honoring the harvest god, Saturn, extended from December 17 through December 24. The Romans, influenced by the concept of the Persian sun god, Mithra, also hallowed December 25 as Mithra's birthday, the *Natalis Solis Invicti* (Birth of the Unconquered Sun), previously established by the emperor Aurelian in 274. The early Roman Church, when it realized that it could not convince the pagans to abandon their customs entirely, decided to Christianize these winter festivals and adopted

December 25 as the date to commemorate the birth of the Son of God. Thus the Church replaced the sun with the "Sun of Righteousness," a prophetic reference to Christ (see Malachi 4:2). It was an act to induce pagans to abandon their gods and superstitions and turn to Christ. But the wild merriment of the Saturnalia and other winter solstice festivals carried over into Christmas celebrations, hence the origin for salutations such as "Merry Christmas" and phrases such as "'tis the season to be jolly."

3. In the year A.D. 350, which pope declared December 25 as the official date to commemorate the birth of Christ?

   A. Pope Julius I
   B. Pope Gregory I
   C. Pope John XXIII
   D. Pope Paul VI

You could narrow your choices down to two by eliminating Popes John and Paul, since they were popes in the mid twentieth century. Pope Gregory I (Gregory the Great) reigned in the late sixth century and was influential in another phase of Christmas, as you will encounter later. That leaves Pope Julius I, whose reasons for choosing December 25 were summarized in the answer to the previous question.

4. Northern European pagans celebrated a winter festival from mid November to mid January. When these barbarians became Christianized, they incorporated these festivals, like the Roman Saturnalia, into Christmas. What was the name of this ancient festival?

   A. Ra
   B. Mithra

C. Bryn

D. Yule

During the period that we now call the winter solstice, ancient Scandinavian tribes held their annual midwinter festival. Although their understanding of equinoxes and solstices was at best rudimentary, they knew enough to celebrate the return of the "burning wheel," or the sun. From the Anglo-Saxon we have various spellings of *hweol* ("wheel"), thought to be the translation of the Norse word *Jul* (hence our "Yule"), which describes this festival. *Jul* may also originate from the Germanic *Geola* ("feast"). And what feasting there was! Because heavy snows barred large portions of livestock from grazing, the barbarians, rather than let the entire herd starve, slaughtered many of them and feasted during the holidays. From this, together with other items comprising Yuletide, such as drinking, fertility rites, divination, and magic, it is understandable that when the Northern barbarians became Christianized, a Merry Yule became a Merry Christmas. Interestingly, there was no mention of Yule as being synonymous with Christmas until the eleventh century.

5. By tradition, what does Epiphany, which occurs on January 6, commemorate in the Western (Roman) Church?

    A. The revelation of Jesus to the Gentiles through the Magi (Wise Men)

    B. Birth of Jesus

    C. The angel's Annunciation to Mary that she would bear the Son of God

    D. Mary and Joseph's betrothal

How long the Wise Men traveled to Bethlehem or the exact date of their arrival are subjects of speculation.

Almost every length of time has been postulated, from twelve days to two years (the latter, perhaps, because King Herod murdered the children in Bethlehem from two years old and under). But only tradition states that they arrived to worship the Christ Child on January 6. Also by tradition, this date commemorates the marriage feast at Cana, where Jesus performed His first miracle (see John 2:1–11). Epiphany in the Eastern Orthodox Church, however, is primarily the traditional anniversary of Christ's baptism, although it, too, observes the marriage feast at Cana at that time.

6. In the fourth century, which Roman emperor erected the Church of the Nativity in Bethlehem over the traditional site of Christ's birth?

   A. Nero
   B. Caligula
   C. Diocletian
   D. Constantine

Whereas the first three emperors persecuted Christians, Constantine the Great was the first Roman emperor to embrace Christianity. Following his conversion, he wished to determine the site where Jesus was born. Familiar with the cave theory, he selected a suitable cave near Bethlehem and erected the Church of the Nativity over it. A Samaritan revolt destroyed the original church in 595, but the Byzantine emperor, Justinian I, rebuilt the church on the same site in the sixth century. Justinian's church remains a world shrine in Bethlehem, Israel, to this day.

7. Tours, France, was an important, early archbishopric. In the year A.D. 567, what did the Council of Tours first proclaim?

A. December 25 would be Christmas Day.
B. The twelve days from Christmas Day to Epiphany, January 6, would be a sacred, festive season.
C. January 6 would be the day for Epiphany.
D. December 21 would be the day of the winter solstice.

The phrase "the twelve days of Christmas" originated from the Council of Tours. This Council also specified that a time of fasting and spiritual reflection should precede these festive twelve days. Alfred the Great issued a similar proclamation for England late in the ninth century.

8. The early Roman Church often made reference to Christmas as the Feast of Lights, a term that was borrowed from which Jewish holiday?

A. Rosh Hashanah
B. Yom Kippur
C. Hanukkah
D. Purim

Known as the Festival of Lights, Hanukkah is an annual Jewish holiday celebrated for eight days in mid December on our present Gregorian calendar. It commemorates the rededication of the Temple in Jerusalem by Judas Maccabee in 165 B.C. after it had been defiled by the army of Antiochus IV Epiphanes, king of Syria. The purification rites required the burning of olive oil in cruses, only one of which was present. According to the Talmud, that one cruse burned miraculously for eight days. Since that time, lights (more specifically candles), one additionally lit on each of eight successive nights, have played a crucial role in commemorating this miracle. And to the early Church, lights at Christmas perfectly symbolized the birth of Christ, the Light of the world, Who came to conquer the darkness of paganism. Thus, two important influences for the evolution of Christmas lights not only included the bonfires of pagan winter festivals, but the lights of Hanukkah as well.

9. Beginning in the 1640s, which group led a movement in England to abolish all Christmas celebrations because they were considered to be rowdy and pagan?

    A. Amish
    B. Catholics
    C. Mormons
    D. Puritans

Although the earliest Christmas celebrations were purely spiritual, human nature, following after the wild, drunken revelry of the Roman Saturnalia, required little time to corrupt Christmas. All through the Middle Ages, people observed this holiday not only with gifts and song, but with recklessness and a complete lack of restraint. Whereas the Protestants had always preferred to observe Christmas quietly, a particularly strict group of them, the Puritans, were determined to do away with Christmas entirely while reforming the Church of England in general. The Puritans accomplished this by gaining control of Parliament in the 1640s. To observe Christmas in any form then became a crime punishable by fines or imprisonment. Work continued as usual, and the town criers gave constant reminders by running through the streets yelling, "No Christmas!" This period reached its zenith with the execution of King Charles I in 1649 and the establishment of a Protectorate in 1653 with Oliver Cromwell as Lord Protector. For its duration, the Protectorate also abolished the English monarchy.

10. The year 1660 saw Charles II ascend the English throne. What impact, if any, did this event have on the English, and ultimately American, Christmas season?

    A. Although the Protectorate was abolished, Charles upheld the ban against Christmas.
    B. Although the Protectorate continued, Charles overrode the ban against Christmas.
    C. The Protectorate was abolished along with the ban against Christmas.
    D. Everything remained the same as before.

With Cromwell's death in 1658, the Protectorate collapsed, and the monarchy, along with Christmas, resumed with King Charles II in 1660. Thus began the British Restoration. The Puritan influence had taken its toll, though, for Christmas observances from that time on were much more sedate than before. The era of "Christmas Restored" was not universal in America, however, for New England continued to exercise the ban until the mid nineteenth century. Thanks to the beautiful traditions brought over by German and Dutch immigrants, though, the USA was soon warming to the delights of Christmas once again.

11. How soon before Christmas is the period called Advent generally observed?

    A. One week
    B. Two weeks
    C. Three weeks
    D. Four weeks

Advent begins on the fourth Sunday before Christmas.

12. The word "Advent" is derived from the Latin *adventus*, which means:

   A. "Coming"
   B. "Praising"
   C. "Birthing"
   D. "Announcing"

Adventus means "coming."

13. Which country first introduced the concept of an Advent season?

   A. England
   B. Spain
   C. France
   D. Germany

In the year 524, the Synod of Lerida, Spain, first introduced the concept of an Advent season as a time to prepare for Christmas. The Council of Tours, France, which later established the twelve days of Christmas in 567, also decreed that Advent would incorporate fasting and spiritual cleansing prior to the festivities of Christmas.

14. All of the following are true concerning Advent, <u>except</u>:

   A. It has been observed since the sixth century.
   B. It begins the ecclesiastical year in Eastern and Western churches.
   C. It begins on December 25 for the Orthodox Church.
   D. Around the year 600, Pope Gregory the Great introduced its four Sundays into the church calendar.

The Advent season in the Orthodox Church (also known as Greek Orthodox and Eastern Orthodox) is longer and begins on November 11, St. Martin's Day. St. Martin was a fourth-century bishop of Tours, France, who was known for his charitable deeds. Pope Gregory the Great decreed that Advent would commence on the fourth Sunday before Christmas, with special masses to be held at that time and on each succeeding Sunday during the four-week period of Advent. The Roman Catholic, Lutheran, Anglican, and Episcopal churches especially observe this period.

15. Each of the four weeks of Advent symbolizes one of the four great "comings" of Christ, which are summarized below. Which one of them is <u>incorrect</u>?

   A. First week: His initial coming in the flesh
   B. Second week: His coming to rebuild the temple in Jerusalem
   C. Third week: His coming at the hour of death to the faithful
   D. Fourth week: His coming at the final Judgment

The second week represents His coming into the hearts of His believers.

16. The terms "Christmas Old Style" and "Christmas New Style" refer to:

   A. An old-fashioned Christmas versus a modern Christmas
   B. Christmas before, versus Christmas after, the Puritan era
   C. Christmas on the Julian (Roman) calendar versus Christmas on the Gregorian calendar
   D. Christmas before, versus Christmas after, the Victorian era

In 1752 when Great Britain adopted the Gregorian calendar over the old Roman calendar, the new Christmas Day (still December 25) came eleven days earlier than before. By long-established custom in the town and all the vicinities around Glastonbury, England, everyone turned out on Christmas Eve to watch the annual blooming of an ancient plant, known as the Glastonbury Thorn. According to legend, the Thorn sprouted from the staff of Joseph of Arimathea (see John 19:38) during the latter's mission to what is now Glastonbury, England, in the first century A.D. To everyone, the blooming of this thorn was the trusted, natural evidence that Christmas had arrived. When the Thorn did not bloom on that new Christmas Eve, no one celebrated "Christmas New Style," as it was known. But eleven days later, on the new January 5 (old Christmas Eve), when the Thorn *did* bloom, everyone celebrated "Christmas Old Style." Today the British occasionally still refer to Epiphany, January 6, as "Christmas Old Style."

17. The revelry of medieval Christmases usually included a group of "mummers" who engaged in "mumming." These words refer to:

  A. Singing carols
  B. Putting up decorations
  C. Performing in pageants
  D. Distributing gifts

Mumming (from German and Greek words for "mask") can be traced back to the Roman Saturnalia, when people dressed in outlandish costumes and caroused the streets. Mumming originally referred to farcical masquerade balls which the medieval nobility held at Christmastime and were governed by a person in the role of a fool. Later, mummers provided the Christmas entertainment by providing exotic plays and skits. The annual Christmas pageants at churches and schools today are vestiges of mumming.

18. Prior to the Puritan ban against Christmas in England, it was customary to ring church bells one hour before midnight on Christmas Eve for two reasons. The first reason took root from the popular belief that Christ had been born at midnight. What was the second reason?

> A. The bells prevented any evil spirits from disturbing Christmas.
> B. The bells alerted the townsfolk that they must fall on their knees and pray.
> C. The bells signaled the hour for lighting the Yule log.
> D. The bells commemorated the belief that Satan had died when Christ was born.

Known as the "Devil's Knell" or "Old Lad's Passing Bell," the English tolled church bells at least one hour before midnight on Christmas Eve to commemorate an old superstition which said that Satan had died when Christ was born. One bell tolled once for each year since the Nativity, with the last toll timed to end at midnight. Then at the stroke of midnight, there came joyful pealing as Christmas descended upon all. The custom originated in the Middle Ages and was widespread throughout Europe, until the Protestant Reformation virtually eliminated it. The custom still survives in Dewsbury in Yorkshire, England.

19. Children in the Middle Ages often received their Christmas gifts in bundles of three, each one representing a distinct theme. Which one of the following was not a theme?

A. Something rewarding
B. Something useful
C. Something for discipline
D. Something comical

With as much riot going on at Christmas during the Middle Ages, it is a wonder that the children's gifts did not reflect something comical. The correct answer is D.

20. The English hid four traditional objects in the Christmas plum puddings of yore, each object portending a significant event in the coming year for the finder. Of those objects listed below, which one is <u>not</u> properly matched with its significance?

A. Coin—wealth
B. Thimble—dexterity
C. Button—bachelorhood
D. Ring—marriage

The thimble portended spinsterhood, not dexterity. A number of other European countries established similar or closely related customs over the centuries.

21. Do you enjoy a cup of hot, spicy wassail on Christmas Eve or with your Christmas dinner? Our word "wassail" comes to us through the Anglo-Saxon words "wes hael," which mean:

A. "Good day"
B. "Good to see you"
C. "Come again"
D. "Your health"

"Wes hael" was a greeting that wished someone good health.

22. Originally taking its root in medieval England, the word "wassail" had no association with Christmas at first and described what kind of event?

    A. A jousting tournament
    B. A drinking party
    C. An execution
    D. A summons to court

Wassail's earliest association was with the drinking to one's health. Around the fifth century, a ritual had arisen whereby the person making a toast took a bowl of strong ale and, saying "wes hael" ("your health"), presented it to the one being toasted. The latter's role was to respond with "drink hail," quaff the bowl of ale, and reciprocate in like turn. By the sixteenth century, the liquor as well as the toast itself had acquired the name of "wassail" (a slurring of "wes hael"), the act of toasting had became "wassailing," and the bowl of ale had become the "wassail bowl." If the toasting became quite excessive, "wassail" also described a drinking binge. To say the least, toasting became a popular, social pastime that eventually played a prominent role during the revelry of holiday feasts, especially at Christmastime. Drawing upon a pagan superstition which held that saluting orchard trees in mid winter would increase the fruit yield, people ceremoniously congregated during the twelve days of Christmas to pour wassail from the wassail bowl over tree roots and trunks. That custom further evolved into bands of carolers wassailing through the streets and singing from door to door, wishing everyone good health. Often households invited them in for a taste of wassail from the wassail bowl, which was a vestige of the bowl that held the salutation mixture for trees. It is interesting to note that our party punch bowls of today are descendants of the wassail bowl.

23. The original wassail of yore consisted not only of strong ale but also a number of other delicious ingredients. Which of these was <u>not</u> generally one of them?

    A. Nutmeg
    B. Cinnamon
    C. Chocolate
    D. Apples

Besides ale, other ingredients generally consisted of cloves, eggs, molasses, ginger, lemon, cinnamon, nutmeg, roasted apples, sugar, and sometimes milk. Chocolate would have been a most unusual ingredient, for wassail was, and is, a spiced drink. The specific amounts of these ingredients was left up to the individual person concocting the potion. The wassail of the present age may consist of similar spices along with wine, beer, or ginger ale, depending on the preferences of your guests.

24. Another medieval holiday beverage quite similar to wassail was served with toast floating on top. This soggy toast resembled a portion of an animal's coat which provided an appropriate name for the drink. What was this name?

    A. Lamb's wool
    B. Sheep's skin
    C. Ram's hide
    D. Ewe's fleece

Some contend that, instead of the toast, roasted apples floating on top resembled lamb's wool and hence the name. Aside from that, it was the floating toast which gave the name to the act of drinking one's health, or "toasting" someone. An old Norse variation on this theme consisted of placing a slice of spiced Yule cake in the wassail bowl and then filling the bowl with warm ale. When the cake rose and floated on top, the bowl was passed around for everyone to partake.

25. A royal medieval Christmas banquet commonly included how many courses?

    A. Twelve
    B. Three
    C. Seven
    D. Five

No doubt about it, the twelve days of Christmas and the number of Christ's apostles had much to do with the number of courses served.

26. Which of these delicacies became a traditional dish at medieval Christmas banquets?

    A. Escargot
    B. Cow's brain
    C. Boar's head
    D. Pig's feet

King Henry VIII of England is said to have instituted the boar's head at Christmas feasts. It arrived at the table with much pomp and ceremony. The custom derived in part from that of pagan Scandinavians, who sacrificed a boar to Freya, a fertility goddess symbolized as a boar, at midwinter festivals. On the other hand, a medieval legend states that this custom arose after a young student at the University of Oxford choked an attacking boar on Christmas Day by cramming a book of Aristotle's allegedly unpalatable philosophy down the boar's throat. The student decapitated the boar, retrieved his copy of Aristotle, returned with the boar's head to Oxford, roasted it, and dined with great festivities. The boar's head theme still survives today in Christmas ceremonies conducted at Queen's College, University of Oxford, with a suckling pig substituted.

27. Along with Christmas itself, which of these foods did the Puritans outlaw because they considered it a symbol of idolatry?

    A. Roast pheasant
    B. Gingerbread cookies
    C. Plum pudding
    D. Mince pie

Also known as Christmas pie, mince pie originally consisted of minced bits of various meats, sweets, and spices, which symbolized the Wise Men's gifts to the Christ Child. Traditionally, the pie was baked in the shape of a manger, and an image of the Christ Child was placed on top. The Puritans considered this image to be idolatrous and outlawed mince pies altogether.

28. Which nursery rhyme not only mentions Christmas pie but is a parody on England's King Henry VIII?

    A. "Little Jack Horner"
    B. "Baa Baa Black Sheep"
    C. "Simple Simon"
    D. "Jack and Jill"

Battling the Roman Catholic Church, Henry VIII commenced seizing the estates of English monasteries in 1532. It is said that Richard Whiting, abbot of Glastonbury Abbey at that time, offered the king several choice estates in return for his abandoning any further seizure. Whiting supposedly smuggled the deeds in a Christmas pie and entrusted them to a servant, Thomas Horner, for delivery. The latter, however, stole several deeds for himself, and Whiting subsequently was hanged for treason. The larceny was immortalized in the nursery rhyme "Little Jack Horner," which altered Horner's first name; the extracted "plum" ("He put in his thumb / And pulled out a plum") represented a stolen deed.

29. What was the collective term for a series of mock-religious festivals in force by the twelfth century, which divisions of the lower clergy, particularly in France, England, and central Europe, observed between Christmas and Epiphany?

     A. Feast of Fools
     B. Feast of Idiots
     C. Feast of Heretics
     D. Feast of Beggars

Designed to be a form of release from the solemnity of Christmas, the Feast of Fools took place within the church itself. The atmosphere assumed an air of clowning and buffoonery with obscene songs, the wearing of bizarre costumes, and the reversed roles of superiors and subordinates. The feast was patterned directly after the Roman Saturnalia. The Church finally succeeded in driving it from its cathedrals by the fifteenth century, although some revelries persisted into the eighteenth.

30. The medieval Feast of Asses, a festival held on January 1 during the Feast of Fools, typically featured a parody on the Holy Family's flight to Egypt (Matthew 2:13–15). Which of the following is not true about this feast?

     A. It Christianized the feast of Epona, Roman goddess of horses, mules, and asses.
     B. A woman holding a child rode into the church on an ass.

    C. At the conclusion of the service, the priest and congregation brayed like an ass.

    D. It evolved from an early church drama that depicted the Old Testament story of Nehemiah and his talking ass.

In keeping with the tradition that Mary rode an ass to Bethlehem as well as during the flight to Egypt, a woman holding a child would ride into the church on an ass, and the priest and congregation alike would bray three times at the conclusion of the service. The Feast of Asses evolved from an early church drama dating to the eleventh century or earlier, which portrayed a series of Old Testament prophets attesting to the future birth of Christ. One of these centered around the biblical story of Baalam, his talking ass, and the angel, as told in Numbers 22:22–38. In that early drama, the person playing the part of Baalam rode on a wooden ass. It became an independent play by the thirteenth century and merged with the year-end revels.

31. During medieval Christmas celebrations, what title was given to the "fool" who was appointed to choreograph all of the revelry and madcap?

    A. The Lord of Misrule

    B. The King of Revelry

    C. The Duke of Hilarity

    D. The Prince of Riot

Before the havoc began, by popular vote, a fool was appointed to supervise all the madness and mayhem, one for the nobility and one for the commoners. This was the Lord of Misrule, and everyone, including the nobility, obeyed each of his ridiculous commands all through the twelve days of Christmas. Also called the King of

Christmas, the Lord of Misrule was equivalent to the *Magister Ludi* ("Master of the Games") of the Roman Saturnalia. In Scotland especially, this leader took the name of the Abbot of Unreason. Dressed in clerical robes, he, like the Lord of Misrule, led the commoners in processions through the streets as people sang, shouted, and gave themselves up to every vice. The atmosphere was more akin to our modern-day Halloween, with everyone dressed in bizarre costumes, sometimes as devils and demons, and often in the skins of wild animals. In short, medieval Christmases kept alive the old traditions of the Roman Saturnalia.

32. Which of these was a favorite medieval Christmas game?

    A. "Hot Cockles"
    B. "Hot Cross Buns"
    C. "Hop Scotch"
    D. "Pin the Tail on the Donkey"

To begin the game of "Hot Cockles," a blindfolded person knelt in the center of the room and placed his head in the lap of another person sitting before him. Placing a hand behind himself with the palm upward, the blindfolded person then said, "Hot cockles, hot!" The other players took turns slapping his palm while he guessed who slapped him. If he guessed correctly, the person who had slapped him then took his place. A wrong guess required some sort of forfeit. Without a doubt, some players took this opportunity to seek a bit of revenge if they had any past grievances with the person blindfolded. Anyone not wishing to play could join the mob in the streets.

33. One of the ingredients for a complete Christmas includes the singing of carols, those ancient, and sometimes mod-

ern, melodies that take us all back to the manger. What did the word "carol" originally describe?

    A. A round dance with singing
    B. A chant
    C. A play
    D. A dramatic reading

"Carol" is derived from the Old French *caroler* and the Latin *choraula* (both of which mean "ring dance"), and from the Greek *choraules* ("ring dance with a reed instrument"). Simply stated, carols are popular, religious folk songs that incorporate the common emotions of man with language and music that is shared by all. At first not restricted to Christmas, carols departed from the somber melodies of the Church by offering a more upbeat form of religious expression, and when the mood was free and happy, there was likely to be dancing. In fact, it has been said that carols ushered in the era of modern music, which has always claimed the dance as its basis. A line from the Preface to *The Oxford Book of Carols* states, "The carol arose with the ballad in the fifteenth century, because people wanted something less severe than the old Latin office hymns, something more vivacious than the plainsong melodies." Carols thrived during the sixteenth century and would have continued through the seventeenth century, had not the Puritan movement suppressed them. They were revived primarily through the separate English carol collections of Davies Gilbert and William Sandys, published in 1823 and 1833, respectively, and the 1871 publication of *Christmas Carols New and Old* by Bramley and Stainer.

34. Who first erected a live Nativity scene using people and animals, and at the same time became the father of the Christmas carol?

A. St. Augustine
B. St. Francis of Assisi
C. Flavius Josephus
D. Constantine the Great

Prior to the thirteenth century, the lay conception of religion was somber, abstract, and certainly lacking in popular appeal. But a time came when the whole of Christianity, and certainly Christmas, was shaped to touch the lives of everyone. In 1223 in a cave near Greccio, Italy, St. Francis erected a live Nativity scene using people and animals, the first of its kind, which brought the wonderful realism of the Nativity to a people previously only familiar with rigid Church dogma. St. Francis also conducted the service, *singing* the Gospel account of the Nativity, and preaching the sermon. From that point, people took note of the touchingly human side of the Nativity as well as the spiritual, for St. Francis had succeeded in binding the common man with the happy humanities of Jesus. And from this new appreciation of the Nativity sprang forth a new type of song which adapted secular tunes to a sacred theme, the Christmas carol.

35. Instituted in 844 by Pope Gregory IV, what was the title of a young boy, annually elected by his peers from the local church or monastery school, who held an ecclesiastical office during the Christmas season?

A. Boy-Pope
B. Boy-Bishop
C. Boy-Vicar
D. Boy-Deacon

After you have made your choice, the answer is found in question 36.

36. Which of the following is <u>not</u> true about the Boy-Bishop?

    A. He was elected on St. Nicholas' Day, December 6, to honor this saint.

    B. He served from December 6 to Holy Innocents' Day, December 28.

    C. His raiment included only sackcloth and ashes to depict humility.

    D. The Council of Basle abolished his office in the fifteenth century.

The Boy-Bishop was arrayed in official vestments and mitre and served in the full capacity of a bishop. His office honored St. Nicholas, the legendary, fourth-century archbishop of Myra in Asia Minor and the patron saint of children, among others. The Boy-Bishop served from December 6 until Holy Innocents' Day, the latter day commemorating those innocent children whom Herod the Great had massacred in Bethlehem. By the eleventh century, Holy Innocents' Day, a subcategory of the Feast of Fools, had become a feast for students and choirboys, and the holiday, including the role of the Boy-Bishop, had degenerated into hedonistic revelry. Although the Council of Basle in what is now Switzerland abolished the Boy-Bishop in 1431 in Europe, the custom survived in England until the reign of Elizabeth I (1558–1603).

Questions 37–43. Please supply either a short answer or fill in the lettered blanks.

37. Advent begins on the Sunday nearest this day, (A) _____, which is the feast day of this saint, (B) _____.

(A) November 30; (B) St. Andrew (However, Advent in the Orthodox Church begins on November 11, St. Martin's Day.)

38. The observance of Epiphany, derived from the Greek *epiphaneia*, which means (A)_____, is actually older than the observance of Christmas. The observance of Epiphany dates from at least the (B) _____ century, whereas the official observance of Christmas dates from the (C) _____ century. The eve of Epiphany is also known as (D) _____, and Epiphany itself is also known as (E) _____. You recall that Epiphany is observed on January 6. In some parts of the world, notably England, a cake with one bean inside was divided among Twelfth Day revelers, and the one receiving the bean became (F) _____. This custom was based on a similar game that Roman children played on the last day of the Saturnalia.

(A) "Appearance"; (B) Second; (C) Fourth; (D) Twelfth Night; (E) Twelfth Day (from the old reckoning of a 24-hour period beginning at evening after sundown. Also remember that Epiphany is the last, or twelfth, day in the twelve days of Christmas); (F) "King for a Day" (from the Three Kings or Wise Men).

39. On Christmas Eve, 1492, this famous explorer, (A) _____, and his crew were the first Europeans to spend Christmas in the New World. In honor of the occasion, he gave the name of (B) _____ to his little Christmas settlement.

On Christmas Eve, 1492, as Christopher Columbus explored portions of the West Indies, his flagship, the *Santa Maria*, ran aground off what is now the coast of Haiti in the Caribbean Sea. Constructing a small fort from the ship's remains and salvaging as much of the cargo as possible, Columbus named his settlement *La Navidad* ("The Nativity").

40. We all have seen and probably used the word "Xmas" at some time during the holidays. Obviously, the "mas" is taken from "Christmas," but whence comes the "X"?

The "X" derives from the Greek letter "Chi," which looks like an "X." It is the first letter in *Christos*, the Greek word for Christ. This letter, combined with "mas" (a contracted form of "mass" in the Roman Catholic usage), becomes "Xmas." Although this abbreviation for Christmas has been in common usage since the twelfth century, there was a later time when those who did not understand the significance of Chi believed that "Xmas" cheapened the season by eliminating Christ or crossing out Christ, so to speak. While that was never the intent of the early Christians, each person must decide which word is more comfortable to use.

41. "Christmas" is derived from the Old English words "Christes Maesse." What do these two words actually mean?

The two words mean "Christ's Mass" or "Mass of Christ." "Mass" is further derived from the closing Latin phrase in the Roman Catholic service, "Ite, Missa Est" ("Go, it is ended"), which dismisses the congregation.

42. An English Christmas Eve party game, popular during the nineteenth century and earlier, featured a large bowl filled with raisins that were covered with brandy. The lights were extinguished, the brandy ignited, and participants each plunged their hands through the flames to grasp a raisin. What was the name of this famous old game?

The participants chanted rhymes during the event, part of which read, "But old Christmas makes him come, / Though he looks so fee! fa! fum! / Snip! Snap! Dragon!" The line contributed to the game's name of "Snap Dragon" or "Snapdragon."

43. The Christmas season is broadly divided into two sections: those days in December preceding Christmas Day are designated as (A) _____, and those days from Christmas Day until Epiphany are designated as (B) _____.

(A) Advent; (B) The Twelve Days of Christmas

Questions 44–53. Within the Christmas season, many churches additionally observe the feast days of certain saints or other religious events. Beside each of the following, place an "A" if it occurs during Advent or a "T" if it occurs during the Twelve Days of Christmas. Answers and comments follow this group.

44. St. Lucia's Day _____

45. New Year's Day _____

46. Holy Innocents' Day _____

47. St. Thomas' Day _____

48. St. John's Day _____

49. St. Barbara's Day _____

50. Epiphany _____

51. St. Stephen's Day _____

52. St. Nicholas' Day _____

53. Feast of the Immaculate Conception _____

Answers to 44–53:   44-T (December 13); 45-T (January 1); 46-T (December 28); 47-A (December 21); 48-T (December 27); 49-A (December 4); 50-T (January 6); 51-T (December 26); 52-A (December 6); 53-A (December 8).

Comments: St. Lucia's Day Christianized a day associated with Hertha, a Germanic goddess of the home, spinning, children, and sometimes death. According to legend, Lucia, a Christian and native of Syracuse on the island of Sicily, once plucked out her eyes to avoid a suitor, after which the Virgin Mary restored her sight. She received martyrdom through a stab to her throat in 304, for which artists have rendered her as a maiden with a throat wound who holds a tray bearing two eyes and a knife. She supposedly returned to rescue Syracuse from famine in the fifth century and to bring food and light to Christians hiding in the catacombs, for which she also is depicted as radiating brilliant light. St. Lucia is the patron saint of Syracuse, Milan, sight, tailors, and blacksmiths. "Lucia Day" also opens the Christmas season in Sweden.

Although the Anglican Church still observes St. Thomas' Day on December 21, the Roman Catholic Church moved it to July 3. Legends state that many years after Christ's death, St. Thomas the Apostle became an evangelist in India, where he found and converted the Wise Men to Christianity. The former British custom of "Thomasing" (begging from door to door) on this date stemmed from another legend: that St. Thomas, endowed with an enormous sum to construct a king's palace, chose instead to distribute it among the poor.

Around the year 93, St. John the Evangelist, also known as St. John the Divine and St. John the Apostle, was exiled for life on the island of Patmos in the Aegean Sea. The Church instituted his feast day around the fifth century. Legend holds that St. John suffered no ill effects after having unwittingly consumed poisoned wine, which led to the belief that drinking blessed wine on this day would stimulate health.

According to legend, St. Barbara, living in Asia Minor in the third century, was beheaded for her faith at the hands of her own father. Because he supposedly was struck down and killed by lightning through the wrath of God, St. Barbara became associated with storms, and she is the patron saint of artillery. Although her feast day was dropped from the Church calendar in 1969, many European countries observe a quaint custom, whereby girls place cherry tree branches, so-called "Barbara branches," in water on this date. If buds bloom by Christmas Eve, the girls will supposedly wed in the coming new year.

St. Stephen was the first Christian martyr (Acts 6:8–15 and all of Acts 7). St. Stephen's Day, primarily observed as "Boxing Day" in the Commonwealth of Nations (Australia, Canada, and Great Britain), became a public holiday through Parliament in 1871. The latter name derived from a medieval English custom in which churches opened their alms boxes or "Christmas boxes" on this date and distributed the funds to the poor. By the seventeenth century, it was customary on this date for members of the working class to seek tips, called "boxes," from those to whom they had rendered services during the year. The custom fell into decline during the nineteenth century. Boxing Day currently remains a holiday for various forms of recreation.

The Feast of the Immaculate Conception commemorates the Roman Catholic dogma that the Virgin Mary, free from all original sin, was immaculately conceived. Although the Eastern

Church had been observing the feast on December 9 as early as the fifth century and the Roman Church since the seventh, Pope Pius IX assigned the feast to December 8 in 1854. The feast also launches the Christmas season in many Roman Catholic countries, particularly in Spain and in Latin America.

54. From what you now know about them, what important fact do St. Stephen's Day (December 26), St. John's Day (December 27), and Holy Innocents' Day (December 28) all share in common?

Falling consecutively, these three feasts all honor some of the earliest people who were persecuted for the sake of Christ. This is a thought worth cherishing forever.

55. What are the traditional colors of Christmas?

    A. Red and green
    B. Blue and purple
    C. Orange and white
    D. Black and gold

The red of ever-present fires at pagan winter solstice festivals symbolized the return of the sun, the promise of Spring, and the waning of winter. Green became synonymous with long or everlasting life, especially the preservation of life through a harsh winter, as symbolized by the evergreen plants used as decorations during the winter festivals. When the Church Christianized these festivals, the special colors also took on religious interpretations. Red then symbolized the blood of Christ; green, the eternal life promised through Christ. More recently, others have advocated white, for Christ's purity; and gold, for His royalty, colors most appropriate for a Chrismon tree (see chapter four).

56. In 1843, John Horsley is reputed to have created what Christmas "first"?

    A. First mass-produced Christmas tree ornaments
    B. First Christmas party favors, called "crackers"
    C. First electric Christmas tree lights
    D. First printed Christmas card

Horsley was an English illustrator, whom a Sir Henry Cole commissioned to design a printed Christmas card, supposedly the first of its kind. Rather than send seasonal notes to his numerous friends, as custom dictated at the time, Cole elected to send cards as a short-cut. Another Englishman, William Egley, also designed a Christmas card, but the date on that card is somewhat obscure, either 1842 or 1849. The first three digits are quite plain, but the last one is marred; if it is actually a 2, then Egley's card would rank as the first printed Christmas card.

57. The first printed Christmas card had the following greeting:

    A. "A Merry Christmas and Happy New Year to You"
    B. "Seasons Greetings"
    C. "Good Health and Long Life"
    D. "Christmas Blessings Upon Ye Merry Folk"

The greeting bid recipients to be merry and happy; that is, A. Until the era of "political correctness" in the 1990s and beyond, Christmas cards traditionally included the phrase "Merry Christmas and Happy New Year" and often featured scenes of the Nativity or Madonna (Virgin Mary) and Child. Today, Christmas cards are becoming more secular with generic winter scenes and greetings that often read "Happy Holidays," "Season's Greetings," or simply "Greetings." The decline of cards featuring "Merry Christmas" and religious emblems is an unfortunate sign of the times.

58. John Horsley's first printed Christmas card of 1843 caused quite a stir because of the scene it depicted:

   A. A large family imbibing wine
   B. The pope playing a round of "Hot Cockles"
   C. The lord mayor of London sipping wine with the queen
   D. The Archbishop of Canterbury portrayed as the Abbot of Unreason

Horsley's first printed Christmas card depicted a large family imbibing wine. Not surprisingly, a number of people criticized the card for promoting drunkenness, which boosted public interest even more. There were also two side panels which illustrated verses from Jesus' Sermon on the Mount (Matthew 25:35–36): feeding the hungry and clothing the naked. R. H. Pease of New York is credited with printing the first American-made Christmas cards in the 1850s.

CHAPTER THREE

Those Who Bring Gifts

Children still wait breathlessly each Christmas Eve around the world for saints, mythical spirits, elves, and other personages of folklore who make their annual appearances with toys and gifts galore. It could be said that the name of Santa Claus represents the very personification of Christmas festivities in many parts of the world. But the world knows of other spirits who bring gifts and good cheer as well, names like the Wise Men, Befana, Babouschka, and the Youngest Camel, for instance. This chapter explores in depth each of these wonderful holiday spirits and more.

1. Although Santa Claus is now one of the world's most celebrated Christmas gift bringers, he was patterned after which historical saint in the early Church?

    A. St. Francis
    B. St. Boniface
    C. St. Nicholas
    D. St. Peter

It is now commonplace to use St. Nicholas interchangeably with Santa Claus.

2. All of the following statements are true about St. Nicholas, <u>except</u>:

    A. His acts of generosity were legendary.
    B. He was an archbishop.
    C. He was penniless all his life.
    D. He became associated with Christmas because of the proximity of his feast day, December 6.

The complete history of St. Nicholas is virtually nonexistent, and almost everything that has been written about him constitutes a legend. The only concrete evidence of his existence lies in the records of the First Council of Nicaea held in the year 325, which show that Nicholas was present. A native of Patara in the district of Lycia (now Demre, Turkey), Nicholas achieved the office of archbishop in the city of Myra. He was reputed to have been quite wealthy and was a secret benefactor to the poor and needy. In time his generosity became legendary to the point that, even after his death, any gift received under mysterious circumstances was automatically attributed to the spirit of St. Nicholas. Although he was originally entombed in Myra, a group of sailors from Bari, Italy, who were familiar with the legends and fearing that Turkish Moslems would desecrate the tomb, moved St. Nicholas' remains to a shrine in Bari in 1087. Following his posthumous canonization to sainthood, the Roman Catholic Church assigned his name to December 6, the traditional day of his death, which became St. Nicholas' Day. Because of the proximity of December 6 to Christmas Day, it was only a matter of time before the beneficent St. Nicholas became a prominent personality at Christmastime.

3. As part of their Christmas season, a number of European countries observe St. Nicholas' Day on December 6. But before its Christianization, December 6 had been a pagan feast day to which god?

    A. Zeus
    B. Hades
    C. Poseidon
    D. Kronos

    Poseidon to the Greeks, Neptune to the Romans, this god was the giver of all good things, and his feast day was December 6. When the early Roman Catholic Church began Christianizing pagan feast days, St. Nicholas, also a giver of good things, was the ideal replacement to be honored on December 6.

4. Of the countless legends that surround St. Nicholas, one, known as "St. Nicholas and the Three Dowerless Maidens," became the basis for which one of our popular Christmas traditions today?

    A. Singing carols
    B. Hanging up stockings
    C. Decorating a Christmas tree
    D. Burning a Yule log

    According to this legend, a father was unable to find suitable husbands for his three young daughters because they lacked dowries. He was about to sell them either as slaves or as prostitutes, when St. Nicholas learned of their plight. To prevent this disaster, St. Nicholas secretly tossed a purse of gold into their house on each of three successive nights, which supplied their dowries. These purses fell not onto the hearth, the intended destination, but into stockings hanging by the chimney to dry. Not only did this legend further the cause of gift-giving at Christmastime, when those in dire need are most especially remembered, but it also became the basis for our tradition of hanging up stockings on Christmas Eve to receive gifts. St. Nicholas is often pictured holding three gold balls, which are variations of the three purses of gold. The Medici family of Florentine bankers adopted these three gold balls on their coat of arms as a symbol of St. Nicholas. In time this symbol became that of lenders, especially pawnbrokers. Thus St. Nicholas is not only the patron saint of maidens (virgins) but also of pawnbrokers. In other legends, he supposedly rescued children from fates worse than death, and really preposterous legends had him restoring life to children who had passed away. And so it is no wonder, then, that St. Nicholas has since had a special identity with children, and never more so than at Christmastime.

5. Santa Claus, as we now picture him, emerged from the writings or drawings of all of the following notable Americans, <u>except</u>:

    A. Washington Irving
    B. Clement Moore
    C. Thomas Nast
    D. Mark Twain

In 1809 the writer Washington Irving, author of such stories as "Rip Van Winkle" and "The Legend of Sleepy Hollow," published his *Knickerbocker History*, a satire about New York and the early Dutch settlers in this country. There, St. Nicholas flew across the skies in a wagon as he brought children their Christmas gifts. According to tradition, his story influenced Clement Moore to write the poem "A Visit from St. Nicholas" in 1822, which drew upon the St. Nicholas traditions of Dutch immigrants as well. In that poem, St. Nicholas became "a right jolly old elf," but flew about in a reindeer sleigh. This poem, in turn, inspired political cartoonist Thomas Nast to portray Santa Claus and all of his now-familiar trappings (red suit trimmed with white fur, buckled shoes, wide belt, pointed stocking cap, reindeer sleigh) in a series of cartoons which appeared yearly in *Harper's Illustrated Weekly* from 1863 to 1900. And from Nast's drawings emerged the Santa that everyone has come to know and love. It may interest you to know that Nast also created the elephant mascot of the Republican Party and the donkey mascot of the Democratic Party. Twain, of course, was not a part of Santa's evolution.

6. From elf size in the nineteenth century, Santa took on full human size through a series of commercial ads drawn by Haddon Sundblom beginning in 1931. For what company were these ads originally created?

    A. Norelco Company
    B. Coca Cola Company
    C. Walt Disney Studios
    D. Pillsbury Bakeries

From these ads came large posters of a smiling, plump, bearded, full-sized Santa dressed in a red suit trimmed with white fur, complete with black belt and black boots, and who held a bottle of Coca Cola. Although Santa's image had become standardized by this time, Sundblom's drawings served even more to popularize a most familiar holiday figure in the twentieth century.

7. What did Norway's *julenissen* and Sweden's *jultomten* help to contribute to the Santa Claus repertoire?

    A. Santa's elves
    B. Santa's workshop

    C. Santa's descent down the chimney
    D. Santa's reindeer

Scandinavian folklore is rich in the concept of elves. *Julenissen* and *jultomten* are mischievous elves living in the attic or barn and are guardians of the household and livestock, according to these two countries' legends. These elves must be placated each Christmas Eve with a bowl of rice pudding to keep them under control.

8. Who first depicted the North Pole as Santa's home?

    A. Washington Irving
    B. Clement Moore
    C. Thomas Nast
    D. Mark Twain

Although Thomas Nast never stated why he specifically chose the North Pole as Santa's home, no doubt Santa's original trappings of the reindeer sleigh and the furry costume, as described in "A Visit from St. Nicholas," were significant influences.

9. Of Santa's familiar habits, which one is said to be derived from Hertha, Norse goddess of the home?

    A. Flying in a reindeer sleigh
    B. Carrying a large sack of gifts
    C. Knowing whether children have been good or bad
    D. Descending into the home via the chimney

During pre-Christian Germanic feasts at the winter solstice, families prepared altars of flat stones in their homes and laid fires of fir boughs. Then it was believed that Hertha descended through the fire and smoke to bring health and good fortune to all. Not only was Hertha a forerunner of Santa's descending through the chimney, but the flat stone altars became our modern hearths of today.

10. How does St. Nicholas arrive in the Netherlands?

    A. By boat
    B. By airplane
    C. By train
    D. By car

According to Dutch tradition, St. Nicholas was born in Spain. Therefore, he arrives in the Netherlands by steamer on the last Saturday in November. He rides a white horse and is accompanied by Black Peter, a moorish demon who is a scourge to naughty children.

11. Befana (or La Befana), the female counterpart of Santa Claus, brings the holiday gifts in Italy. Befana is a:

    A. Little girl
    B. Fair maiden
    C. Queen
    D. Old woman

Make your choice. The answer will be revealed shortly.

12. When does Befana leave her gifts?

    A. On Christmas Eve
    B. On Christmas Day
    C. On New Year's Day
    D. On Epiphany Eve

Make your choice. The answer will be revealed shortly.

13. According to Italian legend, Befana rejected an invitation to go to Bethlehem to see the Nativity. Who had extended this invitation?

A. The Wise Men
B. The Christ Child
C. The shepherds of Bethlehem
D. The Heavenly Host

While traveling to Bethlehem, the Wise Men passed by Befana's home and invited her to accompany them as their guide. But because she was sweeping and had other chores, the old widow Befana rejected the Wise Men's invitation. Hours after they left, Befana had a change of heart. Rummaging around her house, she found a few old toys that had once belonged to her children, who were now grown and gone away. Thinking that the Christ Child might enjoy these little gifts, Befana set out after the Wise Men, hoping to catch up with them before they reached Bethlehem. Alas, she found neither them, Bethlehem, nor the Christ Child. The legend continues in the next question.

14. Because Befana refused the Wise Men, what was her fate?

   A. She would dwell in Purgatory, only to be loosed annually on Epiphany Eve to distribute gifts to children.
   B. She would search forever for the Christ Child by examining the faces of all sleeping children on Epiphany Eve.
   C. She would serve the saints in Heaven but would make an annual pilgrimage to Earth on Epiphany Eve to perform acts of charity.
   D. She would dwell in Heaven, with the exception that she would spend each Epiphany Eve in Purgatory.

Befana descends through the chimneys (much like Santa) on Epiphany Eve to examine all sleeping children, after which she leaves them gifts in their shoes by the fireplace. She hopes that, by leaving such gifts, someday she will have left them to the Christ Child. For the naughty little ones, she leaves ashes, much like Santa again. The name "Befana" is a corruption of *Epiphania* (Epiphany), the traditional date for the Wise Men's visit to the manger. Hence, the legend of Befana centers on that date. Because Befana was sweeping when the Wise Men came upon her, she is pictured as either carrying, or riding on, a broom.

15. Babouschka, Befana's counterpart in Old Russia, forever seeks the Christ Child because she:

    A. Shunned the Wise Men
    B. Failed to believe the Wise Men
    C. Misdirected the Wise Men
    D. Swindled the Wise Men

Babouschka, a name that means "grandmother," not only misdirected the Wise Men, she also refused to shelter the Holy Family during their flight to Egypt. Otherwise, her role on Epiphany Eve and her eternal fate are the same as those of Befana.

16. Father Christmas is another familiar name associated with Christmas gifts. Which of the following is <u>not</u> true about him?

    A. He is the British equivalent of Santa Claus.
    B. He was never a Christian religious figure.
    C. He is derived from a combination of the gods Osiris and Mithra.
    D. He is portrayed as a giant wearing a fur-lined robe.

Father Christmas is derived from a combination of the gods Saturn (a giant god of Rome's Golden Age, who brought joy and revelry to the Saturnalia) and the wild chief of the Scandinavian gods, Odin (to whom sacrifices were made at midwinter festivals, such as Yule). Thus Father Christmas symbolizes those ancient, secular pleasures now Christianized in the merriment of Christmas. In addition to his dress described in the question, he was crowned with holly, ivy, or mistletoe and carried a Yule log and a bowl of Christmas punch. If you review Charles Dickens's *A Christmas Carol*, you'll notice that his description of the Ghost of Christmas Present is virtually identical to that traditionally given to Father Christmas. Take note that a number of countries have gift-givers whose names, when translated into English, mean "Father Christmas." Examples include *Papai Noel* of Brazil and *Père Noël* of France.

17. In modern Russia, Father Christmas disappeared with the rise of the Communist Party. Which figure symbolic of winter replaced him?

    A. Grandfather Frost
    B. Father Snow
    C. Comrade Winter
    D. The Siberian Ice Man

In dress, Grandfather Frost otherwise resembles Santa Claus. He has no religious function and brings gifts on New Year's Day. You will encounter more about this figure in the chapter "Christmas Around the World."

18. The Wise Men's gifts have attained symbolic attributes about Christ. Which of the following symbolisms is correct?

A. Gold—that Christ would be the King of kings
B. Frankincense—that Christ would be the High Priest
C. Myrrh—that Christ would be the Great Physician
D. All of them are correct.

Gold, that most precious of metals, has always represented royalty. Prayers have arisen to Heaven with the burning of sweet incense in ceremonies ancient and modern. And the ointment myrrh has been used not only as a medicinal balm, but as an agent in ancient times with which to anoint the deceased for burying. It seemed to be a portent for Jesus. Thus the correct answer is D.

19. As with the life of St. Nicholas, what has been written about the Wise Men before and after their journey to Bethlehem has arisen entirely from legend. Which of these is not a known legend about the Wise Men?

A. They ascended into Heaven in the same manner as did Christ.
B. They became Christians and were martyred in India for their faith.
C. They journeyed for two years to Bethlehem, during which time they never lacked provisions.
D. They journeyed for twelve days to Bethlehem, requiring neither rest nor provisions, because the time required seemed to be only one day.

Ironically, there have been no stories about the three Wise Men ascending into Heaven. Another legend states that some 300 years after their deaths, their remains eventually came to rest in the cathedral in Cologne, Germany, having been brought there by the emperor Frederick Barbarossa. It was believed that anything touching their skulls was empowered to prevent accidents. A shrine to the Wise Men still exists at Cologne Cathedral.

20. Which of these names does <u>not</u> belong to one of the legendary three Wise Men?

    A. Caspar (also Gaspar and Kaspar)
    B. Ludmior
    C. Melchior
    D. Balthasar

These legendary names first surfaced in the sixth century. A Greek manuscript contained them as did a church mosaic of the same period in Ravenna, Italy. St. Bede the Venerable, the English Benedictine monk and scholar (673–735), also mentioned their names. Various sources have attempted to list other specifics on each one of the three Wise Men, such as their ages, ethnic backgrounds, and the gift which each personally brought to Bethlehem. For example, the Wise Men have been portrayed as the kings of Ethiopia, Arabia, Tarsus (in Turkey), Egypt, Mesopotamia, and Persia. Their ages have been listed as sixty, forty, and twenty. Although different texts list the same generic information, a real problem arises if we attempt to match the names, ages, countries, and gifts all together. There's just too much variation from one source to another. Despite this diversity, the most common of legends assigns the following identities: Melchior, king of Arabia, fair-skinned, white-bearded and elderly, brought gold; Caspar, king of Tarsus, ruddy, young and beardless, brought frankincense; and Balthazar, king of Ethiopia, middle-aged and black, brought myrrh.

21. According to Syrian legend, the Youngest Camel in the Wise Men's caravan suffered the most during the long

journey to Bethlehem. His great desire to see the Christ Child, however, prevented him from giving up. Because of his faith, the Christ Child blessed the Youngest Camel with:

A. Immortality
B. Two humps instead of one
C. The ability to speak
D. The power of divination

The Youngest Camel (sometimes called the Gentle Camel of Jesus) nearly perished from exhaustion, but his faith persevered. And because the Christ Child granted him immortality, it is the Youngest Camel who returns each Christmas to bring the gifts in Syria.

22. The messenger for one of Germany's principal gift bringers is portrayed as a little angelic girl with gold wings who wears a gold crown and carries a small fir tree. This child is the messenger for:

A. The Christ Child
B. St. Nicholas
C. Baboushka
D. Befana

German Catholics adhere to the traditional principle that all Christmas gifts come from the Christ Child, yet it is more specifically His little messenger who actually brings them. In time, the name "Christ Child" referred to this angelic messenger and not to the Baby Jesus. Ironically, this concept arose from the preaching of Martin Luther, initiator of the Protestant Reformation, who admonished that all should revere Christ as the central theme of Christmas and not St. Nicholas, as people were more likely to do. Therefore the Christ Child and His messenger replaced St. Nicholas as the principal gift bringer to German Catholics. The German Protestants adopted the name of *Weihnachtsmann* ("Christmas man") as the replacement for St. Nicholas. The Christ Child figure is also traditional in Austria, Switzerland, and some other parts of Europe. The fir tree which the messenger carries is a symbol of eternal life.

23. Are you familiar with the name "Kris Kringle?" It is actually the corruption of a German word that means:

    A. Christ's Mass
    B. Christ Child
    C. Christ's Love
    D. Christ's Birth

"Kris Kringle" is a corruption of *Christkindlein* ("little Christ Child"). When German immigrants settled in Pennsylvania (the "Pennsylvania Dutch"), they also brought the concept of the little Christ Child (His angelic messenger) who brought the Christmas gifts. Over time, contracting *Christkindlein* lead to *Christkindl*, and mispronouncing the name even further finally produced "Kris Kringle." But today, the name is synonymous with Santa Claus or St. Nicholas, for these names are all used interchangeably for the jolly gift-bringer, at least in the USA. A perfect example is the usage in the film *Miracle on 34th Street*, in which Kris Kringle must prove that he is the one-and-only Santa Claus.

Questions 24–27. Please fill in the blanks or provide short answers.

24. In former days, St. Nicholas was portrayed as riding about on a (A) _____ as he made his nocturnal rounds delivering gifts to children on the eve of his festival day.

Children would set out their (B) _____to receive the gifts, which St. Nicholas dropped into their homes via the (C) _____. Good children received pleasant gifts, whereas naughty children received (D) _____ for their reward. (E) _____ immigrants brought their customs surrounding St. Nicholas and his festival day, (F) _____, with them when they settled in New Amsterdam in America. Eventually the customs of this festival day merged with those of Christmas, because of the close proximity of the two days. St. Nicholas also changed in name and appearance in America. The Dutch name for St. Nicholas, *Sint Nikolaas*, was slurred into *Sinterklaas*, and this became the now-familiar name of (G) _____. The poem titled (H) _____ transformed St. Nicholas into "a right jolly old elf," instead of the ascetic archbishop of Asia Minor, and cartoonist Thomas Nast drew him flying in a (I) _____, which had been depicted in the poem. Whereas the St. Nicholas of European folklore dropped gifts through chimneys, in the American folklore of today it is Santa himself who personally drops in through the (J) _____ to deliver the Christmas gifts. One thing did not change, however, and that was Santa's (K) _____, which descended from the vestments of Archbishop St. Nicholas.

(A) Horse or donkey; (B) Shoes or stockings; (C) Chimneys; (D) Rods, sticks, ashes, or soot; (E) Dutch; (F) December 6; (G) Santa Claus; (H) "A Visit from St. Nicholas;" (I) Reindeer sleigh; (J) Chimneys; (K) Red suit with white fur trim.

25. Name at least three persons or places that claim St. Nicholas as patron saint.

St. Nicholas is the patron saint of Russia; sailors; children; pawnbrokers; virgins; Greece; Sicily; Liège, Belgium; Lucerne, Switzerland; Freiburg, Germany; Laplanders; bankers; scholars; and thieves (believe it or not).

26. Summarize the influences which each of the following had on the giving of gifts at Christmastime:

    A. Roman Saturnalia
    B. Wise Men
    C. St. Nicholas

The Roman Saturnalia was a major year-end festival during which giving gifts was customary. When Christmas Christianized this festival, the gift-giving practice continued. The Wise Men are credited with presenting the first "official" Christmas gifts of gold, frankincense, and myrrh to the Christ Child. (But none of those gifts was the *first* gift of Christmas. This will become more evident later on in the book.) St. Nicholas secretly went about giving gifts to the poor and to those who otherwise were in dire need.

27. If Father Christmas is the British equivalent of Santa Claus, who is the Norwegian equivalent of Santa?

In Norwegian folklore, *Julesvenn* hid barley stalks around everyone's homes during the pagan winter festival of *Jul* (Yule) to symbolize the bountiful harvests that were expected in the following year. *Julesvenn* was the perfect way for Norwegians to infuse the Santa concept into the personage of a national Christmas figure. Yet it is not *Julesvenn* who delivers the gifts, but the *julenissen*, a composite figure of St. Nicholas and the *nisse*, a mischievous elf.

Questions 28–48. The following table pairs countries with mythical spirits that bring gifts. For each country, mark in the third column whether the spirit listed is true or false. If it is false, add the correct spirit in the last column. Answers and comments follow this group. (Hint: Only five of the spirits listed are false!)

Country	Spirit Bringing Gifts	Spirit True or False	Correct Spirit
28. Greece	St. Basil		
29. Denmark	*Julenissen*		
30. Czech Republic	St. Nicholas		
31. Hungary	Wise Men		
32. Old Russia	Babouschka		
33. Spain	Wise Men		
34. Sweden	*Jultomten*		
35. England	Father Christmas		
36. Syria	Magic Mule		
37. German Catholics	*Christkindl*		
38. Croatia	Christ Child messenger		
39. Italy	Virgin Mary		
40. Poland	Star Man		
41. Switzerland	Yule Goat		
42. The Netherlands	St. Nicholas		
43. France	Father Christmas		
44. Costa Rica	Wise Men		
45. Puerto Rico	Wise Men		
46. Brazil	Wise Men		
47. Mexico	Wise Men		
48. Norway	*Julenissen*		

Answers to 28–48: 28-True; 29-False (see comments); 30-True; 31-False (see comments); 32-True; 33-True; 34-True; 35-True; 36-False (see comments); 37-True; 38-True; 39-False (see comments); 40-True; 41-False (see comments); 42-True; 43-True; 44-True; 45-True; 46-True; 47-True; 48-True.

Comments: In Greece, *Agios Vassilis* (St. Basil), one of the Patriarchs of the Greek Orthodox Church, brings the gifts on the eve of his feast day, January 1. In Denmark, it is the *Julemand* ("Christmas Man") who brings the gifts. In Czech Republic, *Svaty Mikulas* (St. Nicholas) descends on a golden cord, accompanied by an angel. In Hungary, the angels bring the gifts. In Syria, it is the Youngest Camel (Gentle Camel of Jesus). In Italy, Befana brings the gifts. Because Switzerland consists of a mixture of German, French, and Italian cultures, the respective gift bringers parallel the parent countries. In Germany, remember that Protestants look to *Weihnachtsmann*, and in France, gifts may also come from *le petit Jésus* ("the little Jesus" or Christ Child) as well as from *Père Noël* ("Father Christmas"). In general, the Wise Men or Three Kings bring gifts on Epiphany, yet children in countries with that custom usually also receive gifts at Christmas from Santa or the Christ Child. In Brazil, the Santa Claus-Father Christmas figure is *Papai Noel*. In the Netherlands, St. Nicholas' Day is the principal day for gifts, brought by the saint himself.

Questions 49–54. According to the folklore of some parts of the world, frightfully popular ogres, all representing Satan, accompany St. Nicholas or other bringers of Christmas gifts for the purpose of punishing naughty little boys and girls and those children ignorant of their catechism. Although St. Nicholas always intercedes on the children's

behalf, he leaves a lump of coal, ashes, or switches instead of gifts. Together, gift bringers and ogres represent good versus evil. Each question in this section describes a particular ogre. From the following list of ogres, match each one with the appropriate description. Answers and comments follow this group.

    A. *Cert*
    B. *Klapparbock*
    C. *Knecht Rupprecht*
    D. *Pelznickel*
    E. *Père Fouettard*
    F. *Swarte Piet*

49. This fur-clad creature appears on December 5 (eve of St. Nicholas' Day) with blackened face, dark beard, long tail, and red, serpentine tongue. He growls, rattles chains, and bears a long whip with which to "beat" children who are ignorant of their catechism. He appears in much of northern and central Europe, particularly Germany and Austria, and carries a sack to kidnap naughty children.

50. This furry creature is popular with the "Pennsylvania Dutch" in the USA.

51. A personification of Satan in the Netherlands, this creature is compelled to walk behind St. Nicholas. He carries the saint's bag of gifts, jumps down the chimneys, and delivers the gifts for St. Nicholas; therefore, he is all sooty. He also carries another bag into which he stuffs naughty children.

52. This stern figure carries a birch rod and accompanies France's equivalent of Father Christmas. He also totes a basket into which he stuffs naughty children.

53. This Danish creature is derived from the mythical goats Gnasher and Cracker which pulled the god Thor's chariot at the winter solstice. A man dresses in goatskins and goes about terrorizing naughty children.

54. This Czech ogre is dressed in black, carries a whip and chains, and accompanies *Svaty Mikulas* (St. Nicholas).

Answers to 49–54: 49-C; 50-D; 51-F; 52-E; 53-B; 54-A.

Comments: *Knecht Rupprecht* ("Servant Rupert") is also known by a host of other names, which include *Grampus*, *Klaubauf*, *Krampus*, Hans Muff, Hans Trapp, *Ruklas* ("Rough Nicholas"), and others. *Pelznickel* is a corruption of the Teutonic being *Pelz Nicholas* ("Furry Nicholas"), which has led to other spellings such as *Belsnickel*, *Pelznichol*, *Bellsniggle*, etc. A wild figure, he not only brings gifts but punishment as well. *Swarte Piet* is Black Peter. *Père Fouettard* ("Father Whipper") accompanies *Père Noël* ("Father Christmas"), and *Klapparbock* means "Goat with Yule Gifts."

CHAPTER FOUR

The Christmas Symbols

I t's beginning to look like Christmas around the house as the Christmas tree in your parlor bids you happiness with its lights, tinsel, and glittering decorations, and the holly wreaths hanging on your front door seem to shout "Merry Christmas!" Mistletoe boughs bid kisses beneath chandeliers and doorways, and your windows glow with the cheeriness of burning candles. And depending on your style of residence, you may even be burning a special Yule log to warm your visitors. Yes, Christmas is well represented by traditional plants and greenery, those natural elements with Christian interpretations, with which you deck your halls for the coming holidays. In addition to greenery, your mantel may feature a Nativity scene with figures of the Holy Family, shepherds, and Wise Men, and special treats for little ones may include candy canes. This chapter focuses on the myriad of symbols which punctuate the Christmas season.

1. Why do evergreen trees and plants, such as mistletoe and holly, have such great significance at Christmastime?

A. As evergreens, they bear fruit at Christmas.
B. As evergreens, they grow only in the Holy Land where Christ was born.
C. As evergreens, they signify a rebirth of the soul at Christmastime.
D. As evergreens, they symbolize the promise of eternal life through Christ.

Always symbolizing nature and long life because they flourish through the winter, evergreens were first sacred to pagans such as the Druids, who wore holly during the cutting of the mistletoe at winter solstice festivals. The Romans decorated homes and images of the god Saturn with holly during the Saturnalia, and some early Christians decked their homes with these plants to escape Roman persecution. Laurel was another plant used, sacred to the god Apollo. With the Christianization of pagan winter festivals, the evergreens came to symbolize the eternal life promised through Jesus Christ. The arranging of evergreens in homes also stemmed from an ancient belief that benign woodland spirits abode in them during the winter. The spirits would then reside in the home as a part of the evergreens.

2. From which civilization did evergreen Christmas wreaths spring?

A. Roman
B. Aztec
C. Arabian
D. Babylonian

By now, it should be rather clear that many of our familiar Christmas traditions descended from the Romans. They decorated statues of various gods with evergreen wreaths at the Saturnalia, and they also wore wreaths on their heads. Wreaths, often bestowed upon the Roman gladiatorial champions, were an emblem of valor and victory over death. Wreaths also symbolized the sun disk, the sun god Mithra, which the Romans adopted from the Persians.

3. Of the following descriptions about the Advent wreath, which is <u>not</u> correct?

    A. It is attributed to Martin Luther, who initiated the Protestant Reformation.
    B. It is a large, evergreen wreath with some thirty candles attached, one for each day of Advent.
    C. The first candle is lit on the first Sunday of Advent.
    D. All candles are lit on the last Sunday of Advent.

The Advent wreath contains only four candles, one for each Sunday of Advent. One additional candle is lit each Sunday, with all four candles burning on the last Sunday. In some wreaths, a large, red candle, symbolizing Christ, is added on Christmas Day. Advent wreaths decorate homes and churches alike, and it is customary to hold a period of devotion after lighting the candles each week.

4. A Mexican legend holds that once a little girl in poverty despaired because she had no gift to place before the altar at Christmas. By the wayside, she saw a small plant which she plucked and presented as her gift. Miraculously, the little weed was transformed into a beautiful, scarlet flower, the *Flor de la Noche-Buena.* Although the literal English translation is "Flower of the Good Night,"

in practical usage, it means "Flower of Christmas Eve." This flower is better known as:

    A. Mistletoe
    B. Holly
    C. Lily
    D. Poinsettia

In another version of the legend, a boy knelt at the altar with no gift, whereupon the poinsettia sprang up at his feet. Dr. Joel Poinsett, the American botanist for whom the flower was named, was also ambassador to Mexico from 1824 to 1829. The poinsettia became a popular Christmas plant after he brought it back to his home in South Carolina. The poinsettia is primarily a tropical plant, native to Central America and Mexico. You may also see white and yellow varieties, besides the familiar type with its large, red bracts. Contrary to popular opinion, the poinsettia is nontoxic.

5.   According to legend, which of these Christmas symbols did Winfrid, St. Boniface, introduce into Germany?

    A. Holly
    B. Mistletoe
    C. Christmas tree
    D. Christmas crib

An English missionary to the Germanic tribes in the eighth century, St. Boniface chose to rid the pagans of their chief symbol, the great oak near Geismar, sacred to the god Thor. He struck the tree, whereupon a great wind splintered the oak into four pieces. Believing that the pagans needed a physical symbol of Christian faith, St. Boniface called their attention to a small fir tree nearby. Because the tree pointed to Heaven and because its evergreen leaves symbolized eternal life through Christ, St. Boniface gave them the fir tree as a replacement, the symbol of the Christ Child. Thus St. Boniface is said to have instituted the first Christmas tree.

6. Another Christmas tree legend focuses on the Nativity itself. Can you pick out that legend among three impostors?

   A. After Jesus was born, the manger hay turned into evergreen sprigs, symbols of eternal life.
   B. From the manger wood sprouted an evergreen tree, a symbol of eternal life.
   C. When Christ was born at midnight, all the trees in the world bloomed, and they still bloom on every Christmas Eve.
   D. When Christ was born, all evergreen trees assumed a shape that pointed to Heaven, and they still do today, because they symbolize eternal life.

This is one of few legends that can be traced to a definitive source. Georg Jacob, an Arabian geographer, first told the story in the tenth century, and soon it had spread all over Europe. It is felt that this legend partly contributed to the custom of decorating trees at Christmastime in imitation of those that supposedly bloomed over 2,000 years ago. Another influential factor stemmed again from the Roman Saturnalia, for it was quite customary for people to decorate their homes and even trees with trinkets, streamers, and images of Saturn during this festival.

7. One of the more popular Christmas tree legends holds that a cold, hungry young boy sought refuge at a poor woodsman's home on Christmas Eve. He was welcomed, given food, and a bed. On Christmas Morning, the boy filled the home with brilliant light, and the family then knew that the boy was really the Christ Child. He rewarded the family's kindness by planting a tiny tree that

would grow and forever bear fruit at Christmas. What type of tree did the Christ Child plant?

    A. Oak tree
    B. Maple tree
    C. Sycamore tree
    D. Fir tree

This legend again links the Christ Child to the fir tree as His symbol.

8. A story about the fifteenth-century German theologian, Martin Luther, helped to establish the Christmas tree in his country. On one Christmas Eve, as Luther contemplated a starry sky through the branches of fir trees, he was so inspired that he brought a small tree home to decorate for his children. What specific items did Luther place on the tree to represent the starry heavens?

    A. Numerous paper stars
    B. Numerous candles
    C. Numerous gold balls
    D. Numerous angel dolls

Although Luther's idea to adorn a tree with candles was not original (the Romans and Druids hung candles and trinkets from sacred trees during their winter festivals), it is believed that his was the first lighted Christmas tree as such.

9. Of the Christmas evergreens, which one "bears the crown"?

    A. Holly
    B. Ivy
    C. Mistletoe
    D. Rosemary

"Of all the trees that are in the wood the holly bears the crown" is a phrase from an old Yule song, "The Holly and the Ivy." For ages holly and ivy have vied against each other in folklore, with sharp holly termed the "man's plant" and clinging ivy the "woman's plant." Holly and ivy have been the subjects of various carols about who would rule the household, the husband or the wife. An early belief held that the plant which was first brought into the home at Yuletide determined who would rule the house in the coming year. The Christian interpretation, on the other hand, has been to view holly as the masculine side of Christ and ivy as the feminine side, the Virgin Mary.

10. Each part of the holly plant has come to symbolize a different attribute of Christ. Which one of the following symbolisms is <u>incorrect</u>?

    A. The white flowers symbolize His resurrection.
    B. The red berries symbolize His shed blood.
    C. The sharp leaves symbolize His crown of thorns.
    D. The bitter bark symbolizes His sorrow over the sins of the world.

The white flowers symbolize Christ's purity.

11. Over the centuries, there have arisen several superstitions about holly. Of the four superstitions listed below, choose the one that did not arise.

    A. Holly near a home would frighten off witches.
    B. "Smooth" (less spiny) holly in the home meant that the husband would dominate; prickly holly meant that the wife would dominate.
    C. Quarrels could be settled under a holly tree.
    D. A holly sprig on a bedpost brought good dreams.

Prickly holly brought into the home at Christmastime meant that the husband would rule the home in the coming year, whereas smooth or less spiny holly meant that the wife would rule. Therefore, domination by the husband or wife could be predicted not only by holly *or* ivy, but also by the two general types of holly.

12. Amid feasting, drinking, and much clamor, one important element at the pagan festival of Yule included a large log, appropriately named the Yule log. From which civilization did the Yule log probably originate?

    A.   Roman
    B.   Greek
    C.   Sumerian
    D.   Egyptian

Some 4,000 years before the birth of Christ, the Yule log is thought to have evolved from the Zagmuk, the Sumerian New Year festival. According to their mythology, their supreme god, Marduk, annually saved the world from destruction by descending into the underworld at this time to battle the monsters of chaos. The burning of wooden effigies of these monsters supposedly aided Marduk in this task, and these are thought to have been the earliest prototypes of Yule logs.

13. Which one of these statements is <u>not</u> true about the Yule log?

    A. Pagans of northern Europe originally burned the log as a symbol of the warmth, light, and life that was anticipated with the coming of Spring.
    B. The log served a dual purpose of light for celebration and a stake upon which criminals were burned.

    C. In medieval days, it was customary to pour wine over the log before lighting it as a libation to deceased family members.

    D. Custom dictated that people wash their hands before touching the log.

To the Teutons, Druids, and other Northern European pagans who celebrated Yule, burning a log, coupled with the din of the celebration itself, warded off demons or mystical spirits which were supposed to have been given free reign during the long period of winter darkness. Particularly at the time of the winter solstice, the veil separating the physical and the spirit worlds was believed to be the most thin. At the same time, families believed that the spirits of their ancestors always resided with them and became manifest in the glowing embers of the log. The medieval custom of pouring wine over the log before lighting it paralleled that superstition by honoring deceased ancestors. Because the Yule log was a venerated object, all who touched it first "purified" themselves by washing their hands. The Yule log was not an instrument of execution.

14. When the Yule log was added to the Christmas repertoire, those pagan customs that had been associated with it came as well, but with a Christian covering. When during the Christmas season did the Yule log burn?

    A. It burned only during the twelve days of Christmas.

    B. It burned during the entire month of December.

    C. It burned only on Christmas Day.

    D. It burned only on Christmas Eve and Christmas Day.

It was most important that the log burn continuously during the twelve days of Christmas, as the next question will address.

15. Why was it necessary to keep the Yule log burning all through the twelve days of Christmas?

    A. According to superstition, the fire kept evil away. If the fire went out, bad luck was in store.

    B. According to superstition, twelve days were required to burn away all the evils of the past.

    C. Each day of burning honored one of Christ's twelve apostles.

    D. The Druid winter solstice festival continued for twelve days.

Although the Christianized form of the superstition held that no demons or witches would ever dare to appear during the holy season of the twelve days of Christmas, it was most difficult to cast off a centuries-old superstition which held otherwise. Therefore the correct answer is A. An interesting variation on keeping the Yule log burning came from the Old South prior to the American Civil War. It was customary on a number of the plantations for the slaves to have a holiday from their work as long as the Yule log burned. Therefore, to keep the log smoldering as long as possible, the slaves would moisten the log beforehand so that it would burn more slowly. Quite original!

16. Not only was it important how long the Yule log burned, but also how the log was lit in the first place. What was the ritual for lighting the log from year to year?

    A. The log was soaked in new wine and then lit.

    B. A piece of the previous year's log was saved to light the new log.

   C. Small twigs were used from the same tree which yielded the log.

   D. Fire was brought from the Eternal Flame at the altar.

Lighting the new log with a piece of the old symbolized the cycling of the log from year to year.

17. When people selected their Yule logs, they frequently turned to a Nativity legend about ash wood as the basis for choosing ash logs. Can you pick out that ash wood legend?

   A. The Christ Child was first washed and dressed by an ash wood fire.

   B. Christ's cross was made of ash wood.

   C. Christ's manger was made of ash wood.

   D. The Christ Child first played with a toy fashioned from ash wood.

This legend also helped to Christianize the Yule log, for its burning symbolized not only that first Christmas fire whereby the Holy Family received warmth, but also Jesus as Light of the world. Therefore, the correct answer is the only one of the four which mentions fire, A.

18. Old superstitions about the Yule log included all of the following, <u>except</u>:

   A. If you beat the log, you could see the evil spirits departing in a shower of sparks.

   B. A barefoot person near the burning log brought good luck.

   C. The ashes, when placed in the clefts of fruit trees, improved crops.

   D. Putting the ashes under a bed kept lightning from striking the house.

A barefoot person, squinting person, or flat-footed woman could not approach the burning log without bringing *bad* luck. Also, if you could not see the head of your shadow cast by the light of a Yule log fire, you were doomed to die within a year's time. Note that, while the spirits of family members were supposedly manifest in the glowing embers, beating the log drove evil spirits away in showers of sparks.

19. It was customary to select the next Yule log on the same day that, for some, marked the end of the Christmas season. What was that day?

    A. Michaelmas
    B. Epiphany
    C. New Year's Day
    D. Candlemas

February 2 marks the day of Candlemas. According to ancient Jewish law, after a woman gave birth to a male child, she was required to spend forty days in purification rites before she was accepted back into society. Candlemas, a date forty days past Christmas Day, commemorates not only this event, but the presentation of the infant Jesus in the Temple in Jerusalem as well. At that time, according to Luke's Gospel, Simeon referred to Jesus as "A light to lighten the Gentiles, and the glory of thy people Israel" (see Leviticus 12:1–4 and Luke 2:22–33). Thus, candle ceremonies play a significant part of Candlemas to symbolize Jesus as Light of the world.

Thought to have been instituted by the Byzantine emperor Justinian I around the year 542, Candlemas Christianized the Roman purification feast of *Februa*, which had been observed originally in mid February. To make

Candlemas fall forty days after Christmas, the date was moved to the second day in February.

Some societies now consider Epiphany to be the end of the Christmas season. But until the Second Vatican Council (1962–1965), Candlemas terminated the Christmas season in the Roman Catholic Church. In medieval times, this was not only the time for families to select their next Yule log, it was the time to burn the Christmas greenery and the remnants of the old Yule log as well, while saving a piece of that log to light the one for the following year. Ritual dictated that each household cut their own log rather than purchase it. The log was kept until spring or summer, when it was set outdoors to dry. An old superstition also said that a sunny Candlemas predicted forty more days of winter weather. Does that sound familiar? It should, for it is the basis for the superstition associated with Groundhog Day, February 2, in the USA.

As a European tradition, the Yule log generally lost favor when modern technology replaced the large, open fireplaces. Of course, the use of Yule logs still pops up today in a number of community Christmas projects in the USA which attempt to recreate the holiday atmosphere of yore. Although department stores may sell so-called Yule logs which emit beautifully colored flames, their relatively small size cannot begin to compare with those monstrous logs which once graced gigantic, medieval fireplaces.

20. Mistletoe is the most romantic of the Christmas evergreens. Wherein lies the origin for kissing under the mistletoe?

    A. In Scandinavian mythology

B. In Greek mythology
C. In Roman mythology
D. In Middle Eastern mythology

From its history and legends, there exists no truly Christianized substitute for the pagan symbolism surrounding mistletoe. According to Scandinavian mythology, Balder, the god of light and son of Odin and Frigga, king and queen of the gods, sensed that he was about to die and pleaded with his mother to intervene. Frigga then exacted a promise from everything animate and inanimate on earth that Balder would not be harmed. Unfortunately, she had overlooked the mistletoe. Balder's only enemy, the evil Loki, then fashioned a dart from mistletoe and, while the gods hurled darts at the seemingly invincible Balder, Loki gave the dart to Balder's brother Hoder, the blind god of war. Hoder shot the dart, and Balder fell dead. Frigga, weeping bitter tears that became the mistletoe's white berries, ultimately revived Balder through acts of love and kindness. In her joy at Balder's revival, Frigga kissed each person passing beneath the tree upon which mistletoe grew, through which acts the mistletoe became the symbol of love and affection. Forevermore would anyone standing under it receive a token of love, that is, a kiss. Among the Celtic Druids, mistletoe was highly sacred, it never touched the ground, and it was considered to be a powerful, external aphrodisiac. It hung in homes as charms against evil and illness, and all who entered doorways overhung with mistletoe received a kiss of friendship.

It should be no surprise that mistletoe, this parasite of trees, this pagan symbol of love and joy, would eventually find its way into Christmas, a celebration literally abounding in love and joy, even though no one ever found a way to Christianize its romantic symbolism as such. In modern times, however, some couples have gone so far as to take the biblical admonition to salute one another with a holy kiss a bit too freely (see Romans 16:16).

Your church may ban mistletoe from its sanctuary and give as its reason the fact that mistletoe symbolized carnal acts that the ancient Druids performed at the winter solstice festival. On the other hand, most evidence shows that mistletoe actually decorated many medieval churches and was variously associated with the ecclesiastical custom of pardoning criminals and other sinners at Christmastime.

As a word of caution, mistletoe berries are quite toxic.

21. From the mistletoe bough, by custom, a gentleman plucked one of its berries for each kiss bestowed upon a lady, then delivered the berry to her. What happened when all the berries had been plucked?

    A. If a couple passed under the bough, the lady slapped the gentleman.
    B. The bough lost its spell, and no more kisses were available.
    C. The bough was removed and burned in the Yule fire.
    D. A lady with berries could kiss any gentleman she wished.

In addition to the bough losing its spell (choice B), another superstition held that any maiden not kissed under the mistletoe would not marry in the coming year.

22. Which Christmas symbol did Princess Henriette of Austria (1816), Princess Helene of France (1840), and Queen

Victoria of England (1841) popularize in their countries?

    A. Yule log
    B. Wassail
    C. Christmas tree
    D. Advent wreath

Christmas trees had arrived in England by the late 1700s, but their future in that country was especially assured when Queen Victoria permitted her consort, the German-born Prince Albert of Saxony, to set one up in Windsor Castle. Because the *crèche* (Nativity scene) had become so well established in France at a much earlier date, however, Christmas trees never did acquire the same popularity there that they did in a number of other European countries.

23. A variety of Christmas tree utilizing only ornaments that specifically symbolize Christ is called a:

    A. Christos tree
    B. Chrismon tree
    C. Christage tree
    D. Chrissus tree

A Chrismon tree converts the conventional Christmas tree into a significantly more religious emblem.

24. Appropriate ornaments for a Chrismon tree would include all of the following, <u>except</u>:

    A. Monograms of "X" (Chi) and "P" (Rho), the first two letters in *Christos*, the Greek word for Christ.
    B. Greek letters "A" (Alpha) and "Ω" (Omega)
    C. Angels
    D. Crosses

Because the word "Chrismon" derives from "Christ" and "monogram," appropriate ornaments originally consisted of monograms that pertained to Christ, such as the Greek letters Chi and Rho. Other acceptable ornaments include Alpha and Omega letters, which respectively signify Jesus as the Beginning and the End; doves, symbolizing the Holy Spirit which descended on Jesus following His baptism; crosses, the emblem of Christ's crucifixion; and anchors, rocks, and lambs, respectively symbolizing Jesus as our Anchor, the Rock of Ages/Rock of our salvation, and the Lamb of God. Angels are specific, heavenly beings that do not symbolize Christ.

25. The only colors suitable for a Chrismon tree are:

    A. Blue and Yellow
    B. Red and Green
    C. Purple and Orange
    D. White and Gold

The white symbolizes Jesus' purity; the gold, His royalty. The tree should only be illuminated with white lights.

26. A variety of Christmas tree utilizing only ornaments that portray the earthly ancestry of Christ or that feature Messianic prophecies is called a (an):

    A. Jesse tree
    B. David tree
    C. Joseph tree
    D. Adam and Eve tree

The concept stemmed from medieval art, which depicted Christ's progenitors springing from a tree rooted in Jesse,

King David's father, with Christ at the top (see Isaiah 11:1). Jesse tree ornaments depict Christ's earthly ancestors (David, Abraham, Isaac, Jacob, etc.) and may include biblical prophecies about the coming Messiah.

27. From which country did the Nativity scene originate?

    A. United States
    B. Germany
    C. Italy
    D. Mexico

From chapter two, you should recall that St. Francis of Assisi first devised the concept of a Nativity scene in Greccio, Italy, in 1223.

28. By tradition, which two stable animals are always present in Nativity scenes to stand watch over the manger?

    A. Ram and ewe
    B. Bull and cow
    C. Ox and ass
    D. Rooster and hen

Portrayals of the Nativity have included ox and ass since the Middle Ages.

29. From the previous question, which passage of Scripture loosely serves as the basis for including these two animals in traditional Nativity scenes?

    A. Numbers 22:21–33
    B. 1 Corinthians 9:9
    C. John 12:14–15
    D. Isaiah 1:3

Ox and ass first appeared as beasts adoring the Christ Child in the Gospel of Pseudo-Matthew in the New Testament Apocrypha, which very loosely derived from the passage in Isaiah. As is clearly evident, however, Isaiah 1:3 mentions nothing about Christ's future Nativity as such.

Questions 30–34. Several other plants have become the subject of Christmas legends. Match each of the numbered legends with the corresponding plant from the list below. Answers and comments follow this group.

A. Christmas Rose; B. Lavender; C. Pennyroyal; D. Rosemary; E. Wild Thyme

30. After Jesus was born, Mary washed His swaddling clothes and laid them on this shrub to dry. At that moment, not only did the plant become wonderfully fragrant, but its flowers, originally white, also turned blue.

31. When Madalon, a little shepherd girl, saw the Wise Men en route to Bethlehem with gifts for the Christ Child, she wept, because she had no gift to give. An angel saw Madalon's grief and brushed away the snow, revealing this beautiful, white, pink-tipped flower.

32. This plant with pale purple flowers acquired its sweet scent when Mary laid Jesus' garments on it to dry.

33. This formed the Virgin Mary's bedding when she gave birth to Jesus.

34. Together with hay, this plant lined the manger and bloomed at the very hour of Jesus' birth.

Answers to 30–34: 30-D; 31-A; 32-B; 33-E; 34-C.

Comments: Its name deriving from the Virgin Mary, the rosemary is a fragrant, evergreen mint shrub that is native to the

Mediterranean region. Spanish folk-lore also had a part in giving the flowers their blue hue. As the Holy Family stopped to rest during their flight to Egypt, Mary laid her blue robe on the shrub. The flowers, originally white, changed into the color of the robe. During the Middle Ages, because rosemary allegedly repelled evil spirits, it was spread on the floor at Christmastime, and those who inhaled its fragrance would receive happiness in the new year.

Another version of the Christmas rose legend holds that the angel brushed away the path, revealing many white flowers. Madalon gathered them for the Christ Child, and where He touched them, there remained tips of pink. The Christmas rose is an evergreen, Eurasian perennial.

The common variety of lavender is an evergreen shrub of the mint family and is native to the Mediterranean region.

Wild thyme and pennyroyal also belong to the mint family. Whereas the former is ubiquitous, the latter is native to southern Europe and western Asia.

This next question briefly summarizes the evolution of the Christmas tree while adding a few new points to challenge you. Try your hand at filling in the missing words.

35. It is generally recognized that the first Christmas trees became firmly established in the country of (A) _____ during the Middle Ages, in part because of

legends surrounding two clerics, (B and C) _____. At first, medieval land ordinances restricted a cut tree to no more than (D) _____ feet in height. This not only conserved trees but allowed the convenience of bringing the tree indoors to be erected on a table. Instead of cutting trunk and all, some families preferred to erect a small "pyramid" and overlay it with fir boughs. Seen prior to the fifteenth or sixteenth century, this pyramid consisted of a decorated, wooden framework with shelves containing gifts, food, or a (E) _____. In time the Christmas tree itself (also pyramid shaped) became much more popular and replaced the pyramid in Germany. A similar structure, known as the (F) _____, continued to survive for a while, particularly in Italy. Another source for the German Christmas tree arose from certain medieval mystery plays which were annually performed on Christmas Eve. Because December 24 had once been the feast day of (G) _____ in the Catholic Church, one such play dealt with the creation of man. On the stage there stood a large evergreen tree, known as the (H) _____, which was decorated with numerous (I) _____ and which symbolized the (J) _____. According to legend, when Adam left the Garden of Eden, he carried away a twig from the (K) _____. This same twig is also said to have sprouted to become the Christmas tree and later the wood for the (L) _____. In 1604 there appeared the first definite reference to decorated Christmas trees as such in the then-German city of (M) _____, wherein the decorations included items such as paper roses, sweets, wafers, and gold foil. By the nineteenth century, Christmas trees had spread to other European countries. It is thought that religious German immigrants, the Moravians, brought the first Christmas trees to America upon their arrival in 1735.

At that time, the Moravians decorated their version of Christmas trees, which were really (N) _____, similar to those described above. Later on, German mercenaries, known as the (O) _____, helped to establish Christmas trees in America by decorating them even during the Revolutionary War. Finally, the first written record that mentioned decorated Christmas trees in the USA appeared in the diary of a Matthew Zahn from Lancaster, Pennsylvania, dated December 20, 1821.

Answer to 35:   (A) Germany; (B and C) St. Boniface and Martin Luther; (D) Four; (E) Nativity scene; (F) *Ceppo*; (G) Adam and Eve; (H) Paradise Tree; (I) Apples; (J) Garden of Eden; (K) Tree of Forbidden Fruit; (L) Cross of Christ; (M) Strassburg (now Strasbourg); (N) Pyramids; (O) Hessians.

Comments: A variety of evergreen trees now serve as the most popular and fragrant of Christmas trees. Long-needled pines include the Scots pine, which is native to Europe, and the white pine, which is found in New York State. Short-needled trees include the Douglas fir from western North America, the white spruce from the northern USA and Canada, and Europe's Norwegian spruce. If you're interested in a true fir, try the balsam fir, found along the North American east coast and in Canada's Northwest Territory, the Fraser fir from Appalachia, or a white fir from the western USA. Then sit back and admire your handsomely decorated tree as your home fills with that heavenly "Christmas scent."

Questions 36–40. Candy canes, hard sugar sticks that now feature red and white stripes with one end bent in a hook, arose in Europe during the seventeenth century as Christmas tree decorations and as pacifiers for children. Over the centuries, the physical features of candy canes have acquired religious interpretations or other inspirational symbolisms. For each characteristic below, briefly describe the associated interpretation. Answers and comments follow this group.

36. The hook

_____

37. Appearance of "J" on turning the cane upside down

_____

38. Red and white stripes

_____

39. Hard texture

_____

40. Peppermint flavor

_____

Answers and comments to 36–40.

The hook shape originated at the cathedral in Cologne, Germany in 1670. The shape was designed to portray a shepherd's crook, which commemorated the shepherds of Bethlehem at the Nativity. Turning the cane upside down resembles a "J," representing Jesus. The stripes themselves signify the stripes of flogging which Jesus suffered just prior to His crucifixion; the red and white colors respectively represent Jesus' blood, shed for the remission of sins, and purity. The hard texture symbolizes Christ as the Rock, the foundation of the Church, and the peppermint flavor is reminiscent of hyssop, an aromatic plant that the ancient Hebrews used during purification rites. One romantic myth about candy canes held that early Christians used them as a secret means of identifying one another to avoid persecution. This could hardly be true, given the candy cane's history.

CHAPTER FIVE

Beloved Carols
and Songs

There is no more fitting language that propels one's soul into the holiness, nostalgia, and beauty of Christmastime than the language of music. From "Silent Night" to "White Christmas," from "The First Nowell" to "Jingle Bells," scores of beloved carols and songs, ancient and modern, have painted for us a complete portrait of Christmas from the manger to the space age. In this chapter, you'll explore the stories behind many of your favorite carols, and you'll make some fascinating correlations about a host of selections from the classical to the contemporary.

1. Which carol, first performed in 1818 by a then-unknown priest and a schoolmaster-organist in Oberndorf, Austria, is probably the best-loved of all sacred carols?

   A. "Hark! The Herald Angels Sing"
   B. "O Little Town of Bethlehem"
   C. "Silent Night"
   D. "Joy to the World"

How this epitome of all Christmas carols initially arose as an anonymous entity is really quite fascinating. According to the traditional story, Father Joseph Mohr served as assistant priest for the Church of St. Nicholas in the little village of Oberndorf, Austria. He and his organist, Franz Gruber, composed the simple but exquisitely reverent "Silent Night" at the last minute to provide some music for their Christmas Eve Midnight Mass of 1818, because the church organ was inoperable. Mohr and Gruber sang their new composition to guitar accompaniment, and the choir came in only for the two-line refrains. As far as everyone was concerned at the time, the song was pretty, and that was the end of it.

In 1995, the discovery of an authentic, autographed copy of "Silent Night" in Father Mohr's hand at a museum in Salzburg dispelled some of the myths regarding the carol's origin. Simply titled "Weihnachtslied" ("Christmas Song") with lyrics arranged for guitar, the manuscript bore an inscription which confirmed Gruber as the musical composer, along with the date of 1816. At that time, Father Mohr was serving at another parish. Authorities dated the manuscript itself to 1820, a year after Father Mohr had left Oberndorf. It has since been concluded that Father Mohr wrote the lyrics to what is now known as "Silent Night" in 1816 and requested Gruber's musical setting in 1818. Although the exact reasons for presenting a new carol with guitar accompaniment during a Roman Catholic Mass are unknown, speculations still include the unplayable organ as well as the decision to present a simple folk carol, a common practice in Germany and Austria at that time.

The story continued some years later, when a Carl Mauracher was brought in to rebuild the organ at

Oberndorf around 1824. While working, he supposedly discovered the manuscript of "Silent Night" nearby, which had remained since the Christmas of 1818. With Gruber's permission, Mauracher carried a copy away and began to familiarize everyone with the charming simplicity of the carol. Apparently neither the original manuscript nor Mauracher's copy bore Mohr's or Gruber's names as the authors, nor a specific title. In time, troupes of folk-singing families from Tyrol, a mountainous province in western Austria, added "Silent Night" to their repertoire as they toured Europe. After one such family gave a rendition in Leipzig, Germany, the first printing of "Silent Night" appeared on the market in 1832, but it was identified merely as an anonymous "Tyrolean Song." This amazing story continues with the next question.

2. In 1839 the Rainers, a European family of touring folk singers, first introduced "Silent Night" into the USA. In which city did they appear?

   A. New York City
   B. Boston
   C. Philadelphia
   D. Chicago

When the Rainers first sang "Silent Night" at the Alexander Hamilton Monument in New York City, they only knew the song by its then-popular title, "Song from Heaven." Either desiring anonymity or simply forgetting to sign their manuscript, Father Joseph Mohr and Franz Gruber at that time were still unknown as the authors. The story continues in the next question.

3. The world may never have known the real story behind "Silent Night," had Frederick William IV, King of

Prussia, not instituted a search for its source in 1854. How did the king get his answer?

A. Father Mohr drew up a letter that detailed everything about "Silent Night" and sent it to the king in Berlin.
B. Franz Gruber drew up the letter.
C. Mohr and Gruber co-wrote the letter.
D. The organ builder Carl Mauracher drew up the letter.

Father Mohr could not have told the story, for he had died in 1848, never having known the outcome of his carol. Gruber had received no word about the profound success of "Silent Night" until 1854, after which he drew up an explanatory letter and sent it to the king in Berlin. But after so many years of not knowing who wrote the song, or when, a skeptical world did not fully accept Mohr's and Gruber's authorship until some time after Gruber's death in 1863. It now seems evident that Mohr and Gruber presented their carol only for the moment, expressly for the Christmas of 1818, with no thought of its ever going beyond their little Austrian village. Born in simplicity like Christ, "Silent Night" forever will be music's supreme expression of Christmas.

4. Whose recording has become the largest-selling, contemporary Christmas song in the world?

A. Elvis Presley: "Jingle Bells"
B. Bing Crosby: "White Christmas"
C. Gene Autry: "Rudolph, the Red-Nosed Reindeer"
D. Perry Como: "I'll Be Home for Christmas"

Bing Crosby first introduced Irving Berlin's "White Christmas" on the Kraft Music Hall radio show which aired Christmas Day, 1941. His subsequent recordings of this immortal piece in 1942 and 1947 have sold over thirty million copies alone, making it the largest-selling, single Christmas recording in the world. Although Irving Berlin wrote "White Christmas" in 1940, Crosby did not make his memorable recording on Decca Records until May, 1942. By March, 1947, the original master disk had worn out from millions of pressings, which made it necessary for him to re-record "White Christmas" at that time. And that's the version with which everyone is most familiar today.

5. Perry Como would have been the first to record "Rudolph, the Red-Nosed Reindeer" by New York City songwriter Johnny Marks, had it not been for one problem with Como's group. What was it?

> A. They wanted too much money.
> B. They wanted to change the reindeer's name from Rudolph to Rudy.
> C. They wanted to make some changes in the lyrics.
> D. They were not sure that a song about an animal could be a hit.

Marks insisted that the song was perfect as written and would accept no changes in the lyrics. He went on to find cowboy star Gene Autry, who recorded the song without demanding any changes. Autry first introduced "Rudolph" during his annual winter rodeo show at New York City's Madison Square Garden in 1949.

6. For many years the music to that glorious carol, "Joy to the World," had been attributed to the genius of German composer G. F. Handel. But it took music scholars 100 years to discover this error. Who was the real composer?

    A. F. J. Haydn
    B. Father Joseph Mohr
    C. W. A. Mozart
    D. We still don't know.

Those who proposed Handel as the composer cited the similarity of the melody of "Joy to the World" to two pieces from his oratorio *Messiah*, "Glory to God" and "Lift up Your Heads." But in 1986, the music for this carol was traced to an anonymous English tune titled "Comfort," which had been published in hymn collections in the early 1830s. Influenced by the erroneous premise that the music was Handel's, the American composer Lowell Mason arranged the "Comfort" tune and published it together with Isaac Watts's lyrics as "Antioch" in 1836. By appending the phrase "from Handel," he unwittingly succeeded in perpetuating the Handel myth. Mason's arrangement has enjoyed widespread popularity in the USA. Therefore, the correct answer is D.

7. What lovable Christmas character did Robert May create in 1939?

    A. A Christmas-stealing Grinch
    B. A winter elf named Jack Frost
    C. A snowman named Frosty
    D. A red-nosed reindeer named Rudolph

An advertising copywriter, May created the Rudolph story as a Christmas sales gimmick for the Montgomery Ward Company. The composer Johnny Marks, May's brother-in-law, carried it further and established Rudolph forever as a part of Christmas with his tune "Rudolph, the Red-Nosed Reindeer." Publishing difficulties delayed the song's release for several years, after which Marks succeeded in having cowboy singing star Gene Autry record it in 1949.

8. Johnny Marks published "Rudolph, the Red-Nosed Reindeer" only after founding his own publishing company. What was the name of his company?

    A. St. Nicholas Music Company
    B. Kris Kringle Music Company
    C. Santa Claus Music Company
    D. Father Christmas Music Company

Amazingly, Marks pitched his tune for years to numerous publishers, none of whom showed the slightest interest in "Rudolph," so Marks started his own publishing company in order to issue the sheet music. Appropriately, he named his firm St. Nicholas Music Company.

9. In "Do You Hear What I Hear?" the story of Christ's birth ascends through four different channels before ultimately reaching all people of the world. Identify the order of those channels specified in the song.

    A. From lamb to night wind to shepherd boy to king to all people
    B. From night wind to lamb to shepherd boy to king to all people
    C. From shepherd boy to king to night wind to lamb to all people
    D. From king to shepherd boy to lamb to night wind to all people

Songwriters Gloria Shayne and Harry Regney created this unusual Christmas ballad for the Harry Simeone Chorale, which produced a successful recording in 1962. Renditions by the Norman Luboff Choir and Bing

Crosby have also been favorably received. The correct answer is B.

10. The feast mentioned in the familiar carol "Good King Wenceslas" implies the feast day of:

    A. St. Peter
    B. St. Andrew
    C. St. Stephen
    D. St. John

The Feast of St. Stephen is December 26 on the Roman Catholic Church calendar. St. Stephen was the first Christian martyr (see Acts 6:8–15 and all of Acts chapter 7).

11. "Cantique de Noël" ("Song of Christmas") is the original French title of which of these favorite carols?

    A. "The First Nowell"
    B. "Silent Night"
    C. "O Holy Night"
    D. "Away in a Manger"

"Cantique de Noël" is better known as "O Holy Night."

12. The subject of "The Coventry Carol" is:

    A. Mary's joy at the Annunciation
    B. The angels' visit to the shepherds
    C. Herod's slaying of Bethlehem children
    D. The Wise Men's visit to the Christ Child

Dating from 1392, a long-running "mystery play" about the life of Christ became quite popular in Coventry, England. In the segment that portrayed the Slaughter of the Innocents, one song arose that has now become known as "The Coventry Carol." Its somber, tragic mood is both a lullaby and a lament for the infants who perished in Bethlehem.

13. Before any of us ever heard of the spritely "Jingle Bells," this holiday favorite first appeared under what original name, until its composer changed it?

    A. "The One-Horse Open Sleigh"
    B. "Dashing Through the Snow"
    C. "A Merry Little Jingle"
    D. "A Sleighing Song"

"Jingle Bells" was born not at Christmastime but at a church Thanksgiving pageant in Boston. James Pierpont of Medford, a community outside of Boston, based this peppy song on the annual sleigh races held in Medford, and his father's class of little Sunday school children first performed it in 1857 at the pageant. By popular demand, they gave an encore performance at Christmastime that same year. The title would probably always have remained "The One-Horse Open Sleigh," had not one of Pierpont's friends commented that his delightful song certainly was "a merry little jingle." That was enough for Pierpont. By changing the title, he bestowed immortality upon "Jingle Bells."

14. The words to which of the following carols came as an inspiration to its writer after he had returned from a sojourn in the Holy Land?

    A. "O Little Town of Bethlehem"
    B. "It Came Upon the Midnight Clear"
    C. "The First Nowell"
    D. "While Shepherds Watched"

A minister in Philadelphia, Phillips Brooks wrote the words to "O Little Town of Bethlehem" for Christmas,

1868, three years after what to him was a profound experience of worshipping in the Church of the Nativity in Bethlehem. When asked about that memory, he stated that his soul was still singing from that incredible moment.

15. Which of these carols is based on a monastic chant?

    A. "What Child is This?"
    B. "While Shepherds Watched"
    C. "O Come, All Ye Faithful"
    D. "O Come, O Come, Emmanuel"

This carol is a thirteenth-century Latin carol based on the antiphonal chants which were sung in medieval monasteries on each of the seven nights leading up to Christmas Eve. Dr. John Mason Neale, a nineteenth-century Anglican priest, translated the verses of "O Come, O Come, Emmanuel," and his associate Thomas Helmore adapted the tune from a plainsong. It is argued that the familiar refrain ("Rejoice! Rejoice! Emmanuel," etc.) was also added at a later time to balance the stanzas, for it supposedly was not a part of the original carol.

16. "And there shall come forth a rod out of the stem of Jesse, and a Branch shall grow out of his roots." This passage from Isaiah 11:1 serves as the basis for which carol?

    A. "O Come, O Come, Emmanuel"
    B. "O Come, All Ye Faithful"
    C. "Lo, How a Rose E'er Blooming"
    D. "From Heaven Above to Earth I Come"

This lovely German carol first appeared in print in 1599, but is believed to be centuries older than that. A few years later in 1609, Michael Praetorius, a German composer and music publisher, harmonized the piece for sacred singing and titled it "Rosa Mystica" ("Mystic Rose"). Today we are familiar with the English version of "Lo, How a Rose E'er Blooming" through the translation made by the late-nineteenth-century American music scholar, Theodore Baker. This carol likens the birth of the Christ Child to the blooming of a fresh, young rose with all its purity: a Branch of Jesse, the father of King David, as Isaiah the prophet foretold in the Old Testament.

17. In 1868 the melody for which of these carols came to its composer in a dream?

    A. "O Little Town of Bethlehem"
    B. "I Saw Three Ships"
    C. "Good Christian Men, Rejoice"
    D. "The Holly and the Ivy"

A hint to the answer lies in the date, 1868, which also appeared a few questions back. Phillips Brooks, the Philadelphia minister who wrote the words to "O Little Town of Bethlehem," asked his church organist, Lewis Redner, to furnish the music for his poem which the children's Sunday school class would be singing at Christmas services. But Redner was unable to compose anything which pleased him until the eleventh hour, so to speak. Redner remarked that on the night before the children were to perform the carol, the music which we all now know came to him in a wondrous dream. And since that Christmas of 1868, "O Little Town of Bethlehem" has been a blessing to everyone who holds Christmastime most dear.

18. "Beautiful Star of Bethlehem" is an allegory in which the Star serves to:

A. Light the path to salvation through Christ.
B. Bring mankind to repentance of sins.
C. Encourage the Wise Men to persevere on their journey.
D. Be a beacon of faith for the poor in spirit.

Tennessee dairy farmer Robert Boyce, who wrote "Beautiful Star" in 1938, originally intended his simple hymn to be sung throughout the year. Yet its popular appeal through gospel, country, and bluegrass genres has bonded it to the Christmas season. In addition to guiding the Wise Men, the Star lights the path to salvation through Christ. Boyce said that it was God Who inspired him to write this hymn.

19. What is the more familiar English title of the Latin hymn, "Adeste Fideles"?

A. "Silent Night"
B. "From Heaven Above to Earth I Come"
C. "The First Nowell"
D. "O Come, All Ye Faithful"

In past eras, there was some controversy regarding the authorship of one of our most sacred carols. John F. Wade, a British scholar and music copyist living in France in the early 1740s, was originally thought merely to have copied or borrowed the text from Latin sources, whereas John Reading, a seventeenth-century English organist, was supposed to have contributed the music. Research in 1947 by Dom John Stéphan of Buckfast Abbey, Devon, England, however, supported Wade as the sole writer of the words and music to "Adeste Fideles." The complete carol as we know it today consists of seven stanzas: Wade's original four, two additional Latin stanzas contributed by a French clergyman, and an anonymous stanza of Gallic origin. In 1841, Frederick Oakley, canon of London's Westminster Abbey, made an initial translation of Wade's stanzas, which opened with "Ye faithful, approach ye." After his conversion to Roman Catholicism in 1852, Oakley made a second translation of only three stanzas, which opened with "O come, all ye faithful," by which words the carol is better known. William Brooke translated the remaining four verses and combined them with Oakley's.

20. In 1743, the joyous pealing of bells on Christmas Morning inspired Charles Wesley to write which of these carols?

    A. "I Heard the Bells on Christmas Day"
    B. "Angels We Have Heard on High"
    C. "Christmas Bells are Ringing"
    D. "Hark! The Herald Angels Sing"

Endeavoring to portray the joy of Christmas bells, the first two lines of Charles Wesley's famous poem originally read "Hark! How all the welkin [heaven] rings / 'Glory to the King of Kings.'" Feeling that such wording was a little too archaic, George Whitefield, one of Wesley's contemporaries, changed these lines in 1753 to "Hark! The herald angels sing: / 'Glory to the new-born King.'" Although Wesley had originally titled his poem "Hymn for Christmas Day," it has since become more popularly known by its altered first line. In 1856, William Cummings, an organist at England's Waltham Abbey, published his adaptation of Wesley's hymn text of 1743 to "God Is Light," a spirited chorus from Felix Mendelssohn's cantata, *Festgesang*. In 1840, Mendelssohn had written this cantata for ceremonies in Leipzig, which commemorated the 400th anniversary of printing press inventor Johann Gutenberg. Cummings' adaptation is the one most frequently sung today.

21. *The Milton Berle Show*, one of television's top comedy-variety shows of the 1950s, first introduced which of these children's novelty songs during the Christmas season of 1955?

> A. "All I Want for Christmas Is My Two Front Teeth"
> B. "Nuttin' for Christmas"
> C. "I Saw Mommy Kissing Santa Claus"
> D. "The Chipmunk Song (Christmas Don't Be Late)"

Written by Sid Tepper and Roy Bennett and sung by five-year-old Barry Gordon, the song summarizes the pranks and mischief a little boy has committed all year, which explains why he is getting "Nuttin' for Christmas." The pranks and misdeeds mentioned in the song were a compendium of those which Tepper's and Bennett's own children had committed at various times.

22. Which of these carols was originally written as a moral poem for children?

> A. "Good King Wenceslas"
> B. "I Saw Three Ships"
> C. "O Come, O Come, Emmanuel"
> D. "The Coventry Carol"

Anglican priest Dr. John Mason Neale wrote "Good King Wenceslas" in 1853 and centered his carol around that historical figure from the tenth century, Wenceslas, the benevolent and generous duke (not king) of Bohemia. And as much as his people loved him, many undoubtedly regarded him as their king. Neale chose Wenceslas as a role model for generosity all through the year, not just traditionally at Christmas. He chose for his musical setting "Tempus adest floridum," a thirteenth- or fourteenth-century Scandinavian spring song, which resided in a 1582 carol collection titled *Piae Cantiones*. Neale may never have set out to write a Christmas carol as such, but "Good King Wenceslas" definitely found its way into the season, probably because the carol's events occur on the feast day of St. Stephen, observed on December 26.

23. Which song is the only selection from a Broadway musical that has become a popular Christmas song?

    A. "White Chistmas"
    B. "We Need a Little Christmas"
    C. "Santa Claus Is Coming to Town"
    D. "Do You Hear What I Hear?"

Written in 1966 by Jerry Herman and set in New York City during the Great Depression, *Mame* revolves around the title character (originally played by Angela Lansbury), an eccentric woman with a youthful approach to life. Hard times are taking their toll on everyone's spirits. To dispel the doldrums, Mame inspires everyone to light the candles and deck the halls to the tune of "We Need a Little Christmas," despite the fact that Christmas itself is still a month away. The musical *Mame* was based on a play by Jerome Lawrence and Robert E. Lee as well as the novel by Patrick Dennis.

24. The legendary Bing Crosby recorded over 70 sacred and secular Christmas songs during his illustrious career. After he signed with Decca Records in 1934, which were the first two Christmas carols that he recorded for that label?

A. "White Christmas" and "The First Nowell"
B. "Jingle Bells" and "Santa Claus Is Coming to Town"
C. "Joy to the World" and "O Holy Night"
D. "Silent Night" and "Adeste Fideles"

At the suggestion of Decca's president, Jack Kapp, Crosby recorded "Silent Night" and "Adeste Fideles" in 1935. But Crosby did not feel comfortable about recording any sacred songs for profit, so he arranged for all proceeds to go to various charities. He kept that policy for the remainder of his recording career.

25. Which of these songs was the only Christmas hit of the rock and roll era to reach the #1 spot on the pop charts?

A. "Rockin' Around the Christmas Tree"
B. "Jingle Bell Rock"
C. "The Chipmunk Song (Christmas Don't Be Late)"
D. "The Little Drummer Boy"

You may be quite surprised, but of all the Christmas hits of the latter 1950s, it was "The Chipmunk Song" that rose to the #1 position on the charts in 1958. Remember those three cute chipmunks named Alvin, Theodore, and Simon? Ross Bagdasarian, Sr. (pseudonym David Seville) created this zoological trio and named them after three executives at Liberty Records. It was also Bagdasarian himself who created the high-pitched voices of the chipmunks by speeding up a recording of his own voice. The mention of a hula hoop in the song gives you a clue to its date, for hula hoops were the Christmas toy rage in the latter 1950s. This piece won three Grammys, one of which was for the best children's recording of 1958.

26. Which of these carols is a testimonial to the Christmas tree?

    A. "Cantique de Noël"
    B. "In dulci jubilo"
    C. "Vom Himmel hoch, da komm' ich her"
    D. "O Tannenbaum"

"O Fir Tree" is the literal German translation, but we know this traditional carol best as "O Christmas Tree." That the tradition of decorating trees at Christmastime arose in Germany is a most logical reason for why that country regards "O Tannenbaum" as one of its most beloved carols. Whereas verse 1 is of folk origin, verses 2 and 3 were contributed by the German poet Ernst Anschütz in 1824. The melody probably arose during the sixteenth or seventeenth century, although it did not appear in print until 1799, paired with lyrics unrelated to Christmas.

27. The only major Christmas ballet being performed today is:

    A. *Swan Lake*
    B. *Sleeping Beauty*
    C. *The Nutcracker*
    D. *Hansel and Gretel*

The first three choices are ballets with musical scores by Russian composer P. I. Tchaikovsky, and the last is an opera by German composer Engelbert Humperdinck. St. Petersburg's Director of Imperial Theatres commissioned Tchaikovsky to supply the musical score for a ballet, the subject of which was a German fairy tale, *The Nutcracker and the Mouse King*. Tchaikovsky, feeling that this story lacked drama as well as emotion, nevertheless completed his task and, through strains now so familiar, carried the story's principal character, Clara, into the fantasy of Christmas Eve and a dream world of sweets where the nutcracker was a prince. With original choreography by ballet-masters Marius Petipa and Lev Ivanov, *The Nutcracker* premiered at the Maryinsky Theatre in St. Petersburg on December 18, 1892. Despite Tchaikovsky's dissatisfaction with his work, performances of *The Nutcracker* have enormously complemented the holidays of untold millions, and annual performances have become a tradition throughout the world.

28. In 1863 the Reverend John F. Young translated three of the original six stanzas of the carol "Stille Nacht" into English. This carol is better known to us as:

    A. "We Three Kings"
    B. "Joy to the World"
    C. "Silent Night"
    D. "From Heaven Above to Earth I Come"

Father Joseph Mohr had originally penned six stanzas to what we know as "Silent Night," but Young, who later became the Episcopal bishop of Florida, only translated three of them (1, 2, and 6) into English. They remain the most familiar of the stanzas.

29. What was the name of the church in Oberndorf, Austria, where "Silent Night" first premiered on Christmas Eve, 1818?

    A. The Church of St. Nicholas
    B. The Church of the Holy Virgin
    C. The Church of St. Joseph
    D. The Church of the Immaculate Conception

The name of the church was mentioned in the answer to the first question in this chapter. Unfortunately, the original Church of St. Nicholas is no longer standing, but a monument to the memory of Father Mohr, Franz Gruber, and "Silent Night" has been erected at the original site.

30. Which one of these carols did the clergy initially denounce?

    A. "The First Nowell"
    B. "Angels We Have Heard on High"
    C. "O Holy Night"
    D. "While Shepherds Watched"

French poet Placide Cappeau of Roquemaure and composer Adolphe Adam of Paris certainly did not set out to anger church elders with their new carol, "Cantique de Noël," better known as "O Holy Night," written in 1847, but that's just what happened. After hearing its performance, the bishop of Paris condemned the carol as totally lacking in musical taste and religious spirit. But as popular as "O Holy Night" has become over the decades with its most inspirational message, the Church's initial reaction was quite puzzling. It is thought that such prejudice against the carol stemmed from the fact that neither Cappeau nor Adam seriously embraced Christianity, and that Adam, then a popular composer, wrote primarily for theatres, which were places of abomination to the Church. The American minister John S. Dwight was responsible for drawing up the English lyrics.

31. To some it may seem ironic, but Christmas carols have temporarily halted the pursuit of war on occasion. Such was the case with the Franco-Prussian War. On Christmas Eve, 1870, above the din of gunfire, one soldier was

heard singing this carol, which brought the battle to a halt:

    A. "Silent Night"
    B. "Angels We Have Heard on High"
    C. "It Came upon the Midnight Clear"
    D. "O Holy Night"

The war was raging outside Paris when, according to the story, a French soldier jumped out of his trench and began singing "Cantique de Noël" ("O Holy Night"). How he managed to be heard is a mystery, but his French comrades as well as the opposing Germans ceased fighting. One German then returned the "favor" with one of his own country's carols, "Vom Himmel hoch" ("From Heaven Above"). Unfortunately, the war resumed after Christmas. There have been similar stories with other carols. For example, in World War I during the Christmas of 1914, Germans along the Western Front sang "Stille Nacht" ("Silent Night") while the British troops opposite them joined in. Perhaps if they had kept on singing, they all would have just laid down their arms and walked away in peace.

32. About which of these songs did its composer comment, "Not only is it the best song I ever wrote, it's the best song *anybody* ever wrote"?

    A. "Adeste Fideles"
    B. "The Little Drummer Boy"
    C. "White Christmas"
    D. "Silent Night"

Hardly modest, Irving Berlin made this comment after having conceived "White Christmas" in January, 1940. Apparently Berlin was unable to read music, for he required the assistance of a musical arranger to provide a score, not only for "White Christmas," but for all of his other famous songs. As Berlin hummed the melody, the arranger would approximate the chords on the piano until Berlin was satisfied with the arrangement. The process was tedious and frustrating, to say the least.

33. Whose recording is the second largest-selling, contemporary Christmas song in the world?

    A. Bing Crosby: "Jingle Bells"
    B. Gene Autry: "Rudolph, the Red-Nosed Reindeer"
    C. Elvis Presley: "Here Comes Santa Claus"
    D. Andy Williams: "The Most Wonderful Time of the Year"

It has sold over twelve million copies alone, not to mention the countless numbers of other artists who have contributed their renditions of "Rudolph." Thus, Gene Autry's original recording in 1949 ranks number two in sales behind Bing Crosby's recording of "White Christmas," which has sold over thirty million copies alone.

34. Which state in the USA would most appreciate the song "Mele Kalikimaka" ("Merry Christmas") by R. Alex Anderson?

    A. Alaska
    B. New Mexico
    C. Utah
    D. Hawaii

Residing in Hawaii gave part-time songwriter Anderson the chance to create a totally different kind of Christmas tune, one which strongly contrasted with the snow-and-sleigh themes of other contemporary songs.

His little tune informs us that Christmas on the islands will always be sunny, green, and bright, and the palm trees will sway on Christmas Day. Bing Crosby and The Andrews Sisters recorded this delightful tune in 1950.

35. On December 17, 1965, which recording did NASA play at the request of Gemini 7 astronauts Frank Borman and James Lovell as they returned to earth?

    A. "White Christmas"
    B. "Sleigh Ride"
    C. "I'll Be Home for Christmas"
    D. "Home for the Holidays"

Borman and Lovell specifically requested Bing Crosby's 1943 recording of "I'll Be Home for Christmas" as they returned to earth after having completed 206 orbits. People in the Armed Forces during World War II often spent Christmas in places far removed from home and loved ones. That's why "I'll Be Home for Christmas" had such special meaning, for it promised the family waiting back home that, even if their father, mother, son, or daughter couldn't physically be with them for Christmas, they would still be with them in their dreams. Written by Walter Kent, Kim Gannon, and Buck Ram in 1943, one of their friends got Crosby interested, who then made the first recording of this tender ballad in that same year.

Questions 36–50 are also of the multiple choice type, except that now they get a little tougher, because these questions all have <u>more than one correct answer</u>. Two, three, or even all four answers may be correct, in any combination. Take a few deep breaths and dive in!

36. If not for the influence of spouses, some of our cherished, holiday classics would never have become known

to us. Which of the following celebrities' spouses persuaded them to introduce now-famous tunes?

    A. Ernest Tubb
    B. Gene Autry
    C. Johnny Marks
    D. Eddie Cantor

Although Gene Autry initially was not very impressed with Johnny Marks's new tune, "Rudolph, the Red-Nosed Reindeer," his wife Ina loved it and persuaded him to make a recording. As she did with "Rudolph," Ina also urged him to record "Frosty the Snowman," which he did in 1951.

Singer/comedian Eddie Cantor was a popular radio personality back in the 1930s when he received a pitch from Haven Gillespie and J. Fred Coots regarding their new tune, "Santa Claus Is Coming to Town." Although they had written the tune in 1932, publishers initially were not interested. Cantor also rejected the song, yet it appealed to his wife, who convinced him to sing it on his radio program just before Thanksgiving, 1934. The most popular rendition has been the recording made in 1943 by Bing Crosby with The Andrews Sisters.

37. In which of the following classics do the events occur on Christmas Eve?

    A. Tchaikovsky's *The Nutcracker*
    B. Humperdinck's *Hansel and Gretel*
    C. Puccini's *La Boheme*
    D. Liszt's *Weihnachtsbaum* (*Christmas Tree*)

Of the choices listed, only *The Nutcracker* ballet revolves entirely around Christmas Eve. Based on the fairy tale by the Brothers Grimm, *Hansel and Gretel* is an opera which has nothing to do with Christmas as such, yet its fantasy is an ideal companion to the mystique of Santa. Whereas Christmas Eve is the setting for the first two acts of the opera *La Boheme*, the holiday is only incidental to the opera's principal theme. Not a stage production, *Weihnachtsbaum* instead is Hungarian composer Franz Liszt's arrangement of twelve hymns and carols for piano solo.

38. *The Nutcracker* ballet, in part, features certain national dances which symbolize different beverages, and these entertain Clara with beautiful choreography in the Kingdom of Sweets. Which beverages and national dances are properly paired?

   A. "Spanish Dance" symbolizes hot chocolate.
   B. "Russian Trepak" symbolizes milk.
   C. "Chinese Dance" symbolizes tea.
   D. "Arab Dance" symbolizes coffee.

All are paired correctly except the "Trepak," which has no specific symbolism in this ballet.

39. Which of these statements describe the lyrics to "Do You Hear What I Hear?"

   A. The night wind sees a star with a tail as big as a kite.
   B. The lamb hears a voice as big as the sea.
   C. The shepherd boy knows that a Child shivers in the cold.
   D. The king calls for people everywhere to pray for peace.

This contemporary retelling of the Nativity story passes first from the elements, then to an animal, then to a child, then to an adult, then to all humanity. All of the statements are correct.

40. The musical score for the first performance of "Silent Night" on Christmas Eve, 1818, did not include a part for the church organ, because it was supposedly damaged. For whom or what did composer Franz Gruber score this carol?

   A. Tenor
   B. Bass
   C. Guitar
   D. Choir

While playing a guitar, Father Joseph Mohr sang tenor, Gruber sang bass, and the choir joined in only for the two-line refrain which followed each stanza. The answer to a previous question revealed all this information.

41. Which of these reindeer names appear in "Here Comes Santa Claus"?

   A. Prancer
   B. Vixen
   C. Donder
   D. Blitzen

Two years before his smash hit "Rudolph," Gene Autry had scored another hit with "Here Comes Santa Claus," which he had written in 1947 with Oakley Haldeman, a friend who also managed his music publishing company. Vixen and Blitzen are the token reindeer mentioned.

42. A taste for pumpkin pie pops up in which of these favorites?

   A. "Home for the Holidays"
   B. "Rockin' Around the Christmas Tree"
   C. "Over the River and Through the Woods"
   D. "Jingle Bells"

Hearts turn to home for Christmastime and the appeal of love, warmth, good cheer, and pumpkin pie. As the title of Robert Allen's and Al Stillman's 1954 hit sums it all up, "(There's No Place Like) Home for the Holidays."

Back in the 1950s, when rock and roll music dominated every teenage dance party, or "hop," Christmas was no exception, and "Rudolph" writer Johnny Marks in 1958 created just the tune for a Christmas hop, "Rockin' Around the Christmas Tree." After the dancing comes pumpkin pie, carols, and holiday sentiment.

Although originally associated with Thanksgiving, "Over the River and Through the Woods" has since taken on the Christmas spirit as well. Because an old-fashioned sleigh ride to the grandparents' house for a grand feast is a delight with either holiday, the words "Thanksgiving Day" or "Christmas Day" in verse two are easily substituted for the appropriate occasion. Then there are cheers for the pudding and the pumpkin pie. The lyrics originated as a poem written in 1844 by Lydia Maria Child of Medford, Massachusetts, which she originally titled "A Boy's Thanksgiving Day." The composer of the musical setting remains anonymous. There is no reference to pumpkin pie in "Jingle Bells."

43. Which of these people had a hand in creating or promoting "Blue Christmas"?

   A. Billy Hayes
   B. Jay Johnson
   C. Ernest Tubb

D. Elvis Presley

"Blue Christmas" had surfaced in 1948 after songwriters Billy Hayes and Jay Johnson found a way to work the theme of lost love and "blue" emotions into Christmas, but the song just didn't go anywhere until Ernest Tubb turned it into a country hit in 1949. A variety of other recorded versions have appeared, including those by Elvis Presley, Johnny Cash, and Dean Martin, but "Blue Christmas" has remained country all the way.

44. If you're looking for a list of many secular things that make Christmas so special, you'll find it in "Christmas Is," a 1966 favorite by Percy Faith and Spence Maxwell. Which of these are included on that list?

    A. Sleigh bells, sharing, holly, and caring
    B. Memories of the children to keep
    C. A world as bright as tinsel
    D. A time when wishes come true

According to the lyrics, Christmas is not only a time for all of the above, it is also a time for warm carols and children jumping into bed to wait for Santa. Johnny Mathis (1971) and Tom T. Hall (1979) made two of the first vocal recordings of the song. As comforting as the lyrics are, they, as do many other popular Christmas songs of the twentieth century, seem to ignore the most important reason for Christmas, and that is Jesus Christ.

45. What do "Jingle Bell Rock" and "Rockin' Around the Christmas Tree" have in common?

    A. Rock and roll music
    B. Johnny Marks
    C. A one-horse sleigh
    D. A Christmas "hop"

Whereas both songs feature the rock and roll theme of the 1950s and mention "hops" (teenage dance gatherings at the time), "Rockin' Around the Christmas Tree" was the 1958 creation of Johnny Marks. Young Brenda Lee's recording made it the top Christmas hit of 1960. In 1957, Joe Beal and Jim Boothe wrote "Jingle Bell Rock," a modern sleighing song complete with jingling bells, snow, and a one-horse sleigh. When you think about it, "Jingle Bell Rock" is merely a contemporary version of "Jingle Bells" with a rock gimmick. Rocker Bobby Helms's recording made it the top Christmas hit of 1957.

46. Which of these phrases or statements apply to "I Heard the Bells on Christmas Day"?

    A. It derives from a poem originally titled "Rejoice, Ye Merry Bells."

    B. Words by Henry Wadsworth Longfellow, music by Johnny Marks

    C. Lyrics include the line "Hate is wrong and mocks the strong."

    D. God is not dead, and the right shall prevail.

To soften his despair following his wife's death in 1861, American poet Longfellow published a poem titled "Christmas Bells" in 1867. At first bitter and filled with hate toward God after losing his wife, Longfellow described how the pealing of Christmas bells beckoned him to abandon his feeling that "hate is *strong* and mocks the *song*" of the Nativity. God is indeed not dead, and, according to the lyrics, "The wrong shall fail, the right prevail." Longfellow's poem subsequently became a carol that was initially sung to the tune of "Waltham," written in 1872 by English organist John Baptiste Calkin. But it was Christmas songwriter Johnny Marks who, in 1956, gave us the song "I Heard the Bells on Christmas Day" by adapting Longfellow's words and composing the more familiar tune that we now sing.

47. Which of these people were initially associated with the bluegrass tune "Christmas Time's A-Coming"?

    A. Bill Monroe
    B. Tex Logan
    C. Dolly Parton
    D. Patsy Cline

"Christmas Time's A-Coming" is considered to be the best known of bluegrass Christmas songs. Having grown up savoring the sounds of Bill Monroe and the Blue Grass Boys in the 1940s, Tex Logan became proficient on the "fiddle" and played with various country groups while he worked on a Ph.D. degree in electrical engineering at the Massachusetts Institute of Technology. Although he wrote "Christmas Time's A-Coming" in 1949 specifically with Bill Monroe in mind, he wasn't able to pitch it to Monroe, whom he had never met, until 1951. Logan's band, along with a number of other big-name country stars, including Monroe, had completed a country concert in Baltimore during the fall of that year. Backstage, Logan played "Christmas Time's A-Coming" for Monroe, who agreed on the spot to record it in time for the Christmas sales. It is thought that Logan borrowed the tune for his song from an earlier one titled "Christmas Time Will Soon Be Over," which a celebrity known as Fiddlin' John Carson had recorded in 1927.

48. Which of these often-sung carols are wassailing songs that came to us from medieval England?

A. "We Wish You a Merry Christmas"
B. "Here We Come A-Caroling"
C. "Deck the Halls"
D. "God Rest Ye Merry, Gentlemen"

Traveling about in groups to announce news or the time, and especially to wish everyone "wes hael" ("be well," hence our word "wassail") at Christmastime, the "Waits" of medieval England also added singing to their duties of well-wishing. These people acquired the name of Waits because, "wassailing" from door to door with their merry melodies, they waited to see if proprietors would favor them with some little gift in the way of money, food, or beverage. And at least three of their more popular holiday melodies have survived from that time period. Of the four traditional carols listed, only "Deck the Halls" is not believed to have a medieval birth. While the tune derives from a Welsh traditional dance-carol, the lyrics are anonymous, possibly from nineteenth-century America.

49. A particularly popular Christmas legend states that, because of their service to the Christ Child at His birth, animals are empowered with speech at midnight on Christmas Eve. "The Friendly Beasts," a traditional, twelfth-century carol from England, is based on the legend, for in it certain animals recite the gifts which they give to Mary and the Christ Child. Which animals and gifts are properly paired?

A. The donkey's gift is to carry Mary to Bethlehem.
B. The cow's gift is her manger and hay.
C. The sheep's gift is his wool for a blanket.
D. The dove's gift is to coo Jesus to sleep.
E. The camel's gift is in the Wise Men's pack.

Even if you are totally unfamiliar with this carol, the gifts as listed are quite appropriate for each animal. According to another medieval legend, stable animals carry on a dialogue in Latin: the rooster crows, "Christus natus est" ("Christ is born"); the raven, "Quando?" ("When?"); the crow, "haec nocte" ("This night"); the ox, "Ubi?" ("Where?"); the lamb, "Bethlehem;" the ass, "Eamus" ("Let us go").

50. Americans wrote which of the following holiday standards?

    A. "It Came Upon the Midnight Clear"
    B. "O Little Town of Bethlehem"
    C. "Up on the Housetop"
    D. "We Three Kings"

Edmund H. Sears was a young minister from Massachusetts when he published one of his early poems, "It Came Upon the Midnight Clear," in *The Christian Register*, a church periodical, in 1849. It gained rapid popularity and was eventually adapted to a melody by Richard S. Willis, a music critic and composer in New York City, which he had included in his *Church Chorals and Choir Studies* of 1850.

Brooks and Redner wrote "O Little Town of Bethlehem," as you recall.

"Up on the Housetop" came to us from Ohio composer Benjamin R. Hanby. First published in 1866 under the title of "Santa Claus," it must have taken some inspiration from the poem "A Visit from St. Nicholas" ("Twas the Night Before Christmas"), for it relates a similar theme of Santa's landing on the roof, jumping down the chimney, and bringing lots of goodies for children.

An instructor of church music, the Reverend John H. Hopkins composed "We Three Kings" for an elaborate Christmas pageant held in 1857 at New York City's Episcopal General Theological Seminary. His carol accompanied the performance of the Wise Men in this pageant.

Questions 51–61: "Odd Man Out." In this most challenging format, each question consists of a group of four names, titles, objects, or phrases. Three of those within each group share something in common, regarding Christmas music, while the remaining one does not. Choose the <u>one</u> which does <u>not</u> belong, then state what the other three share in common. Here's a general example: In the group Piano - Organ - Violin - Dog, Dog does not belong, because the other three are all musical instruments.

51. A. Yellow
    B. Blue
    C. Red
    D. White

There are actually two correct answers. If you discarded "yellow," the other three are colors that appear in the titles of familiar Christmas songs: "Blue Christmas;" "Rudolph, the Red-Nosed Reindeer;" and "White Christmas." If you discarded "white," the other three are the colors that Nellie wants to see in her box of paints in the children's favorite, "Jolly Ole St. Nicholas."

52. A. "The Coventry Carol"
    B. "Silent Night"
    C. 1818
    D. Handel's *Messiah*

Coincidence or fate, "Silent Night" and *Messiah* both had debuts of a kind in 1818. "Silent Night" had its first performance on Christmas Eve in Oberndorf, Austria, and *Messiah* had its first *full* performance in the USA on Christmas Day, 1818, in Boston. It should be noted, however, that excerpts from *Messiah* had been played in New York in 1770. Discard A.

53. A. "Frosty the Snowman"
    B. "Winter Wonderland"
    C. "Jingle Bells"
    D. "Silent Night"

The first three are all secular Christmas songs with themes of snow, sleighing, and winter games, whereas "Silent Night" is a sacred carol. Through the years, these first three songs have come to be associated with Christmas, yet their themes do not center upon Christmas at all, in contrast to "Silent Night," which is the musical epitome of Christmas. Among other favorites, almost every Christmas album will feature a rendition of Felix Bernard's and Dick Smith's peppy tune of 1934, "Winter Wonderland," which Guy Lombardo and His Royal Canadians introduced that same year. In 1946, two recordings of this tune, one by The Andrews Sisters with Guy Lombardo's band, the other by Perry Como, became bestsellers. For reasons that will become obvious, comments about "Frosty the Snowman" appear with the next question.

54. A. "White Christmas"
    B. "Frosty the Snowman"
    C. "Here Comes Santa Claus"
    D. "Rudolph, the Red-Nosed Reindeer"

The last three songs have Gene Autry in common, for he was the first to record them, having written "Here Comes Santa Claus" as well. You'll recall that Bing Crosby first recorded "White Christmas." Since its appearance in 1950, "Frosty the Snowman" has appealed to the young and young-at-heart alike, with its tale of a talking snowman who runs and plays with children, until he melts away. Written by Steve Nelson and Walter E. "Jack" Rollins, "Frosty" became a legend with Gene Autry's recording that same year, and the Frosty character has been featured in several animated productions for television.

55. A. "Caroling, Caroling"
    B. "Some Children See Him"
    C. "The Star Carol"
    D. "Gesu Bambino"

The first three are part of the collection known as the Alfred Burt Carols. This designation applies to fifteen carols, the music for which was composed by American jazz trumpeter Alfred S. Burt, with lyrics by his minister-father, Bates G. Burt, until the latter's death in 1948. Thereafter, a family friend, organist Wihla Hutson, served as lyricist. Since 1922, Bates Burt had pursued his annual tradition of composing an original carol and sending out copies as Christmas "cards" to friends, and Alfred joined the project in 1942. The final work, "The Star Carol," was completed just four days prior to Alfred's untimely death in 1954 at the age of 33. All of the Alfred Burt Carols were published later that same year, including a Columbia recording titled *The Christmas Mood*. The remaining Alfred Burt Carols are: "Ah, Bleak and Chill;" "All on a Christmas Morning;" "Carol of the Mother;" "Christ in the Stranger's Guise;" "Christmas Cometh Caroling;" "Come, Dear Children;" "Jesu Parvule;" "Nigh Bethlehem;" "O Hearken Ye;" "This Is Christmas;" "We'll Dress the House;" and "What Are the Signs?" Contrary to Burt's ties to jazz, his carols manifest deep, simple reverence and often a quick-spirited, medieval flair.

"Gesu Bambino" ("The Infant Jesus"), which does not belong with this group, is the best-known composition of the Italian-American organist and composer, Pietro A. Yon (1886–1943). Applying metaphorical attributes to the Christ Child, the carol closes each verse with the familiar refrain to the carol "Adeste Fideles."

56. A. "Nuttin' for Christmas"
    B. "Suzy Snowflake"
    C. Songwriters Roy Bennett and Sid Tepper
    D. Songwriters Sammy Cahn and Jule Styne

Bennett and Tepper collaborated on both songs, writing "Suzy Snowflake" in 1951 and "Nuttin' for Christmas" in 1955. "Suzy Snowflake" was dedicated to Tepper's baby daughter, Susan, and you'll recall that the children of both songwriters had actually committed a number of pranks which were reproduced in "Nuttin' for Christmas." Songwriters Cahn and Styne do not belong in this group.

57. A. "Flow Gently, Sweet Afton"
    B. James R. Murray
    C. Adolphe Adam
    D. Over forty musical settings

The carol "Away in a Manger" has in common A, B, and D. The words to the first two verses of this carol originally appeared in *Little Children's Book for Schools and Families*, a Sunday school collection which the Evangelical Lutheran Church had published in Philadelphia in 1885. The text then appeared two years later with music in a publication edited by James R. Murray, titled *Dainty Songs for Little Lads and Lasses*. Although Murray supplied the musical setting there, he attributed the lyrics to Martin Luther under the heading "Luther's Cradle Hymn." It would appear that he borrowed the 1885 text and, idolizing Luther, gave him undue credit, much in the same way that Lowell Mason did with Handel and "Joy to the World." Research in 1945 concluded that the first two verses originated as an anonymous poem taken from a series of American Lutheran children's dramatic presentations which, in 1883, honored the 400th anniversary of Luther's birth. By 1892, the carol had acquired a third anonymous verse. There have been over forty musical settings to "Away in a Manger," the two most popular being Murray's and the tune to the Scottish poem "Flow Gently, Sweet Afton." You recall that Adolphe Adam wrote the music to "O Holy Night."

58. A. James Montgomery
    B. "In dulci jubilo" ("In Sweet Jubilation")
    C. "News! News! / Peace! Peace! / Joy! Joy!"
    D. Dr. John Mason Neale

"Good Christian Men, Rejoice," which has in common B, C, and D, is the English title for the German macaronic carol "In dulci jubilo." It is macaronic by virtue of the fact that the verses mix a vernacular language with Latin phrases. This carol is attributed to the Dominican monk Heinrich Suso, who in 1328 claimed that a company of angels visited him and engaged him in joyous dancing to a tune which began as "In dulci jubilo." In 1853, the Anglican priest, Dr. John Mason Neale, discovered a Swedish-Latin version of the carol in the 1582 collection, *Piae Cantiones*, and provided the English translation, with the exception that he omitted the Latin phrases. Neale's associate, Thomas Helmore, transcribed the music and mistook two short notes for ones of longer duration. Neale then adjusted the lyrics by adding a two-word phrase to each verse as an exclamation, which accounts for the "News! News!" etc.

Not belonging to this group is James Montgomery, a journalist living in Sheffield, England, who penned "Angels, from the Realms of Glory" for the Christmas Eve edition of his newspaper, *The Iris*, in 1816. In 1866 Henry Smart, a London organist, provided the musical setting (originally titled "Regent Square") which we know today.

59. A. "Go Tell It on the Mountain"
    B. "The Little Drummer Boy"
    C. "Mary's Little Boy Child"
    D. "Sweet Little Jesus Boy"

Christmas favorites of African American origin are A, C, and D. Whereas some contend that "Go Tell It on the Mountain" arose as an anonymous slave song in the early 1800s, others attribute it to John Wesley Work, Jr. (1871–1925), an African American instructor of Greek and Latin at Fisk University in Nashville, Tennessee. According to the Reader's Digest Association, however, the Jubilee Singers of Fisk University introduced "Go Tell It on the Mountain" in 1879, and it became a popular spiritual through the Singers' tours of the USA and Europe. Work's authorship remains uncertain.

Christmas takes on the calypso flavor of the West Indies with "Mary's Little Boy Child," written by African American songwriter Jester Hairston in 1956. Popularized by Harry Belafonte's top Christmas recording that same year, this piece is a rhythmic narrative of the Nativity.

Christmas Eve, 1932, found African American songwriter Robert MacGimsey in a plaintive mood in New York City when he wrote the lullaby "Sweet Little Jesus Boy."

Christ is born lowly and comes to save the world, but everyone casts Him away, because "we didn't know who You was."

Harry Simeone, Katherine Davis, and Henry Onorati re-worked Davis's original 1941 "Carol of the Drum" and changed the title to "The Little Drummer Boy" in 1958. The definitive recording by the Harry Simeone Chorale appeared the same year. In this classic tune, a poor little boy's only gift to the Christ Child is the music which he plays on his drum. A similar but much older theme is found in the Burgundian traditional carol, "Pat-a-Pan," which features two boys playing the flute and drum as instruments of praise.

60. A. "The Christmas Song"
    B. "Let It Snow! Let It Snow! Let It Snow!"
    C. "Jingle Bells"
    D. "Sleigh Ride"

With the exception of C, which was written in the nineteenth century, the other three were written during the twentieth century during summer heat waves at that. On the other hand, you could eliminate A, the lyrics of which mention nothing about snow, whereas those of B, C, and D do.

Conjuring up the most pleasant scenes, thoughts, and aromas of Christmastime, "The Christmas Song" ranks close to "White Christmas" in conveying the nostalgia of the season. Written by Mel Torme and Robert Wells in 1946, it became a most popular addition to the Christmas repertoire with Nat "King" Cole's recording in the same year. Suffering from summer heat and trying to cool off mentally, Wells jotted down some wintry remembrances. His list began with chestnuts, which his mother had used to stuff the Christmas turkey. "The Christmas Song" is a compendium of those remembrances.

Rejecting cold drinks or a run to the beach, songwriters Sammy Cahn and Jule Styne plunged into the cooling depths of a winter song and created "Let It Snow!" during the summer heat wave of 1945. In their opinion, that was the best way to cool off. Vaughn Monroe's recording made it the top Christmas song that same year.

Leroy Anderson, an arranger for The Boston Pops Orchestra, found himself in a similar situation three years later when he wrote "Sleigh Ride" during the miserable August heat of 1948. He originally scored the piece for orchestra only, and The Boston Pops with conductor Arthur Fiedler first introduced live audiences to it, with all the sleigh bells, horse clip-clops, and other marvelous sound effects that Anderson had inserted into his masterpiece of wintry imagery. The Boston Pops first recorded "Sleigh Ride" in 1949. Although Mitchell Parish added lyrics a year later, orchestral renditions alone still provide for a much superior performance today.

61. A. Candy canes abound, and silver lanes are aglow.
  B. The five-and-ten is glistening once again.
  C. Jack Frost nips at your nose.
  D. Holly hangs on your front door.

Three sure signs of Christmas are A, B, and D as mentioned in "It's Beginning to Look Like Christmas." Written in 1951 by Meredith Willson, of *The Music Man* fame, this song paints a merry scene as the signs of Christmas spring up everywhere. And with all the children's excitement, it will be a delight to parents when their little ones are back in school again. The concept of Jack Frost nipping at your nose is depicted in "The Christmas Song," which doesn't belong in this group.

For questions 62–73, fill in the blanks or provide short answers.

62. In 1741 a composer created a monumental work of music, portions of which are often performed at Christmastime. Just after completing one particular selection from that work, the composer claimed to have seen all Heaven before him and the Great God Himself.

    A. Name the composer.
    B. Name the piece that he had just completed.
    C. Name the major work that featured that piece.

    G. F. Handel had just completed the "Hallelujah Chorus" from his oratorio *Messiah*. This title often is mistakenly rendered as *The Messiah*.

63. The horse's name in "Jingle Bells" is (A) _____, and the name of the person who is "seated by my side" in verse two is (B) _____.

    Actually, the horse's name is *not* specifically mentioned. At one time, it was thought that "Bobtail" was the name, but the lyrics only read "bells on bobtail ring . . ." The word "bobtail" is not capitalized, indicating that it is not the horse's name, only a horse with a bobtail. "Miss Fannie Bright" is "seated by my side."

64. What legend about the three Wise Men serves as the basis for the English carol "I Saw Three Ships"?

    After their deaths, legend holds that the remains of the three Wise Men eventually came to rest in Cologne Cathedral in the twelfth century. Some versions of the carol depict three ships sailing up the Rhine River to Cologne, each one bearing the skull of a Wise Man. Because of this rather somber picture, later versions have the ships bearing "Our Savior Christ and His Lady [the Virgin Mary]." Over the centuries, other interpretations of the three ships have included their representing the Father, Son, and Holy Ghost; faith, hope, and charity, and so forth. Many variant versions of lyrics and tunes exist, the earliest of which was published in 1666.

65. What three things do "Santa Claus Is Coming to Town" and "Rudolph, the Red-Nosed Reindeer" have in common?

One, both mention Santa Claus and his reindeer. Two, the celebrities who first introduced them (Gene Autry for "Rudolph" and Eddie Cantor for "Santa Claus Is Coming to Town") had initial misgivings and only yielded to their wives' persuasions. Three, believing that so-called "kiddie tunes" wouldn't sell, publishers initially rejected both songs. How wrong they were!

66. According to the lyrics to "I Saw Mommy Kissing Santa Claus:"

   A. What is the name of the little boy who spies his mother kissing Santa?
   B. To whom does he tell his "secret"?
   C. Where does he see Mommy kissing Santa?

"Little Johnny" confides to his teddy bear that he saw mommy kissing Santa "underneath the mistletoe." A child peeks a little at Santa on Christmas Eve and draws some innocent conclusions. If you want that mirthful innocence conveyed in your song, have a child sing it. And that's just what British songwriter Tommie Connor arranged with twelve-year-old Jimmy Boyd, who first introduced this song on Frank Sinatra's television variety show in 1952. A recording contract shortly followed with Columbia Records, which, at that time, made Jimmy the youngest artist to record a top Christmas song. It sold over 2.5 million copies.

67. Drawing their subjects from events in the Gospels, "mystery plays" were quite popular during the Middle Ages and were often sponsored by various trade guilds. The Guild of the Shearmen and Tailors sponsored one such play about the life of Christ. What famous carol arose from the Nativity segment of that play and is still sung today?

   The Shearmen and Tailors pageant comprised a portion of the Coventry Plays, an annual performance given in Coventry, England, on the Feast of Corpus Christi. Although these plays are believed to date from 1392, the oldest known manuscript of dialogue alone dates from 1534, the transcription work of a Robert Croo. Initially, the pageant songs were handed down in folk fashion, but in 1591, a Thomas Mawdyke added them to Croo's manuscript. Recalling that "The Coventry Carol" is a lament over the Slaughter of the Innocents, few carols today address as dark an issue as does this carol.

68. "While Shepherds Watched Their Flocks by Night" is an adaptation of the Nativity story by English poet Nahum Tate and is usually sung to an aria from *Cyrus, King of Persia*, an opera by which famous German-born composer?

   Nahum Tate, collaborating with Nicholas Brady, published his adaptation of "While Shepherds Watched" in 1700. Of the scores of musical settings that have been used for this carol, the one most commonly sung in the USA is from G. F. Handel's opera, *Cyrus*. Another popular setting is "Winchester Old," an anonymous, sixteenth-century English tune.

69. In March of 1892, Russian composer P. I. Tchaikovsky was working on a large-scale musical production and apparently forgot that he had previously committed himself to conducting another concert at that time. Having composed no music expressly for the occasion, he bailed himself out by compiling eight pieces from this unfinished work and presented them in a concert on March 19 in St. Petersburg. By what name do we now know this collection of holiday pieces?

We know the collection as *The Nutcracker Suite*. Although Tchaikovsky completed *The Nutcracker* ballet, of which the suite constitutes a small part, in April of 1892, the ballet's premiere performance in St. Petersburg was delayed until December of that year to coincide with Christmas. Performances of the complete ballet are now holiday traditions around the world, yet the *Suite* remains the most familiar sampling of this classic.

70. And speaking of *The Nutcracker Suite*, here's your chance to arrange its eight pieces in the order in which they are performed. Beside each piece, indicate its number in the *Suite*.

    A. "Arab Dance" _____
    B. "Waltz of the Flowers" _____
    C. "Miniature Overture" _____
    D. "Chinese Dance" _____
    E. "Dance of the Sugar-Plum Fairy" _____
    F. "March" _____
    G. "Russian Trepak" _____
    H. "Dance of the Reed Pipes" _____

A-5; B-8; C-1; D-6; E-3; F-2; G-4; H-7. Bear in mind that, with the exception of the "Miniature Overture," these pieces do not appear in the same order in performances of the ballet. Whereas the "March" accompanies the children's entrance in Act I, the other pieces appear in the middle and latter parts of Act II as follows: "Arab Dance," "Chinese Dance," "Russian Trepak," and "Dance of the Reed Pipes" (sometimes called "Dance of the Shepherds"). Between this latter piece and "Waltz of the Flowers" is "Mother Gigogne" (not included in the *Suite*) followed by "Dance of the Sugar-Plum Fairy," the second of two *pas de deux* variations.

71. What unique feature sets "Jingle Bell Rock" apart from all other popular Christmas songs?

"Jingle Bell Rock" was the first song to blend the rock and roll style with Christmas. After rocker Bobby Helms introduced this hit in 1957, other holiday tunes with a similar flair began to appear, among them "Rockin' Around the Christmas Tree" in the following year.

72. How did "Here Comes Santa Claus" acquire its title?

Gene Autry provided a first-hand account in his autobiography *Back in the Saddle Again*. In 1946 Autry, riding his horse Champion, served as the grand marshal for the annual Hollywood Christmas parade, which proceeded along Hollywood Boulevard. Some distance ahead of Santa's float, Autry had reached a certain section of the route known to local merchants as "Santa Claus Lane," when he heard throngs of children shouting from the sidelines, "Here comes Santa Claus!" With Santa Claus Lane right there, and with children unwittingly yet prophetically shouting a new song title, Autry must have had the song arranged in his head by the end of the parade. Recorded in 1947, "Here Comes Santa Claus" was Autry's first Christmas release.

73. When country music's Eddy Arnold teamed up with Jenny Lou Carson in 1949, they gave us "C-H-R-I-S-T-M-A-S," a song that teaches the true meaning of Christmas by associating each letter in "Christmas" with a significant part of the season. Beside each of those letters below, fill in the corresponding symbols from the song. The "C" is completed for you as an example.

C: _____ Christ Child _____
H: _____
R: _____
I: _____
S: _____
T: _____
M: _____
A: _____
S: _____

"H" for the herald angels; "R" for the Redeemer; "I" for Israel; "S" for the Star that guided the Wise Men; "T" for the three Wise Men; "M" for the manger; "A" for all that Christ means; "S" for the shepherds.

For questions 74–89, determine whether each statement is true or false. Answers and comments follow this group.

74. In addition to marshmallows, the lyrics to "A Marshmallow World" liken a snowy winter to whipped cream and sugar dates.

75. When Nat "King" Cole recorded "The Christmas Song" in 1946, he became the first African American to introduce an American Christmas standard.

76. 1950s recording star Brenda Lee was only six years old when she popularized "Rockin' Around the Christmas Tree" with her 1958 recording.

77. Burl Ives made "A Holly Jolly Christmas" quite popular when he first sang it in the 1964 made-for-television animated cartoon, *Santa Claus Is Coming to Town*.

78. The big band of Guy Lombardo and His Royal Canadians first introduced "Winter Wonderland" in 1934 and also backed up The Andrews Sisters for their recorded rendition of the same song in 1946.

79. Oddly, when Eddie Cantor first introduced "Santa Claus Is Coming to Town" on his radio show in 1934, it was not at Christmastime but during the week before Thanksgiving.

80. "Carol of the Bells" is also known as "The Moravian Carol."

81. "Christmas in Killarney" is patterned after an Irish jig.

82. "The Christmas Song" is also known by its first line, "Chestnuts Roasting on an Open Fire."

83. The words to "Joy to the World" are based on Psalm 98:4–9.

84. "The First Nowell" depicts the angels' glad tidings to the shepherds and contains a Latin refrain which translates as "Glory to God in the highest."

85. Irving Berlin is considered to be the most prolific writer of Christmas music in the twentieth century.

86. "What Child is This?" is sung to the English folk tune of "Greensleeves."

87. The Jimmy Dorsey Orchestra provided the musical back-up for Bing Crosby when he first recorded "White Christmas" in 1942.

88. Hearing how Rudolph's peers ostracized him because of his bright, red nose, Ina Autry, Gene Autry's wife, was moved with compassion because the song reminded her of "The Ugly Duckling" fairy tale by Hans Christian Andersen.

89. With their New Year's Eve radio broadcast of 1929, Guy Lombardo and His Royal Canadians first popularized "Auld Lang Syne" as the song to close out the old year and welcome the new.

Answers to 74–89 (if false, see comments):

74-True; 75-True; 76-False; 77-False; 78-True; 79-True; 80-False; 81-True; 82-True; 83-True; 84-False; 85-False; 86-True; 87-False; 88-True; 89-True.

Comments:

"A Marshmallow World," written by Carl Sigman and Peter DeRose in 1949, does not mention Christmas, yet its bubbly portrayal of winter playfulness makes it a charming addition to the season's repertoire of sleigh-and-snow songs. Bing Crosby, Vic Damone, Arthur Godfrey, and Vaughn Monroe all recorded the song in 1950. But of those, only Crosby's recording made the charts.

Brenda Lee recorded "Rockin' Around the Christmas Tree" at the age of 13.

Burl Ives popularized "A Holly Jolly Christmas" in *Rudolph, the Red-Nosed Reindeer* in 1964.

"Carol of the Bells" is also known as "The Ukrainian Carol." It is based on a Slavic legend which holds that when Christ was born, all the bells throughout the world pealed in joyous spontaneity. The carol is further based on *Shchedryk*, a choral work by Ukrainian composer Mykola Leontovich, which was first performed at Kiev University in 1916. In 1936, the American composer Peter Wilhousky added English lyrics and titled the combination "Carol of the Bells." The best performances of this spine-tingling carol are those of Wilhousky's choral arrangement, which simulates the rapturous pealing of silvery Christmas bells.

"Christmas in Killarney" was written in 1950 by three Irish-Americans, John Redmond, James Cavanaugh, and Frank Weldon. Dennis Day, another Irish-American and the tenor who was noted for his appearances on the hit radio-television program, *The Jack Benny Show*, first introduced it with his popular recording of 1951. According to the Irish, who won't hand you any blarney, there's nothing like Christmas in Killarney (a town in southwestern Ireland) "with all of the folks at home."

In 1719, English hymn writer Isaac Watts published his *Psalms of David*, a paraphrased, modern-English translation of the biblical text for that era. His hymn "Joy to the World" is based on the last six verses of his version of Psalm 98, which calls for everything in the earth to sing praises and make a joyful noise unto the Lord Who is to come. The lyrics originally began with "Joy to the earth," but in time "world" replaced "earth."

"Angels We Have Heard on High" is the carol that contains a Latin refrain, "Gloria in excelsis Deo," which translates as "Glory to God in the highest." Therefore, it is macaronic; that is, it consists of a mixture of a vernacular language with Latin. Because it is completely anonymous, speculations widely vary concerning its origin. The verses are thought to be based on a very old French traditional carol, "Les anges dans nos campagnes" ("The Angels in Our Company"), and the music for the verses is probably from the eighteenth century. Speculations about the Latin refrain include that it originated from a carol commissioned by Bishop Telesphorus of Rome in the year 129 or that it originated from a late medieval Latin tune, a setting which shepherds in the hills of southern France used to call the "Gloria" to one another as greetings on Christmas Eve. "Angels We Have Heard on High" served as the basis for James Montgomery's carol, "Angels, from the Realms of Glory" (1816). The former carol first appeared in print in Louis Lambillotte's collection, *Choix de cantiques sur des airs nouveaux* (Paris, 1842). The English version most often sung today has been adapted from James Chadwick's translation of 1860.

John D. (Johnny) Marks is considered to be the most prolific writer of Christmas music in the twentieth century. He published some 175 songs, most of them with Christmas themes. Although he is best known for "Rudolph, the Red-Nosed Reindeer," some of Marks's other treasures include "Rockin' Around the Christmas Tree;" "A Holly Jolly Christmas;" "Everyone's a Child at Christmas;" "The Night Before Christmas Song;" "When Santa Claus Gets Your Letter;" "I Heard the Bells on Christmas Day;" "Jingle, Jingle, Jingle;" "The Most Wonderful Day of the Year;" and "Silver and Gold."

From dance tune to love ballad to an accompaniment for medieval executions, "Greensleeves" has had quite a few applications over the centuries. The composer is unknown, although some candidates have included King Henry VIII and a Richard Jones of the late sixteenth century. How this tune became "What Child Is This?" was the work of William C. Dix. The manager of a marine insurance company in Bristol, England, Dix wrote a poem around 1865 titled "The Manger Throne." Three of his verses were subsequently taken and published together with the tune of "Greensleeves" in 1871 under the title of "What Child Is This?"

Jimmy Dorsey and his orchestra had been with Bing Crosby on the Kraft Music Hall radio show until 1937, at which time Dorsey departed. Crosby then brought in John Scott Trotter to handle the musical arrangements, not only for his Kraft radio show, but also for his recordings with Decca Records, the label which first produced "White Christmas."

For many in the USA, New Year's Eve has become the last night of the Christmas season. And at midnight, when we greet the new year while treasuring the memories of the one waning, it has now become customary to sing the Scottish traditional tune, "Auld Lang Syne" ("Old Long Ago"), thanks to Guy Lombardo's band. The Scottish poet Robert Burns brought "Auld Lang Syne" to prominence and contributed two additional verses to the song's original three. The familiar tune paired with "Auld Lang Syne" today is a Scots country dance, known by various titles as "The Miller's Wedding," "The Miller's Daughter," etc. George Thomson, a Burns contemporary, selected the piece and in 1799 published it with Burns's lyrics in *Select Scottish Airs* three years after Burns's death. Using the same melody but fashioning lyrics that combined Christmas with New Year sentiment, Frank Military and Mann Curtis produced "Christmas Auld Lang Syne" in 1960, which teen idol Bobby Darin successfully introduced.

Questions 90–99 are for those who particularly appreciate classical music. The following are a series of statements that draw comparisons between two often-performed holiday oratorios, Handel's *Messiah* and J. S. Bach's *Christmas Oratorio* (BWV 248). For each statement, determine whether it applies to A-*Messiah* only, B-*Christmas Oratorio* only, or C-both of them. Answers and comments follow this group.

90. The work is based entirely on the events surrounding the Nativity.

91. It is scored for soprano, alto, tenor, bass, chorus, and orchestra.

92. Its "Evangelist" and "Angel" are the only soloists that actually sing biblical passages.

93. Although the work comprises 53 individual pieces, it is broadly divided into three principal parts.

94. It incorporates two famous German carols, "Vom Himmel hoch, da komm' ich her" ("From Heaven Above

to Earth I Come") and "Brich an, o schönes Morgenlicht" ("Break Forth, O Beauteous Heavenly Light").

95. The composer collaborated with another to compose the text.

96. The idea for the work did not originate with the composer.

97. Ironically, the text for the section portraying Christ's birth is based primarily on Old Testament prophecies.

98. Its German composer wrote the work in England, but it premiered in Ireland.

99. Originally designed to have one of its parts performed on each of the three festival days of Christmas, then one on the Feast of the Circumcision, one on the first Sunday of the new year, and finally one on Epiphany, it is now generally performed as a single work.

Answers to 90–99:   90-B; 91-C; 92-B; 93-A; 94-B; 95-B; 96-A; 97-A; 98-A; 99-B.

Comments: *Christmas Oratorio* consists of 64 selections arranged into six individual cantatas or parts, each portraying specific events of the Nativity. Part One portrays the birth of Christ. In Part Two, the Heavenly Host appear to the shepherds and proclaim that Christ is born. Part Three centers around the shepherds' visit to the manger. Part Four takes place eight days after Jesus is born, at the time of His circumcision. In Part Five, the Wise Men seek the birthplace of Jesus from King Herod. And in Part

Six, the Wise Men worship Jesus at the manger. These cantatas originally were intended to be performed on the days outlined in question 99. The text is composed primarily of free verse, which is scored for the chorus and other soloists. Some passages are taken directly from the Bible, and it is the "Evangelist" alone who sings them, except for one solo by the "Angel" who sings that passage from Luke's Gospel, "Fear not; behold, I bring you good tidings of great joy," etc. Although there are no specific designations for a "Mary," "Joseph," or other characters, the context of each selection clearly identifies those people who play principal roles in the Nativity.

Bach incorporated parodies of his other works (new text set to previously established music) as well as established carols for *Christmas Oratorio*. The two carols mentioned in question 94 are the best known of those which Bach used. "From Heaven Above" (created by Martin Luther in 1534) is the musical setting used for the closing chorale of Part One. "Break Forth" appears in Part Two and depicts the annunciation of the heavenly host to the shepherds. It was the creation of Johann Rist (lyrics), a physician and pastor, and Johann Schop (music), Rist's friend and the editor for the collection titled *Himmlische Lieder*, which published "Break Forth" in 1641.

Bach often collaborated with Christian Friedrich Henrici (pseudonym Picander), a poet friend, in writing the texts for his cantatas, and this applies to *Christmas Oratorio* as well. This is not to say that Picander wrote *for* Bach, but rather *with* Bach, because Bach had as much to do with the final draft of the text as did Picander.

In contrast, *Messiah* portrays the life of Christ. The entire text is composed of biblical passages which emphasize spiritual concepts rather than specific events. Therefore, biblical characters are not represented in any form. Its Part One depicts the prophecies of Christ's coming as well as His birth. Part Two depicts His passion, resurrection, and the spreading of the Gospel. Part Three concludes with the promise of redemption through Christ at the Final Judgment.

Charles Jennens, one of Handel's eccentric friends, often supplied him with the ideas and biblical texts for his oratorios, and *Messiah* was no exception. Jennens compiled a series of scriptural passages about the life of Christ and presented Handel with the idea for yet another oratorio. Handel was so immensely receptive to this subject that he completed all of *Messiah* in less than a month.

Handel first presented *Messiah* in Dublin at the request of William

Cavendish, Lord Lieutenant of Ireland, who had asked Handel to give a series of benefit concerts there. *Messiah* premiered at the New Music Hall, Fishamble Street, on April 13, 1742. Its first London performance took place at Covent Garden in March, 1743.

Questions 100–103. The motion picture industry and the Broadway stage have produced four classic, American standards in Christmas music. For each of the following productions, name the song associated with it. Answers and comments follow this group.

100. *Holiday Inn* (1942) _____

101. *The Lemon Drop Kid* (1951) _____

102. *Mame* (1966) _____

103. *Meet Me in St. Louis* (1944) _____

Answers to 100–103. 100-"White Christmas;" 101- "Silver Bells;" 102-"We Need a Little Christmas;" 103-"Have Yourself a Merry Little Christmas."

Comments: Although Bing Crosby had included "White Christmas" on his Kraft Radio Show of 1941, it received its film debut in *Holiday Inn* with Crosby again delivering the rendition.

"Silver Bells" is just about the only song that accents the lights, stores, and bustle of the holiday season. And that's pretty much how composer Ray Evans originally summed up this classic, which he wrote with Jay Livingston in 1950. Although the song had its film debut in *The Lemon Drop Kid*, sung there as a duet by stars Marilyn Maxwell and Bob Hope, Bing Crosby and Carol Richards had recorded their duet version in 1950.

Playing a much older sister to child star Margaret O'Brien in *Meet Me in St. Louis*, Judy Garland was supposed to make their imminent move from St. Louis to New York City less distressing through the song "Have Yourself a Merry Little Christmas," by Ralph Blane and Hugh Martin. Garland found the original lyrics, which mentioned that this could be their last Christmas, too depressing to sing to a young child, however, and requested that they be altered, rather than abandon the number entirely. She recorded the song in 1944 and in 1954, neither of which were charted. Nevertheless, "Have Yourself" remains a classic piece of Christmas nostalgia.

Questions 104–128 primarily constitute a review with a few new challenges. The following table presents 25 of the best known and most frequently performed Christmas songs that were composed in the twentieth century. Based on the information given and from what you already have gleaned, complete those sections which are missing. "Artist or Production" refers to those people who first brought these songs to prominence or, in one case, the stage production by which this was accomplished. Answers and comments follow this group.

	Title	Composer(s)	Artist or Production	Year
104.		Coots / Gillespie	Eddie Cantor	1934
105.	"Winter Wonderland"	Bernard / Smith		1934
106.	"Carol of the Bells"	Leontovich		1936
107.	"White Christmas"		Bing Crosby	1942
108.		Kent / Buck / Ram	Bing Crosby	1943
109.		Blane / Martin	Judy Garland	1944
110.		Cahn / Styne	Vaughn Monroe	1945
111.	"The Christmas Song"	Torme / Wells		1946
112.		Autry / Haldeman	Gene Autry	1947
113.	"Blue Christmas"		Ernest Tubb	1949
114.	"Rudolph, the Red-Nosed Reindeer"		Gene Autry	1949
115.		Anderson / Parish	The Boston Pops	1949
116.	"Frosty the Snowman"	Nelson / Rollins		1950
117.		Evans / Livingston	Crosby & Carol Richards	1950
118.		Meredith Willson	Perry Como	1951
119.	"I Saw Mommy Kissing Santa Claus"		Jimmy Boyd	1952
120.	"The Christmas Waltz"	Cahn / Styne		1954
121.		Allen / Stillman	Perry Como	1954
122.		Beal / Booth	Bobby Helms	1957
123.	"The Chipmunk Song"	Bagdasarian, Sr.		1958
124.	"The Little Drummer Boy"		Harry Simeone Chorale	1958
125.	"Rockin' Around the Christmas Tree"	Marks		1960
126.		Marks	Burl Ives	1964
127.	"We Need a Little Christmas"	Herman		1966
128.	"Feliz Navidad"		José Feliciano	1970

Answers to 104–128: 104- "Santa Claus Is Coming to Town;" 105-Guy Lombardo; 106-Peter Wilhousky; 107-Irving Berlin; 108-"I'll Be Home for Christmas;" 109-"Have Yourself a Merry Little Christmas;" 110-"Let It Snow! Let It Snow! Let It Snow!" 111-Nat "King" Cole; 112-"Here Comes Santa Claus;" 113-Hayes / Johnson; 114-Marks; 115-"Sleigh Ride;" 116-Gene Autry; 117-"Silver Bells;" 118-"It's Beginning to Look Like Christmas;" 119-Tommie Connor; 120-Frank Sinatra; 121-"(There's No Place Like) Home for the Holidays;" 122-"Jingle Bell Rock;" 123-Ross Bagdasarian, Sr.; 124-Davis / Onorati / Simeone; 125-Brenda Lee; 126-"A Holly Jolly Christmas;" 127-*Mame*; 128-José Feliciano.

Comments: The songwriting team of Cahn and Styne created "The Christmas Waltz" expressly for Frank Sinatra. Wondering how to compose a song after Bing Crosby's rendition of "White Christmas" had dominated the scene since 1942, Styne sat at the piano and began his usual warm-up by playing a tango and a Viennese waltz. Then a marvelous idea hit Cahn. Since it had never been done before, why not write a Christmas waltz? So Styne slowed down his waltz a bit, and Cahn tacked on a few light lyrics about gleaming candles, painted candy canes, Santa, and wishes coming true at Christmas.

Blindness did not quell José Feliciano's enthusiasm for music or for Christmas. Voted Best New Artist of 1968, this Puerto Rican-American went on to a successful recording career. His Christmas album of 1970 featured his own Spanish composition, "Feliz Navidad" ("Merry Christmas").

Questions 129–156. With your best book of carols and songs on hand, see how many of these favorites you can identify from descriptions about them, from "snips" of their lyrics, or from exaggerated, "politically correct" titles for you to decipher.

129. The unborn baby Jesus performs a miracle by ordering a fruit tree to bow and yield its fruit to Mary.

This is a three-part English traditional carol, thought to have arisen during the fifteenth century and may have evolved from one of the Coventry Plays, a cycle of mystery plays presented in Coventry, England, during the Middle Ages. Based on an apocryphal story, Part I of "The Cherry Tree Carol" portrays the prenatal journey to Bethlehem. Passing by a cherry orchard, Mary bids Joseph to pluck some of the fruit for her. Joseph, an old man with reservations about Mary's pregnancy, brusquely responds with, "Let him pluck thee a cherry that brought thee with child." At this, the unborn Jesus commands the orchard to bow its limbs and yield its fruit to Mary, whereupon Joseph repents. In Part II, also apocryphal, the angel provides Joseph with prophecies concerning Jesus' imminent birth, and in Part III, the young Jesus predicts the redemption of mankind through His own death, burial, and resurrection.

The carol's immense popularity over the centuries has generated countless folk versions, such that no two are exactly alike.

130. Decipher: "First Person Singular Pronoun Requests Double Restitution of Anterior, Durable Elements of Mastication As Sole Yuletide Endowment."

A little-known group, The Satisfiers, first introduced "All I Want for Christmas Is My Two Front Teeth" on Perry Como's radio show. Written by Don Gardner in 1946, the song didn't satisfy the public until Spike Jones and His City Slickers, known for their outrageously comical musical performances, recorded it and made it the top Christmas song of 1948. There, George Rock portrayed a child longing for his missing two front teeth so that he could wish everyone a Merry Christmas without lisping.

131. This dreamy, sentimental piece made popular by The Carpenters features the phrase, "I'm Christmasing with you" and is the 1970s equivalent of "I'll Be Home for Christmas."

Although a young couple cannot be together for the holidays, according to the lyrics, the lady, sitting alone by the fire and the glittering tree on Christmas Eve, sends a mental wish of Merry Christmas to her darling; hence, the title of "Merry Christmas, Darling." Though apart, they will still share Christmas ("Christmasing") in their dreams. This lovely sentiment parallels the theme in the 1943 classic, "I'll Be Home for Christmas," where loved ones separated by the distance of war will celebrate Christmas at home, "if only in my dreams."

The Carpenters, the popular brother-and-sister team of Richard and Karen, were students at the Long Beach campus of California State University when Richard wrote "Merry Christmas, Darling" with Frank Pooler, the university's director of choral studies. But it was Karen's unequaled, melancholy solo that really stole your heart in their recorded single of 1970 and again in their 1978 album, *Christmas Portrait*, which became the number one Christmas album that year.

132. The introduction to one of the most famous of all Christmas songs is seldom ever sung. The lyrics paint a balmy Christmas Eve setting in Los Angeles, yet there is a greater desire to be up North in traditional Christmas weather.

Even Bing Crosby didn't sing the introductory bars when he recorded it, because such an introduction just didn't quite blend with the nostalgic sentiment expressed in "White Christmas."

133. This carol traditionally begins the Festival of Nine Lessons and Carols on Christmas Eve at King's College, University of Cambridge, England.

Mrs. Cecil Frances Alexander, wife of the bishop of Ireland, published "Once, in Royal David's City" in a collection of her poems in 1848. She wrote the poem to instruct her godsons in their catechism. It serves not only as a simple narrative of the Nativity story, but also as an elementary treatise on the divinity of Christ as both man and the Son of God. The musical setting is Henry J. Gauntlett's tune, "Irby," which appeared together with Mrs. Alexander's lyrics in the second edition of her poems (1858).

The Festival of Nine Lessons and Carols evolved from a small Christmas Eve service in 1880 in Cornwall, which featured nine appropriate biblical texts with carols compiled by the Rev. Edward Benson, who subsequently became Archbishop of Canterbury. The concept became popular and spread to other churches. The most noted of these services is that which has been annually held at King's College since 1918, and which has traditionally opened with "Once, in Royal David"s City" since 1919. Just prior to the service, a single choirboy is chosen to sing the first verse of the carol *a cappella*. With the exception of 1930, the Festival at King's has enjoyed annual BBC broadcasts by radio since 1928 and by television since 1963. Although the carols for each lesson may vary from year to year, the Lesson texts remain constant: (1) Genesis 3:8–15, 17–19; (2) Genesis 22:15–18; (3) Isaiah 9:2, 6, 7; (4) Isaiah 11:1–4, 6–9; (5) Luke 1:26–35, 38; (6) Luke 2:1, 3–7; (7) Luke 2:8–16; (8) Matthew 2:1–12; (9) John 1:1–14.

134. "Come to Bethlehem and see / Him whose birth the angels sing; / Come, adore on bended knee / Christ the Lord, the newborn King."

This is an excerpt from "Angels We Have Heard on High."

135. "From God our Heavenly Father / A blessed angel came. / And unto certain shepherds / Brought tidings of the same, / How that in Bethlehem was born / The Son of God by name."

This is an excerpt from the English traditional carol, "God Rest Ye Merry, Gentlemen." This carol, a narrative of the Nativity based on Luke's Gospel, probably arose during the sixteenth century, although printed versions did not appear until the nineteenth century.

One of the oldest tangible settings is found in *The Roxburghe Ballads*, a manuscript collection of verses and tunes which resides in London's British Museum. Although variant lyrics and tunes exist, including the refrain, those commonly sung today were published in separate carol collections, the lyrics in William Sandys's of 1833, the melody in that of Henry Bramley and John Stainer, 1871. The entire verse two, beginning "In Bethlehem in Jewry," is sometimes omitted, possibly to maintain political correctness; or if it is retained, that first line is modernized to "In Bethlehem in Israel." Omitting verse two, which ties in the manger, would leave an unfortunate gap in the Nativity story. Archaic words in the title have also caused misinterpretations. "Rest" does not signify repose but "Keep," and the "Ye" often is modernized to "You." "Merry" has been interpreted as "Good Spirits" and as "Mighty." In either case, "Merry" does not signify merry-making as at a feast; hence, a comma should follow "Merry." Thus the title now reads "God Keep You in Good Spirits (or Mighty), Gentlemen." The carol was undoubtedly used as a wassailing song, as Charles Dickens's *A Christmas Carol* attests: Scrooge threatens to throttle a young boy for singing the carol outside his office door on Christmas Eve.

136. "The star drew nigh to the northwest, / O'er Bethlehem it took its rest; / And there it did both stop and stay, / Right over the place where Jesus lay."

An English traditional carol from the fifteenth century, "The First Nowell" is similar to most ancient carols in that it retells the Nativity story. The word "Nowell" (from the French *Noël* or *Nouvelle*, meaning "new") is freely used to denote Christmas in many English-speaking countries. Sometimes the French word *Noël* is actually substituted in the title, which provides the misconception that the carol is French. The English-men Davies Gilbert and William Sandys first published this carol in their separate carol collections of 1823 and 1833, respectively.

137. "Come and worship, come and worship, / Worship Christ the newborn King."

This is the refrain to "Angels, from the Realms of Glory."

138. "Of peace on earth, good will to men."

This reiterates the latter half of the angelic chorus of Luke 2:14 and is the refrain to "I Heard the Bells on Christmas Day."

139. "Led by the light of faith serenely beaming, / With glowing hearts by His cradle we stand. / So led by light of a star sweetly gleaming, / Here came the Wise Men from Orient land."

An excerpt from "O Holy Night."

140. Decipher: "Vertically Challenged Adolescent Percussionist."

This is a politically correct title for "The Little Drummer Boy."

141. "Still through the cloven skies they come / With peaceful wings unfurled, / And still their heavenly music floats / O'er all the weary world: / Above its sad and lowly plains / They bend on hovering wing / And ever o'er its Babel sounds / The blessed angels sing."

A verse from "It Came Upon the Midnight Clear."

142. "O holy Child of Bethlehem, descend to us we pray; / Cast out our sin and enter in: be born in us today. / We

hear the Christmas angels the great glad tidings tell; / O come to us, abide with us, our Lord Emmanuel."

This is a verse from "O Little Town of Bethlehem."

143. Decipher: "Advance, the Entire Assembly of Those Maintaining Loyalty in Their Belief."

A politically correct title for "O Come, All Ye Faithful."

144. "Rejoice! Rejoice! Emmanuel / Shall come to thee, O Israel."

This is the refrain to "O Come, O Come, Emmanuel."

145. "O Star of wonder, Star of night, / Star with royal beauty bright, / Westward leading, still proceeding, / Guide us to thy perfect light."

This is the refrain to "We Three Kings of Orient Are."

146. "Mild, He lays His glory by, / Born that man no more may die, / Born to raise the sons of earth, / Born to give them second birth."

An excerpt from "Hark! The Herald Angels Sing."

147. "Love and joy come to you, / And to you glad Christmas too, / And God bless you and send you a Happy New Year, / And God send you a Happy New Year."

This is the refrain to "Here We Come A-Caroling" (or "Here We Come A-Wassailing"), also known as "The Wassail Song."

148. Decipher: "First Person Plural Pronoun Desires for Second Person Singular/Plural Pronoun a Jovial Yuletide."

A politically correct title for "We Wish You a Merry Christmas."

149. "The people keep a-coming and the train done gone."

This is the refrain to the popular African American spiritual "Mary Had a Baby." Thought to have originated in South Carolina during the nineteenth century, this spiritual presents a synopsis of the Nativity. Each of its twelve verses consists of one line that is repeated three times, with the seemingly spontaneous phrases of "Oh, Lord!" or "Oh, my Lord!" interrupting the repetitions. The verse sequence is: 1. "Mary had a baby;" 2. "Where did she lay Him?" 3. "Laid Him in a manger;" 4. "What did she name Him?" 5. "Name Him Jesus;" 6. "Who heard the singing?" 7. "Shepherds heard the singing;" 8. "Star keep a-shining;" 9. "Moving in the elements;" 10. "Jesus went to Egypt;" 11. "Traveled on a donkey;" 12. "Angels went around Him." The incongruous refrain has been described as "theologically provocative;" that is, its significance remains to be determined.

150. The lyrics to this African American spiritual take some liberties regarding the biblical account of the shepherds and the Star in the East.

Collected during the American Civil War and published in 1867, "Rise Up, Shepherd, and Follow" urges shepherds to forsake their flocks and follow the Star in the East to Bethlehem. The liberties taken with Matthew's and Luke's accounts of the Nativity are obvious. The title derives from the repetitive phrase traditionally sung by a choir in response to a soloist's rendering of the verses. The African American soprano Dorothy Maynor (1910–1996) popularized this spiritual in the USA.

151. "Therefore, Christian men, be sure, / Wealth or rank possessing, / Ye who now will bless the poor, / Shall yourselves find blessing."

From the concluding verse of "Good King Wenceslas."

152. One of the first carols to be printed, it is traditionally sung at Christmas ceremonies which serve the boar's head at Queen's College, University of Oxford, England.

The anonymous text for "The Boar's Head Carol" derives from the fifteenth century and appears in Jan van Wynkyn de Worde's *Christmasse Carolles* (1521), the oldest collection of printed carols extant. The tune derives from the eighteenth century. The verses are macaronic (mixture of Latin and vernacular English), in which Latin not only comprises the last line of each verse, but the entire refrain as well. The latter reads, "Caput apri defero / Reddens laudes Domino" ("I bring in the boar's head / Giving thanks to the Lord"). Since the Middle ages, Queen's College, Oxford, has served a boar's head (now that of a suckling pig) at Christmas services, the origin of which is a matter of legend as presented in chapter two. Whereas "The Boar's Head Carol" is more convivial than religious, Richard Smert's "The Exeter Boar's Head Carol," also from the fifteenth century, reveres the boar's head as a symbol of Christ.

153. Considered to be Canada's first Christmas carol, it was originally written in the language of the Huron Indians in 1641 and remains as one of Canada's most beloved carols.

A Jesuit priest serving in Canada to Christianize the Huron tribe of Ontario, Father Jean de Brébeuf created "Jesous ahatonhia" ("Jesus Is Born"), a poem in the Huron language, which adapted the Nativity story to an equivalent concept in the Huron culture. Thus, it is Gitchi Manitou (God), who sends the angelic Heavenly Host to proclaim to wondering hunter braves (shepherds) that Jesus is born. Coming to a lodge of "broken bark" (stable), they find the Christ Child wrapped in ragged rabbit skins (swaddling clothes), and three chiefs (Wise Men) present gifts of fur skins (gold, frankincense, myrrh). Father Brébeuf set his narrative to "Une jeune pucelle" ("A Young Virgin"), a sixteenth-century folk tune. The Hurons kept the carol in their oral tradition until 1649, when raiding bands of Iroquois murdered the Father and scattered his flock of converts. After escaping to Quebec, the Hurons revived Father Brébeuf's carol about a century later. The popular English version known today, beginning with the words "'Twas in the moon of wintertime," was translated by J. E. Middleton and published in 1942. The carol is also known as "The Huron Christmas Carol."

154. John Jacob Niles, a folksinger and songwriter, based this plaintive song on a melody that he heard while touring the Appalachian Mountains of North Carolina.

A native of Kentucky, Niles began collecting American folk music at an early age. Although he had studied classical music in Paris and in Cincinnati following World War I, he journeyed to New York during the Depression to pursue a folk music career. There he met and became a guide for famed photographer Doris Ulmann, who was undertaking a project in the southern Appalachian Mountains. While they were touring

North Carolina in 1933, Niles happened to hear a young girl singing a most haunting, melancholy melody not unlike that of a spiritual, and this became the basis for "I Wonder As I Wander." It was first published in 1934 as single sheet music and also in Niles's anthology *Songs from the Hill Folk: Twelve Ballads from Kentucky, Virginia, and North Carolina, Collected and Simply Arranged with Accompaniment for Piano.*

155. This song made the *Guinness Book of World Records* when a radio station in Godfrey, Illinois, once played it 310 consecutive times on the air.

According to the lyrics to "Grandma Got Run Over by a Reindeer," Santa's reindeer sleigh accidentally runs down Grandma on Christmas Eve. Whether you consider Randy Brooks's little composition of 1979 to be warped holiday comedy or outright sacrilege, it must have appealed to quite a few folks, for it hit the top of the Christmas singles charts in 1983, thanks to the recording team of "Elmo & Patsy" (Dr. Elmo Shropshire, a former veterinarian, and Patsy Trigg). It was the first time in thirty years that a Christmas song had received more air time and more sales in one year (ten thousand copies in one week alone) than Bing Crosby's recording of "White Christmas." The lyrics nevertheless created a storm of protest from some, including the Gray Panthers, who once picketed an Elmo & Patsy performance with signs that read "What's so funny about a dead grandma?" Elmo & Patsy responded by producing a music video in 1983 in which Grandma survived the accident. "Grandma," in addition to its status as number one on the Christmas hits charts from 1983 to 1987, has consistently remained a Top Ten Christmas hit. A spin-off album, *Dr. Elmo's Twisted Christmas,* not only features "Grandma," but also a series of sequel novelties such as "Grandma's Gonna Sue the Pants Off of Santa," "Grandma's Spending Christmas with the Superstars," "Grandma's Killer Fruitcake," and "Please Don't Make Me Play That 'Grandma' Song Again."

156. This carol's erroneous sobriquet is "The Portuguese Hymn."

The sobriquet arose after Samuel Webbe, chapel organist for the Portuguese embassy in London, provided a rendition of "O Come, All Ye Faithful" there in 1795. Much impressed, the Duke of Leeds further introduced the carol at a series of concerts, which he patronized in 1797. Through these concerts came the erroneous assumption that "O Come, All Ye Faithful" had arisen in Portugal.

Questions 157–168. Some of our most beloved Christmas carols arose from all over the world. For each title listed below, identify the foreign country from which it originated, if known. Answers and comments follow this group.

157. "Vom Himmel hoch, da komm' ich her" ("From Heaven Above to Earth I Come")

158. "Stille Nacht" ("Silent Night")

159. "Cantique de Noël" ("O Holy Night")

160. "O Tannenbaum" ("O Christmas Tree")

161. "Les anges dans nos campagnes" ("Angels We Have Heard on High")

162. "Adeste Fideles" ("O Come, All Ye Faithful")

163. "Veni, Veni, Emanuel" ("O Come, O Come Emmanuel")

164. "Es ist ein Ros' entsprungen" ("Lo, How a Rose E'er Blooming")

165. "W zlobie lezy" ("Infant Holy, Infant Lowly")

166. "Jesous ahatonhia" ("Jesus Is Born")

167. "Hajej nynej" ("Rocking," also known as "Rocking Carol" and "Little Jesus, Sweetly Sleep")

168. "Canzone d'i Zampognari" ("Carol of the Bagpipers")

Answers to 157–168: 157-Germany; 158-Austria; 159-France; 160-Germany; 161-France; 162-France; 163-unknown, possibly France; 164-Germany; 165-Poland; 166-Canada; 167-Czech Republic; 168-Italy.

Comments: A traditional carol, "Infant Holy, Infant Lowly" is considered to be the best known and the earliest significant carol from Poland. Thought to date from the thirteenth or fourteenth century, its English titles have also included "Jesus Holy, Born So Lowly;" "Baby Jesus, in a Manger;" and "He Is Sleeping in a Manger."

Thought to be the oldest of carol lullabies, "Rocking" originated between the fourteenth and sixteenth centuries.

The verses mimic cradle rocking, especially through the repetitious phrase, "We will rock you, rock you, rock you;" the melody resembles that of "Twinkle, Twinkle, Little Star." Cradle-rocking ceremonies once constituted a part of Christmas vespers throughout all of Europe during the Middle Ages, wherein the priest rocked a cradle containing an image of the Christ Child to a cradle song. "Rocking" most likely was numbered among the repertoire of those songs.

The best known of Italian traditional carols, "Carol of the Bagpipers" arose in Sicily during the seventeenth century. A few days before Christmas, it was customary for the *pifferari* (Calabrian shepherds) to play this carol and others like them on their bagpipes before statues of the Virgin for, according to superstition, the droning music eased the discomfort of her impending labor. G. F. Handel incorporated Italian bagpipe melodies into his oratorio *Messiah*, more specifically in the "Pifa" ("Pastoral Symphony") and in the aria "He Shall Feed His Flock." The latter melody is closely based on that for "Carol of the Bagpipers."

Questions 169–180 pertain to "The Twelve Days of Christmas." English Roman Catholics devised this counting song/carol around the sixteenth century as an underground memory device to teach children their catechism. Thus, the increasing numbers of daily, secular gifts actually symbolize the religious elements of the catechism. In the table below, list each of the gifts for the corresponding days, then briefly indicate the religious symbolism of each. "On the first day of Christmas" is completed for you as an example.

	Day	Gifts from "My True Love"	Religious Symbolism
169.	1	A partridge in a pear tree	One God in Christ
170.	2		
171.	3		
172.	4		
173.	5		
174.	6		
175.	7		
176.	8		
177.	9		
178.	10		
179.	11		
180.	12		

Answers and Comments to 169–180:

One God in Christ is the "True Love" of all Christians. The phrase "partridge in a pear tree" has acquired multiple symbolisms. In one sense, for example, it recalls Jesus' lamentation over Jerusalem (Matthew 23:37); in another, it likens the partridge to Satan, for the bird, according to legend, told King Herod where the Virgin Mary had hidden the Babe and herself from the soldiers that were raiding Bethlehem. The pear tree also represents the cross, the "tree" upon which

Christ was crucified. Thus the partridge and pear tree represent the battle between good and evil.

"Two turtle doves" represent the Bible's Old and New Testaments as well as the two turtle doves sacrificed when the infant Jesus was presented in the Temple (Leviticus 12:8 and Luke 2:24).

"Three French hens" represent the virtues of Faith, Hope, Charity (1 Corinthians 13:13); also gold, frankincense, and myrrh (Matthew 2:11); and the Holy Trinity of Father, Son, and Holy Ghost (1 John 5:7).

"Four calling birds" represent the four Gospels and the Evangelists (Matthew, Mark, Luke, John).

"Five gold rings" symbolize the Pentateuch, the first five books of the Old Testament (Genesis, Exodus, Leviticus, Numbers, Deuteronomy).

"Six geese a-laying" represent the six days of creation.

"Seven swans a-swimming" represent the seven gifts of the Holy Spirit: prophecy, ministry, teaching, exhorting, ruling, giving, and mercy (Romans 12:6–8) as well as the seven sacraments of the Roman Catholic faith: baptism, confirmation, Eucharist, penance/reconciliation, anointing the sick, holy orders, and matrimony.

"Eight maids a-milking" represent the eight Beatitudes from Jesus' Sermon on the Mount: the poor in spirit, they that mourn, the meek, those who hunger and thirst after righteousness, the merciful, the pure in heart, the peacemakers, and those who are persecuted for righteousness' sake (Matthew 5:3–10).

"Nine ladies dancing" represent the nine fruits of the Holy Spirit: love, joy, peace, longsuffering, gentleness, goodness, faith, meekness, and temperance (Galatians 5:22–23).

"Ten lords a-leaping" represent the Ten Commandments.

"Eleven pipers piping" represent Jesus' eleven faithful disciples who did not betray Him as did the twelfth, Judas Iscariot.

"Twelve drummers drumming" represent the twelve points of doctrine in the Apostles' Creed.

CHAPTER SIX

A Christmas Carol

First published in 1843, it's probably the best loved and most frequently read Christmas story in the history of literature, second only to the Nativity story in the Bible. The immortal story *A Christmas Carol* reminds us that anyone can be caught up in the compassion, magic, and wonder of the season, even those with former hearts of stone.

1.   Who wrote *A Christmas Carol*?

     A.   Charles Darwin
     B.   Charles, Prince of Wales
     C.   Charles Dickson
     D.   Charles Dickens

Financially strapped at the time, British author Charles Dickens wrote this story strictly for cash. His situation created feelings of guilt in one who had always championed the poor, love for family and community, and simple virtues despite poverty.

2. What kind of story is *A Christmas Carol*?

    A. A ghost story
    B. A romance
    C. A mystery
    D. A comedy

The formal title provides the answer: *A Christmas Carol in Prose: Being a Ghost Story of Christmas.* During Dickens's time, families traditionally gathered in their homes around the crackling fire amidst the eerie light and told ghost stories on Christmas Eve. It is not surprising, then, that ghosts play key roles in most of Dickens's Christmas works. The tradition of telling ghost stories at Christmastime is a vestige of the ancient pagan superstition that spirits roamed the earth at the winter solstice.

3. What is the principal theme of *A Christmas Carol*?

    A. A good man reforms greedy ghosts.
    B. Ghosts convince a good man to perform more good works.
    C. Ghosts reform a greedy man.
    D. Ghosts fail to reform a greedy man.

Ghosts convince a spiteful, greedy man to change his ways.

Questions 4–11. Provide the names of each principal character in the story based on the following descriptions about them. Answers follow this group.

4. The miser who initially despises Christmas:

    _____.

5. The miser's poor but good-spirited clerk:

    _____.

6. The clerk's handicapped little boy: _____.

7. The miser's deceased business partner: _____.

8. The person to whom the miser was apprenticed when he was a youth: _____.

9. The miser's fiancée who rejected him because of his greed: _____.

10. The miser's nephew: _____.

11. The miser's little sister: _____.

Answers to 4–11: 4-Ebenezer Scrooge; 5-Bob Cratchit; 6-Tiny Tim; 7-Jacob Marley; 8-Mr. Fezziwig; 9-Belle; 10-Fred; 11-Fan.

12. Dickens described several ideal conditions for reading the *Carol*. Which of these is <u>not</u> one of them?

    A. The story should be read by candlelight.
    B. The story should be read aloud.
    C. The story should be read in a cold room.
    D. The story should be read by the fireside.

    Although they all would contribute an especially eerie atmosphere to this ghost story, Dickens's recommendations did not include a warm fire.

13. How many ghosts haunt Scrooge and how many nights do they require to complete the haunting?

    Scrooge receives visits from four ghosts. Although the first ghost says that a spirit will haunt Scrooge on each of three successive nights, they all come on Christmas Eve.

14. Name all the ghosts that haunt Scrooge in the order of their appearance.

Ghost of Jacob Marley, Ghost of Christmas Past, Ghost of Christmas Present, Ghost of Christmas Yet to Come

15. All of the following are true about the Ghost of Christmas Past, <u>except</u>:

    A. It appears as a little child.
    B. It holds a branch of fresh, green holly in its hand.
    C. It wears a white tunic, for its arms and legs are bare.
    D. From the crown of its head springs a bright jet of light.

This Ghost appears as a diminutive, old man with long, white hair.

16. Which of these does <u>not</u> apply to the Ghost of Christmas Present?

    A. It appears as a jolly giant wearing a wreath of holly.
    B. It has icicles in its hair.
    C. It wears a blue mantle trimmed with white fur and carries a scepter.
    D. It sits with bare feet and bare chest atop a large pile of delicious, holiday delights.

Its mantle is green, and it carries a torch. Wearing an old, rusty scabbard without a sword, it personifies Father Christmas.

17. The Ghost of Christmas Present dispenses two items from his torch: (A) _____, which he sprinkles over the meals being prepared at a baker's establish-

ment; and (B) _____ to be sprinkled on people to make them more pleasant, should they begin to quarrel on Christmas Day. Scrooge discovers two wretched children hidden within the Ghost's mantle, a boy named (C) _____ and a girl named (D) _____. As time passes, the Ghost grows visibly older. His existence normally spans the (E) _____, but for Scrooge, the Ghost's "life" ends at (F) _____ on Christmas Eve.

(A) Incense; (B) Water; (C) "Ignorance;" (D) "Want;" (E) Twelve Days of Christmas; (F) Midnight.

18. Indicate whether each of these statements about the Ghost of Christmas Yet to Come is true or false:

   A. The Ghost is hooded in solid black. _____
   B. The Ghost's face shows two bright red eyes. _____
   C. The Ghost never speaks. _____
   D. The Ghost directs Scrooge with one outstretched arm. _____

A-True; B-False (the Ghost never reveals its face); C-True; D-True. The Ghost's silence makes it even more terrifying by keeping Scrooge in perpetual suspense.

Questions 19–33. Since most of the story's events occur during each of the Ghosts' separate visits, this section requires you to associate some of those key events or remarks with the particular Ghost involved. From the lettered list of Ghosts below, match the one that is associated with each of the numbered events or quotes which follow them. Quotes do not necessarily originate from the Ghosts, and a Ghost may be selected more than once. Answers and comments follow this group.

    A. **Ghost of Jacob Marley**
    B. **Ghost of Christmas Past**
    C. **Ghost of Christmas Present**
    D. **Ghost of Christmas Yet to Come**

19. In order for the Ghost to transport Scrooge through the visions, Scrooge must place his hand over the Ghost's heart.

20. After the Ghost shows him the first of many Christmases when he was forced to remain alone at school for the holidays, Scrooge recalls the boy singing a carol outside his door and wishes that he had given the boy something.

21. Scrooge is horrified to see his own tombstone.

22. Bells ring loudly prior to the entrance of this Ghost, which drags a chain made of cash boxes, keys, padlocks, ledgers, deeds, and heavy steel purses. They are symbols of the burden it forged in life.

23. In order for the Ghost to transport Scrooge through the visions, Scrooge must touch the Ghost's robe.

24. "For it is good to be children sometimes, and never better than at Christmas, when the mighty Founder was a child himself." It is Dickens, and not the Ghost, who makes this remark regarding the parlor games that Fred, Scrooge's nephew, plays with his family at their Christmas party.

25. A husband brings his wife the news that their creditor has died. They now allow themselves to hope that their new creditor will be more merciful.

26. In order for the Ghost to transport Scrooge through the visions, Scrooge must step into its shadow.

27. Two businessmen remark that "Old Scratch," a nickname for the Devil, has finally claimed his own. It implies that the deceased has gone to hell.

28. When Bob Cratchit and Tiny Tim return home from church on Christmas Day, Bob relates Tiny Tim's sentiment about being a cripple: "Somehow he gets thoughtful sitting by himself so much, and thinks the strangest things you ever heard. He told me, coming home, that he hoped the people saw him in the church, because he was a cripple, and it might be pleasant to them to remember upon Christmas Day, who made lame beggars walk and blind men see."

29. As Belle, Scrooge's fiancée, breaks their engagement because she can no longer tolerate his obsession with wealth, she states, "Another idol has displaced me . . . a golden one."

30. The Ghost itself shows great remorse over having walked among its fellow beings with eyes averted, never once considering the Star which led the Wise Men to a poor boy's home. It is a remorse that comes too late.

31. Scrooge notes that the power of an employer over his employees actually lies in intangibles such as words and looks, and that the happiness which Mr. Fezziwig gives to his employees is just as great as if it had cost a fortune.

32. "Are there no prisons? Are there no workhouses?"

33. "If he be like to die, he had better do it, and decrease the surplus population."

Answers to 19–33: 19-B; 20-B; 21-D; 22-A; 23-C; 24-C; 25-D (the deceased creditor is Scrooge); 26-D; 27-D (the deceased is Scrooge); 28-C; 29-B; 30-A; 31-B; 32-C; 33-C.

Comments: The sentiment in question 31 is Scrooge's reply to a mocking question from the Ghost as they observe the employee Christmas party which Mr. Fezziwig, Scrooge's former employer, throws for his employees. The Ghost had asked Scrooge why Fezziwig's employees should love and praise him, since he probably spent no more than a few pounds for their enjoyment. When Scrooge reflects on his own answer, he wishes that he could say a kind word to his clerk, Bob Cratchit, at that moment.

In question 32, the Ghost throws Scrooge's own cruel words back in his face. Earlier on Christmas Eve, before the hauntings began, two gentlemen had solicited funds for the poor from Scrooge at his office. Scoffing, Scrooge had replied with these remarks. In Dickens's day, those who were too poor to pay their debts were either thrown into "debtors' prison," or they went to a workhouse until they worked off the debt. At the close of the second vision, after Scrooge discovers the two wretched children, Ignorance and Want, clinging to the

Ghost's robe, he asks, "Have they no refuge or resource?" The Ghost's reply mocks Scrooge with his own words.

In question 33, the Ghost again echoes Scrooge's words. Referring once more to the earlier scene in his office, when the gentlemen soliciting funds had stated that some of the poor would rather die than go to a workhouse, Scrooge had responded with, "If they would rather die, they had better do it, and decrease the surplus population." At the Cratchit home during the second vision, the Ghost predicts that Tiny Tim will die if the present course is not altered. At Scrooge's remonstration over such news, the Ghost hurls a paraphrased version of Scrooge's quote back at him. Dickens then writes, "Scrooge hung his head to hear his own words quoted by the Spirit, and was overcome with penitence and grief." Of course, this episode and the one in the previous question serve to teach Scrooge, as well as us all, that no man has the right to determine what person shall live or die outside of the law. For all he knows, Scrooge may be far less fit to live in the sight of Heaven than this "poor man's child."

34. After recovering from his nightmare, Scrooge loses no time in showing his generosity to mankind on Christmas Morning and bestows four principal gifts. List each

person or persons and their gift(s) in the order that
they are actually received.

First:
_____

Second:
_____

Third:
_____

Fourth:
_____

First is the poulterer, who brings the prize turkey to
Scrooge's house. After paying for the turkey, Scrooge
generously hires a cab so that the poulterer can deliver
the turkey to Bob Cratchit's home with ease. The second recipient is a street boy. Beforehand, Scrooge had
promised a shilling to the boy if he could bring the
poulterer back with him, or half a crown if they came
back in five minutes. After finishing with the poulterer,
Scrooge compensates the boy. Interestingly, we are not
told whether the boy receives the shilling or half a
crown. But with Scrooge's new outlook, I believe the
boy receives *both*. Bob Cratchit is the third recipient,
who receives the prize turkey anonymously. On the
following day, Scrooge also raises Cratchit's salary. The
poor in general are the final recipients. While out for a
Christmas stroll, Scrooge encounters the same gentlemen who had solicited a donation for the poor on
Christmas Eve. Scrooge whispers a large sum in their
ears and then urges them to come and see him about it.
It can only be inferred that Scrooge wishes for them to
come on the next business day.

35. Dickens based many of his works on the experiences
in his own life, and the *Carol* is no exception. In fact,

the following four characters in this story are the embodiments of Dickens's own blood relatives. For each character, explain how they "relate" to Dickens.

A. Ebenezer Scrooge

_____

B. Tiny Tim

_____

C. Little sister Fan

_____

D. Nephew Fred

_____

Scrooge was the embodiment of Dickens himself. Whereas Scrooge was obsessed with obtaining wealth, Dickens himself did not really possess that trait. Instead, feelings of guilt about the need to make money tortured him, which explains why, in many of Dickens's works, including the *Carol*, themes of virtue and close family ties supplant monetary gain. Also like Dickens, Scrooge experienced an unhappy childhood and was compelled to go to work before reaching his teens. Tiny Tim was a composite character drawn from two people: Frederick, Dickens's brother, and young nephew Harry Burnett, the crippled son of Dickens's elder sister Frances, nicknamed Fanny. She, in turn, became the basis for Fan, Scrooge's little sister. And you immediately see how brother Frederick became the model for Fred, Scrooge's nephew.

36. What name did Dickens initially consider for Bob Cratchit's ailing little boy, and why did he choose "Tiny Tim" instead?

Dickens had considered a nickname which his brother Frederick had acquired at the age of two, "Tiny Fred."

He settled instead on "Tiny Tim," because it sounded more diminutive and more suitable for a sickly child.

Questions 37–46 pose significant names and phrases regarding the *Carol*. For each, state its significance or how it relates to the story.

37. The Bible

    The *Carol* sold some six thousand copies in the first five days of its publication, figures which actually outsold copies of the Bible.

38. "God bless us, every one."

    This is Tiny Tim's famous line that makes him an especially endearing character. It is also the last line of the story.

39. "God Rest Ye Merry, Gentlemen"

    Scrooge threatens to throttle a little boy for singing this carol outside his door.

40. Crippled and walks with a crutch

    Tiny Tim's handicap compounds the Cratchit family's hardship of poverty, magnifies Scrooge's heartlessness toward the poor, and tugs on the reader's heartstrings.

41. "A Merry Christmas to you"

    After his reform, these are the words that are the most blithe to Scrooge's ears.

42. Fifteen shillings a week

    Scrooge raises Bob Cratchit's weekly salary from a paltry fifteen shillings to an unspecified amount.

43. "Bah! Humbug!"

    Before his reform, these two words aptly express Scrooge's feelings about Christmas.

44. The Pierpont Morgan Library in Manhattan, New York City

    The original manuscript of *A Christmas Carol* currently resides there.

45. "The Story of the Goblins Who Stole a Sexton"

    Dickens patterned the *Carol* after this earlier short story, which he published in 1837.

46. *The Pickwick Papers*

    Dickens's first novel of 1837 contains "The Story of the Goblins Who Stole a Sexton" in chapter 29. There, Christmastime sees Mr. Pickwick and his colleagues on a holiday at Manor Farm, the estate of their friend, Mr. Wardle. In chapter 28, the ladies and gentlemen present have wiled away Christmas Eve by drinking wassail and playing traditional parlor games, and now midnight approaches. When the time is right, Mr. Wardle further entertains his guests by telling them the sexton ghost story in chapter 29.

Questions 47–53 ask you to identify similarities between *A Christmas Carol* and "The Story of the Goblins Who Stole a Sexton." For each of the following statements about the sexton story, describe the parallel, if any, that exists in the story of Scrooge.

47. Gabriel Grub, the sexton, is a mean-spirited, hateful old man, who takes no pleasure in anyone's happiness.

Scrooge is an old miser who is also sour on the world.

48. The story takes place on Christmas Eve as Grub digs a grave.

    The principal events of the *Carol* occur on Christmas Eve. Scrooge's final vision from the Ghost of Christmas Yet to Come unfolds in a cemetery, when he sees his own grave.

49. Grub knocks a young boy on the head for singing a Christmas carol.

    Scrooge threatens a boy for singing a carol in the street near his office.

50. Troops of goblins flood the cemetery, playing leap-frog over tombstones.

    Other than spirits haunting both men, there is no further parallel. The four spirits that haunt Scrooge have been sent to save him from his own fate.

51. The goblin king escorts Grub into an underground cavern and forces him to drink a glass of "liquid fire" to begin his punishment.

    There is no parallel here.

52. In the cavern, the goblins show Grub visions of a simple, loving family, whose youngest boy eventually dies.

    Through the vision of the Ghost of Christmas Present, Scrooge observes Bob Cratchit's poor but very happy family at Christmastime. The Ghost of Christmas Yet to Come reveals the Cratchits' bitter anguish, should they lose Tiny Tim.

53. Grub learns that those who snarl at the happiness of others are the "foulest weeds on earth." Having fallen asleep in the cemetery, he awakens from his nightmare on Christmas Day a changed man.

Scrooge's nightmare also ends on Christmas Day, and he awakens clutching his own bedpost. From his ordeal, he launches into a new life of kindness and generosity throughout the year.

CHAPTER SEVEN

"'Twas the Night Before Christmas"

This best-loved of all American Christmas poems was first published anonymously in 1823. With fantasy that appeals to children and adults alike, it will forever remain a timeless classic.

1. By tradition, who is listed as the author?

    A. Daniel DeFoe
    B. Edgar Allan Poe
    C. Clement Clarke Moore
    D. Robert Louis Stevenson

For fourteen years from initial publication, no one's name was associated with the poem until 1837, when the *New York Book of Poetry* cited Clement Clarke Moore as the author. Moore, a poet and professor of Greek and Oriental literature at the Episcopal General Theological Seminary in New York City from 1821 to 1850, subsequently claimed authorship in 1844, when he included it in his own *Poems.* He attributed his long silence to embarrassment over his "trifle." That Moore is the legitimate author is now in question, for research conducted in 2000 at Vassar College not only suggests that the real author is Henry Livingston, Jr. (1748–1828), a cartographer and amateur poet from Poughkeepsie, New York, it also suggests that Moore simply plagiarized Livingston's poem. A small sample of the host of evidence cited include the fact that Livingston's poems were almost universally light and frequently written in anapestic meter (the meter of "'Twas the Night Before Christmas"), whereas Moore, a religious pedant not given to frivolous verse, rarely wrote in this meter. Certain phraseologies peculiar to Livingston are also evident in this poem, such as "Happy Christmas" in the closing phrase instead of "Merry Christmas" and "Dunder and Blixem," which became "Donder and Blitzen," the names for Santa's last two reindeer (see question 3). Livingston died long before Moore ever claimed authorship, yet since the latter 1800s, the Livingston family has maintained a claim upon the poem.

2.   Although the first five words of this poem form the now-familiar popular title, under what title did it appear when it was first published?

   A. "The Midnight Visit of St. Nicholas"
   B. "The Jolly Old Elf of Christmas Eve"
   C. "Santa and His Reindeer"
   D. "Account of a Visit from St. Nicholas"

Make your choice, then see the answer to the next question.

3.   The poem first appeared in which publication on December 23, 1823?

A. *Atlantic Monthly*
B. *Harper's Illustrated Weekly*
C. *Boston Herald*
D. *Troy Sentinel*

According to popular accounts, Clement Moore wrote the poem during the Christmas of 1822 for his children. While visiting the Moore family, Harriet Butler, daughter of the rector of St. Paul's Episcopal Church in Troy, New York, supposedly copied down the poem while Moore read it to his children. In 1823, Orville Holley, editor of the *Sentinel*, Troy's newspaper, received an anonymous copy of the poem from an unnamed woman (thought to be Ms. Butler) and published it under the heading "Account of a Visit from St. Nicholas" (which was later shortened to "A Visit from St. Nicholas"). The family of Henry Livingston contends, however, that when Livingston introduced his own children to his own poem, a female guest was present who later became a governess for Clement Moore's children, and that it was she who supposedly brought the poem to the *Sentinel*. Popular accounts further hold that, at the first printing, Santa's last two reindeer erroneously appeared as "Dunder and Blixem," not "Donder and Blitzen," as Moore had supposedly intended, and that Moore corrected the error in subsequent printings. The Vassar research contends, however, that Livingston's original words repeated his favorite exclamation, "Dunder and Blixem," that the *Sentinel* instead printed "Donder and Blitzen" in error, and that Moore, in plagiarizing the poem, perpetuated the error. Unfortunately, no original copy of the poem has ever surfaced to put the matter to rest. With or without error, the poem was an instant success and became a featured item in the *Sentinel* for several Christmases.

4. St. Nicholas calls out the names of his reindeer in a particular order. Fill in the missing names: (A) _____, (B) _____, Prancer, Vixen, (C) _____, (D) _____, Donder, Blitzen.

(A) Dasher; (B) Dancer; (C) Comet; (D) Cupid.

5. Of the names for Santa's reindeer, which two are actually foreign names which mean, respectively, "thunder" and "lightning"?

The respective German-American equivalents for "thunder" and "lightning" are "Donder" and "Blitzen," as opposed to the Dutch-American equivalents of "Dunder" and "Blixem." Conversant in German but not Dutch, it is understandable that Clement Moore would prefer the former pair of names; whereas Henry Livingston, of Dutch descent, would prefer the latter pair.

6. What reindeer name often appears instead of "Donder"?

   A. "Donner"
   B. "Donnar"
   C. "Dannar"
   D. "Donnor"

The correct German word for "thunder" is "Donner." This name change became more frequent in printings and parodies of the poem during the early twentieth century. For example, Donner appears in *Santa's Workshop*, a Walt Disney animated cartoon short of 1932; in Robert May's short story, "Rudolph, the Red-Nosed Reindeer," written in 1939 for the Montgomery Ward

Company; and in Johnny Marks's lyrics to the 1949 hit song of the same title. The latter especially is supposed to have contributed to Donner's popularity. The exact origin for the substitution is obscure but probably stems from publishers' confusion over foreign words with similar sounds, both meaning "thunder."

7. True or false: This poem was the first piece of literature to depict Santa traveling about in a reindeer sleigh.

In 1821, Arthur Stansbury, a Presbyterian minister, created a small, eight-page picture book which he illustrated himself, titled *The Children's Friend: Number III. A New-Year's Present to the Little Ones from Five to Twelve.* In this book, which is believed to be the first printed Christmas book in the USA, Stansbury depicted Santa sitting in a sleigh pulled by a single reindeer. Stansbury's publisher was William Gilley, who just happened to be a friend of Clement Moore.

8. By what name(s) does the poem actually refer to the jolly gift bringer?

   A. St. Nicholas
   B. Santa Claus
   C. St. Nick
   D. A and C
   E. A, B, and C

The name "Santa Claus" never appears in this poem. Therefore, answer D is correct.

9. Besides reindeer, what two other animals are mentioned in the poem?

   A. Dog and cat
   B. Rat and squirrel

C. Mouse and eagle

D. Horse and donkey

Recall the lines, "Not a creature was stirring, not even a mouse" and "More rapid than eagles his coursers they came."

10. What type of storm is mentioned?

A. Tornado

B. Snowstorm

C. Hailstorm

D. Hurricane

Recall: "As dry leaves that before the wild hurricane fly . . ."

11. How many times does St. Nicholas whistle?

Recall: "And he whistled, and shouted, and called them by name;" and "He sprang to his sleigh, to his team gave a whistle."

12. According to the poem, all of these words describe St. Nicholas, <u>except</u>:

A. Chubby

B. Plump

C. Jolly

D. Gnome

Recall: "He was chubby and plump, a right jolly old elf."

13. What did "I" do when "I" saw St. Nicholas?

A. Stared

B. Laughed

    C. Screamed
    D. Scowled

Recall: "And I laughed when I saw him, in spite of myself."

14. Which two of St. Nick's actions are reassuring signs?

    A. He nods to mamma and pets the mouse.
    B. He sneezes and coughs.
    C. He smiles and yawns.
    D. He winks his eye and twists his head.

Recall: "A wink of his eye and a twist of his head, / Soon gave me to know I had nothing to dread."

15. What two things does St. Nick do just before going back up the chimney?

    A. Lays his finger beside his nose and gives a nod
    B. Waves and smiles
    C. Dons his hat and buttons his coat
    D. Hums a tune and puts on his boots

Recall: "And laying his finger aside of his nose, / And giving a nod, up the chimney he rose."

16. What is St. Nick's farewell message?

    A. "Happy Christmas to all, and to all a good night."
    B. "Merry Christmas to all, oh it's been a great night."
    C. "Joyful Christmas to all, and I'm pulling out of sight."
    D. "Thank goodness it'll be another whole year before ole St. Nick comes back around here."

You'll need to read the poem to find the answer.

Questions 17–30 are word associations. For each numbered object in the left column, match the lettered word in the right column which is best associated with it in the poem. Each word is used only once. Answers follow this group.

17. Sleigh _____   A. Miniature

18. Visions_____   B. Merry

19. Mamma_____   C. Sugarplums

20. Cheeks_____   D. Snow

21. Nose _____   E. Wreath

22. Teeth _____   F. Lively

23. Smoke_____   G. Twinkle

24. Beard_____   H. Pipe

25. Belly_____   I. Bow

26. Mouth_____   J. 'Kerchief

27. Eyes_____   K. Cherry

28. Dimples_____   L. Jelly

29. Stockings_____   M. Chimney

30. Driver_____   N. Roses

Answers to 17–30: 17-A; 18-C; 19-J; 20-N; 21-K; 22-H; 23-E; 24-D; 25-L; 26-I; 27-G; 28-B; 29-M; 30-F.

CHAPTER EIGHT

A Treasury of Literary Masterpieces

Nostalgia, sentiment, loving kindness, people turning over a new leaf in life. These are just a few of the myriad subjects which inspired authors have woven into some of the most classic, heart-warming stories and novels of the season. The previous two chapters focused on two of the most beloved pieces of Christmas literature since the Nativity. This chapter explores a host of other literary classics with which you are probably familiar. But if they are new to you, use the answers to become better acquainted, then get copies of these works and plunge into some of the best reading you'll ever encounter. You will then have a greater appreciation for Christmas as never before.

1. After listening to the testimonies of her doubting little friends, eight-year-old Virginia O'Hanlon needed some strong evidence to support her faith in Santa Claus. In 1897, she wrote the editor of a newspaper in her home town and asked, "Is there a Santa Claus?" On September 21, the paper responded with the now-classic editorial, "Yes, Virginia, There Is a Santa Claus," by Francis

P. Church. In which newspaper did this editorial appear?

    A. *New York Sun*
    B. *New York Times*
    C. *Boston Herald*
    D. *Chicago Tribune*

Virginia was prompted to write the *New York Sun*, because her father had always told her, "If you see it in the *Sun*, it's so." A prominent editorial writer for the *Sun*, Church deftly handled a most delicate topic, especially regarding impressionable young readers. His response was masterfully analytical, yet it truly gave all readers cause to pause and reflect on the good that could come from believing in the spirit of St. Nicholas, which would always make happy the heart of childhood.

2.   Although the works of American novelist William Dean Howells often reflect his keen interest in the problems of a developing, industrial America, they also include a volume of children's stories, published in 1892. In his classic tale, "Christmas Every Day," a little girl loves Christmas so much that she wishes that *every* day was Christmas. Of the following statements about the story, one is <u>incorrect</u>.

    A. The Christmas Gremlin grants the little girl's wish.
    B. Everyone becomes poor quickly from buying presents every day.
    C. People lose their voices from saying "Merry Christmas" without end.
    D. On the 4th of July, all patriotic orations turn into Christmas carols.

It is the Christmas Fairy that sets the ball rolling for a year of Yuletide cheer. But the little girl soon regrets her wish when mountains of the same presents and candy pile up in homes and on street corners week after week. After all, new presents must be given and received each day. Loathing Christmas this way, she begs the Fairy to abolish the holiday altogether when the year is spent. Soon, however, the Fairy convinces her to accept the original once-a-year Christmas that has always touched the hearts of humanity ever since Christmas began. The story teaches "everything in moderation."

3. In this short story, a loving couple, Jim and Della Young, find themselves facing Christmas with no ready cash for gifts. In desperation, Della sells her long, beautiful hair to buy Jim a platinum fob for his gold watch. But, unknown to her, Jim sells his watch to buy Della a set of gorgeous, tortoise-shell hair combs. In short, they sacrifice their most prized possessions for each other.

    A. "The Homecoming"
    B. "The Other Wise Man"
    C. "The Gift of the Magi"
    D. "The Treasured Gifts"

Published in 1905, "The Gift of the Magi" is one of the best-known short stories of the early twentieth-century American writer, William Sydney Porter, who wrote under the pseudonym of O. Henry. Jim and Della both manifest unselfish spirits, yet the story ironically describes them as "foolish children" for having sacrificed unwisely. But that is how the world would sum up the situation. Because Jim and Della have given their gifts in the manner of the Wise Men or Magi, however, they are the wisest of all.

4. In this most touching short story by Henry Van Dyke, Artaban spends his remaining days searching for Christ.

    A. "The Little Drummer Boy"
    B. "The Other Wise Man"
    C. "The Christmas Miracle"
    D. "The Five Shepherds"

    Unable to rendezvous with the caravan going to Bethlehem, Artaban, the other Wise Man, misses seeing the Christ Child and passionately begins a lifelong search for Him. He possesses precious gifts intended for the Babe, yet he ultimately sells them in order to provide for those in dire need, whom he encounters along the way. One day many years later in Jerusalem, he suffers a mortal wound and finally meets the Spirit of Christ, Who comes as a gentle Voice, commending him for his charity over the years. It is the day that Christ is crucified.

5. In "The Other Wise Man," Artaban sells his possessions and purchases as gifts for the Christ Child all of these precious stones, except:

    A. Sapphire
    B. Pearl
    C. Diamond
    D. Ruby

    Make your choice, for the answer lies in the answer to the next question.

6. Artaban unknowingly presents his three gifts to Christ through a lifetime of compassion and love. Which statement about his gifts is correct?

    A. Unavoidably detained when the other Magi depart for Bethlehem, Artaban secures another caravan with the sapphire.

    B. Artaban bribes a soldier with the ruby during King Herod's raid on Bethlehem, thereby saving a mother and her baby.

    C. Just before his death in Jerusalem, Artaban redeems a girl from slavery with the pearl.

    D. All of them are correct.

These good works are all selfless acts, and therefore, all are correct.

7.   Which story or book quotes from Matthew 25:40, ". . . Inasmuch as ye have done *it* unto one of the least of these my brethren, ye have done *it* unto me"?

    A. *The Littlest Angel*

    B. "The Other Wise Man"

    C. "The Gift of the Magi"

    D. *A Christmas Carol*

For all his years of good deeds while searching for Christ, this is the blessing that Artaban, the other Wise Man, receives from the Lord. A Presbyterian minister in New York City, Henry Van Dyke first delivered "The Other Wise Man" in 1896 as a sermon to his congregation. He is noted for his short stories, poems, and essays.

8.   "The First Christmas Tree," another short story by Henry Van Dyke, retells which classic legend?

    A. St. Boniface introduced the Christmas tree to Germanic pagans.

    B. Martin Luther introduced the lighted Christmas tree with candles.

    C. The Christ Child planted a fir tree that would always bear fruit in winter.

    D. Trees of the world all bloomed and bore fruit at the Nativity.

Van Dyke also used the St. Boniface story as one of his sermons in 1897.

9. In 1915, the English novelist and poet, Thomas Hardy, penned "The Oxen," the verses of which portray a Christmas Eve fireside scene at midnight. Upon what ancient legend does the poet muse?

    A. The oxen kneel at midnight on Christmas Eve.

    B. The oxen low softly at midnight on Christmas Eve.

    C. The oxen miraculously speak at midnight on Christmas Eve.

    D. The oxen turn toward the East at midnight on Christmas Eve.

While musing before the fire, the poet has no doubts that the oxen are kneeling at that very moment. To be realistic, he admits that such a "fancy" would not be accepted today if it was a newly-created idea. Yet if someone bid him to see it all for himself, he would still go, truly hoping that he would witness the miracle.

10. Through his writings, which author almost single-handedly revived Christmas out of its slump following the British Reformation?

    A. Robert Louis Stevenson

    B. Nathaniel Hawthorne

    C. Daniel Defoe

    D. Charles Dickens

Please recall from chapter two that, after the fall of Oliver Cromwell's Protectorate in England, celebrating Christmas recommenced, albeit on a more subdued level than before. Dickens, desiring his nation to return to those holidays of mirth, frolic, and good cheer of yore, instilled Christmas into the hearts and minds of his readers through many of his beloved works which incorporated that theme.

11. Besides the book *A Christmas Carol*, Dickens wrote another work to which he assigned the same title. What was the format of that work?

   A. A poem
   B. A play
   C. An essay
   D. A short story

The poem "A Christmas Carol" also appears in *The Pickwick Papers* in chapter 28, which describes the Christmas Eve party at Mr. Wardle's Manor Farm. Later, the poem itself was set to a popular tune of the time.

12. In that same poem, how does Dickens compare the Christmas season with the other seasons of the year?

   A. Though it comes but once a year, Christmas is a season for all mankind.
   B. Though it arrives in winter, the Christmas season warms the heart the most.
   C. None of the other seasons can compare with Christmas, the King of seasons.
   D. Christmas is the simplest of seasons, for we become children again.

As Christ is King of kings, so Christmas is the King of seasons.

13. If you're familiar with any of Dickens's other Christmas books, you can quickly see as much of the supernatural woven into them as you can in *A Christmas Carol*. What common theme do three other books, *The Haunted Man and the Ghost's Bargain*, *The Chimes*, and *The Cricket on the Hearth*, all share that's a little different from the theme of the *Carol*?

   A. Good people convince spiteful spirits to change their ways.
   B. Spirits assist good people in performing good works.
   C. Spirits reform the flawed philosophies of basically good people.
   D. Spirits fail to reform wicked people and leave them to their vices.

The Haunted Man describes a Mr. Redlaw, a kind, yet unhappy chemist, who is haunted by the memory of past sorrows. Whereas a servant remarks that his memories of previous happiness are greatest at Christmastime, Redlaw can only mull over his sorrows at this season. Redlaw's unhappy ego appears as a Phantom, whom Redlaw petitions to abolish all memory of past injustices. Complying, the Phantom additionally stipulates that those who meet Redlaw will lose similar memories. While this seems merciful, Redlaw rapidly learns that the inability to recall sorrow or injustice produces a cold, callous behavior devoid of compassion. When he repents of his wish, the Phantom reverses the spell. Redlaw then understands that, at Christmastime, the memory of every remediable sorrow and wrong should be especially active, for we remember Christ, Who suffered wrong for us and redeemed us. And as Christ forgave those who wronged Him, it is proper to remember those who wrong us, that we may also forgive them.

Toby Veck, a poor ticket porter in *The Chimes*, initially manifests an optimistic outlook on life, despite his station, and imagines that the hourly pealing of the church bells signifies good omens. When, however, harsh words from the upper classes suggest that the poor have no place in the upcoming new year, Toby's self-esteem falls, and he imagines that even the chimes mock him. Wallowing in self-pity, Toby meets the Goblin of the Great Bell, who berates him for actually thinking that the working class and the poor are born bad. The Goblin paints a futuristic scene of a world without Toby's positive influence and the devastating consequences if others, like his dear daughter, Meg, abandon all hope of rising above their stations. At the moment when Meg is about to commit suicide rather than remain destitute, Toby awakens from what had been a nightmare at midnight on New Year's Eve. He no longer doubts his capabilities, having learned this "from the creature dearest to his heart."

The characters in *The Cricket on the Hearth*, also a New Year's Eve tale, are plagued with a series of doubts and deceptions. In particular, John Peerybingle, a carrier, reasons that his much younger wife, Dot, has deprived herself of a young and active life by marrying him and now only feigns affection for him. His discovery of Dot's secret meeting with a young man disguised as one much older would seem to support his theory. Additional deceptions complicate the story and interconnect the characters: Caleb Plummer, a poor toymaker, has deceived his blind daughter, Bertha, from birth regarding their lifestyle. Believing that she lives in luxury,

Bertha falls in love with Mr. Tackleton, her father's sarcastic employer. To shield Bertha from Tackleton's blistering words, Caleb convinces Bertha that Tackleton only jests, because he is quite fond of her. Tackleton in turn is about to marry Dot's friend, May Fielding, but May's heart pines for an old flame, Edward Plummer, Caleb's son, who is presumed dead. Years earlier, John Peerybingle had provided Edward with the means of going abroad, but when Edward learned that May would marry, he returned, disguised as an old man determined to know the truth. Dot recognizes him and conspires to keep his secret. Mistaking their intentions, John is about to end his marriage, whereupon a fairy emerges from a cricket on the hearth and bids John to think twice and consider all the good that Dot has done for him, only because her love for him is genuine. They are reconciled, and Caleb eventually confesses his deception to Bertha, who forgives her father's misplaced intentions. And for a sunny ending, Edward and May marry on New Year's Eve.

The correct answer to the question is C.

14. Through his writings, Charles Dickens had become practically the embodiment of Christmas during the Victorian era. Upon his death, a poor girl likened Dickens to another personage of Christmas and asked if he also was going to die. Who was that other personage?

    A. Santa Claus
    B. Father Christmas
    C. St. Nicholas
    D. Kris Kringle

You should recall that in England, Father Christmas is the equivalent of Santa Claus in the USA. This little episode demonstrates that not much is required for people to misplace the real focus of the season.

15. Who created the glorious Christmas celebration at Bracebridge Hall?

   A. Charles Dickens
   B. O. Henry
   C. Washington Irving
   D. T. S. Eliot

An American author, Washington Irving created such memorable tales as "Rip Van Winkle" and "The Legend of Sleepy Hollow." These, together with Irving's Bracebridge Hall Christmas celebration, appear in *The Sketch Book of Geoffrey Crayon, Gent*, published 1819–1820. There, Irving provides five Christmas short stories or "sketches," which describe an old-time British Christmas celebration at the fictitious Bracebridge Hall. These sketches are titled "Christmas," "The Stage Coach," "Christmas Eve," "Christmas Day," and "The Christmas Dinner." These contributions are most significant for two reasons. One, they especially reminded the British to review those old-time Christmas traditions which were about to die from long neglect. And two, they greatly influenced and paved the way for Charles Dickens, whose later genius did so much to revive Christmas altogether on both sides of the Atlantic Ocean.

16. Which enchanting Christmas fairy tale did E. T. A. Hoffmann create?

   A. "Hansel and Gretel"
   B. "The Nutcracker and the Mouse King"

      C. *Amahl and the Night Visitors*
      D. "The Little Match Girl"

This fanciful story later became the world-renowned ballet, *The Nutcracker*, with music by Tchaikovsky, as discussed in chapter five.

17. Which of William Shakespeare's plays is the only one with a passage that refers to Christmas?

      A. *As You Like It*
      B. *Othello*
      C. *Macbeth*
      D. *Hamlet*

Near the end of Act 1, scene 1 (lines 158–164), the ghost of Hamlet's father vanishes at dawn as the rooster crows. That reminds the officer Marcellus of a legend which holds that the rooster crows all night at Christmastime ("The bird of dawning singeth all night long"), and that the holy period prevents the occurrence of any other supernatural events: ". . . then no planets strike, / No fairy takes, nor witch hath power to charm."

18. In Louisa Mae Alcott's novel *Little Women*, "Marmee," Mrs. March, receives a Christmas gift from each of her four daughters. The daughters are paired below with the gifts they give. One pair is <u>incorrect</u>:

      A. Beth—Nightgown
      B. Jo—Slippers
      C. Amy—Cologne
      D. Meg—Gloves

Marmee receives handkerchiefs from Beth.

19. The beloved American poet, Robert Frost, composed "Christmas Trees" in 1916. Here, a city buyer approaches a New England farmer about purchasing all the fir trees on his property for a Christmas enterprise. Of the following statements about this work, one of them is <u>incorrect</u>.

  A. The farmer sees his property as a place filled with fir "churches" that have spires.
  B. The would-be buyer estimates a thousand trees on the farm and offers the farmer $30 for the whole bunch (three cents per tree).
  C. In the city, Christmas trees sell for $5 apiece.
  D. The farmer figures that his trees are worth three cents more to give away than to sell.

At that time, Christmas trees sell for $1 apiece, according to the poem. Describing this poem as a "Christmas circular letter," Frost portrays nature pitted against materialism, holiday sentiment against commercialism. The farmer wishes that he could send all his friends a tree wrapped in a letter to wish them a Merry Christmas.

20. The children's Christmas books by American author Charles Tazewell are perennial favorites that present endearing messages of inspiration. Which of these is <u>not</u> one of his titles?

  A. *The Littlest Angel* (1939)
  B. *The Littlest Tree* (1997)
  C. *The Littlest Snowman* (1955)
  D. *The Small One* (1947)
  E. *The Polar Express* (1985)

Make your choice. The next question will reveal the correct answer.

21. In Chris Van Allsburg's *The Polar Express*, a little boy boards a special train for Santa's abode at the North Pole, where Santa grants the boy's request to receive one silver bell from the reindeer sleigh. Not only does the bell become the first gift of Christmas that year, but what else is special about the little bell?

     A. It rings only when Santa laughs.
     B. It rings only on Christmas Day.
     C. It rings only for those who believe in Santa Claus.
     D. It rings only when your Christmas wish comes true.

Back home, although the boy and his little sister can clearly hear the bell, their parents cannot. After several years, the bell falls silent for the sister as well, but never for the boy, because the boy has never failed to believe in Santa Claus.

22. In Rumer Godden's book, *The Story of Holly and Ivy* (1958), which of the following groups become Christmas gifts for each other?

     A. A crippled dog, a blind cat, and an elderly couple
     B. A mouse, a blind cat, and an elderly couple
     C. A doll, an orphan girl, and an elderly couple
     D. Twin girls and an elderly couple

Not quite a parody on the tune "The Holly and the Ivy," this sweet little children's story pairs up Holly, a doll left alone in a toy store on Christmas Eve, with Ivy, a little orphan girl. Holly wishes that a child would take her home for Christmas and hold her, while Ivy wishes to have a real home and a grandmother for Christmas. Not far away, an elderly, childless couple wish that they could share their holiday feast and Christmas tree with someone. Since all good wishes seem to come true at Christmastime, the loving and joy that flood from this story will more than make your days merry and bright.

British author Rumer Godden's fiction principally centers around foreigners in exotic lands, particularly India, where she resided for many years. Her children's books, however, quite often feature dolls in worlds of their own.

Earl Hamner's book, *The Homecoming: A Novel About Spencer's Mountain,* is a family-oriented tale set in rural Virginia during the Great Depression. It became the basis for the 1971 made-for-television special, *The Homecoming: A Christmas Story,* which in turn, led to the television series, *The Waltons.* Questions 23–28 pertain to Hamner's book.

23. On Christmas Eve, 1933, what actual event in Hamner's life inspired this novel?

    A. His father was simply late coming home.
    B. His little sister had run away and had finally returned.
    C. Previously separated, his father and mother were reconciled.
    D. His family gathered together at the old homestead in Schuyler, Virginia.

    The first choice is correct.

24. When does the story principally take place?

    A. One week before Christmas
    B. On Christmas Eve
    C. On Christmas Day
    D. The story only specifies "Christmastime."

Clay and Olivia Spencer, together with their eight children, Clay-Boy, Becky, Shirley, Matt, Luke, John, Mark, and Pattie-Cake, struggle to make ends meet during lean years, for jobs are scarce. Clay works all week in a machine shop forty miles away and returns home only on Friday evenings. It's now Friday, Christmas Eve, and Olivia anxiously awaits for Clay's return. But as the evening wears on, there is still no sign of Clay. About 1 AM, Clay finally returns, having missed his bus. He is loaded with gifts and explains to his children that he "wrassled" an old burglar in a red suit outside their home and grabbed an armload of presents from his sleigh before the old man escaped.

25. What holiday confection does Olivia bake?

    A. Plum pudding
    B. Mincemeat pie
    C. Applesauce cake
    D. Raisin pudding

The third choice is correct.

26. As Clay-Boy reminisces about his recent childhood with his siblings, what does he remember putting out for Santa and his reindeer on Christmas Eve?

    A. Milk, cookies, and hay
    B. Corn flakes and carrots
    C. Cookies and sugar cubes
    D. Wheat cakes and oats

The second choice is correct.

27. Who sings a solo rendition of "O Holy Night"?

    A. Clay-Boy

    B. Ep Bridges, the sheriff
    C. Emma and Etta Staples, the elderly neighbors
    D. Hawthorne Dooly, the African American minister

When Olivia can no longer endure waiting for Clay to return, she sends Clay-Boy out to look for him. Since the boy knows that sometimes his father plays poker at odd hours with his white friends in a church established by African Americans, his search begins there. To his surprise, he finds a Christmas Eve service in progress. Clay-Boy has never socialized with black people before, and he certainly feels no welcome, until Hawthorne Dooly, the minister, kindly invites him to share their service. Besides singing favorite carols and enjoying a children's Nativity pageant, Clay-Boy listens spellbound as Rev. Dooly reverently delivers his version of "O Holy Night."

28. Neighbors Emma and Etta Staples are two old-maid sisters who make an alcoholic concoction for "medicinal" purposes as well as for Christmas gifts. By what term do they refer to this brew?

    A. "The Tonic"
    B. "The Recipe"
    C. "The Formula"
    D. "The Family Secret"

Being a worldly man, Clay periodically pays a call on the Staples sisters to partake a little of "The Recipe," and Clay-Boy next directs his search there. Thinking that the boy is making a social visit, the sisters earnestly strive to entertain him with old stories about Ashley Longworth, a lost love, records on the Victrola, and three glasses of eggnog spiked with The Recipe, of course. When he's quite numb, not from the cold, however, they drive him back home around midnight in a one-horse sleigh.

Continuing with *The Homecoming*, after Clay-Boy brings home the Christmas tree, each of his brothers and sisters decorate it with their own very simple yet very personal ornaments. Questions 29–35 present statements about each sibling's decoration. From the following list, insert the appropriate words in the blanks. Answers follow this group.

A. Key   E. Coal   I. Black-eyed peas
B. Chain   F. Cotton
C. Turkey   G. Pine cones
D. Silver bells H. Blue jay

29. John contributes _____ varnished with gold paint.

30. Mark produces an antique, brass _____.

31. Shirley makes a _____ from construction paper.

32. Matt creates a red flannel Santa with _____ for eyes, a lump of _____ for a nose, and a beard made of _____.

33. Luke fashions _____ from tinfoil.

34. Becky brings in a _____ nest containing one speckled egg.

35. Pattie-Cake hangs a cutout of a paper _____ left over from Thanksgiving.

Answers to 29–35: 29-G; 30-A; 31-B; 32-I, E, F in that order; 33-D; 34-H; 35-C.

Questions 36–44 recall some Christmas episodes from several different titles. Please provide short answers.

36. Written during the Christmas of 1629, "On the Morning of Christ's Nativity" was this young man's first great English poem, composed just a few weeks after his twenty-first birthday. Who was he?

   One of the foremost poets of English literature, John Milton placed this poem first in his *Poems*, published in 1645. "Christ's Nativity" begins with a short prelude of six stanzas, which ponders the paradox between the Babe's divine power versus His mortality. Then follows The Hymn, the principal work of twenty-seven stanzas. Rather than elaborate directly upon the Gospel texts of Matthew and Luke, Milton views the Nativity as creating a closer harmony between heaven and earth (Nature), which the music of the angels and the planets herald. But compared with the earthly Advent of the Creator, Nature regards herself as most inconsequential. Peering into the future, the poem's latter stanzas emphasize the Incarnate's redemption of mankind through the recovery of righteousness and the overthrow of idolatry, followed by the Day of Judgment. The final stanza returns quietly to the manger and the sleeping Babe, with angels and the Star in attendance nearby.

37. Two small portions of Milton's "On the Morning of Christ's Nativity" appear as an epigraph in which epic novel by General Lewis Wallace?

   From the prelude, Wallace first quotes the first two lines of the fourth stanza. Then follows the entire fifth stanza of The Hymn. These lines grace *Ben-Hur: A Tale of the Christ*.

38. On Christmas Morning in *Little Women*, Marmee returns from visiting the Hummel family, whose mother is ill and whose six children suffer from hunger and cold. What does Marmee suggest that she and her daughters do for the Hummels?

   Marmee suggests that she and her daughters sacrifice their breakfasts to the Hummels, which they do.

39. Henry Wadsworth Longfellow was one of America's most popular poets of the nineteenth century. His poem, "The Three Kings," provides a narrative account of the Wise Men's journey to Bethlehem. Of their gifts mentioned in the poem, which one is intended for the "Paraclete"?

   Since the Paraclete is the Holy Spirit, a gift that would be used in Eastern worship services would be most appropriate. Thus, the gift is frankincense.

40. In which classic children's book does Babar, the elephant king, relieve Father Christmas on Christmas Eve while the latter takes a vacation in Babar's land?

   Jean de Brunhoff, an early twentieth-century French author of children's books, created the popular *Babar* series, which included *Babar and Father Christmas*. When the elephant children wonder why Father Christmas never comes to their country, king Babar sets off to find Father Christmas and persuades him to take a vacation in Babar's kingdom. So that he can deliver the gifts on Christmas Eve, Father Christmas provides Babar with a red suit which enables him to fly to all the elephant children's homes.

41. In Charles Tazewell's precious book, *The Littlest Angel*, a little boy enters Heaven, only to find himself not quite

prepared to cope with his new environment. But as the time for the birth of the Son of God draws near, the Littlest Angel fulfills the biblical phrase "the last shall be the first," as far as heavenly Christmas gifts are concerned. What gift does the Littlest Angel present to God to honor Christ's birth?

The Littlest Angel's only possession is a rough, unsightly little box that contains a collection of small treasures from his life on earth. But he gladly parts with his treasures for the sake of Christ.

42. The following items would be of interest to a little boy. Four of them are found in the Littlest Angel's treasure box, which he gives to God, while the other two are not. Indicate which items belong in the box.

    A. Butterfly_____
    B. Pop gun_____
    C. Bird's egg_____
    D. Stones_____
    E. Baseball card_____
    F. Dog collar_____

In his box are a golden-winged butterfly which he captured on the hills above Jerusalem; a sky-blue egg from a bird's nest in an olive tree; two white stones from a muddy river bank; and a tooth-marked, leather collar which his mongrel dog had worn.

43. According to the story, how does God regard the Littlest Angel's gift?

When the Littlest Angel steps forth with his seemingly meagre little box, most of the angels present scorn the gift and regard it as a complete insult to the Son of God. But God, seeing that the little box contains things of the earth and of men, remarks that this gift is the most pleasing. Because His Son will be King of both, He will know and love these things. Regretfully, He will leave them behind when He departs the earth and returns to Heaven.

44. After God completely accepts the Littlest Angel's gift, what happens to it?

The little box soars into the heavens and becomes the brilliantly shining Star of Bethlehem.

Questions 45–52 pertain to "A Christmas Memory," a particularly endearing Christmas short story written in 1956 by the American author, Truman Capote. An autobiographical sketch of his early life at the age of seven, it recalls one special Christmas which he spends with an elderly yet child-like cousin, Miss Sook Faulk. Answers follow this group.

45. Throughout the story, Capote affectionately refers to Miss Faulk as (A) _____, while she calls him (B) _____ in memory of a boy who had been her best friend in childhood.

46. As their way of opening the Christmas season, Buddy and his cousin bake thirty _____ late in November.

47. They take pure joy in giving these confections to those who have touched their lives in some tender way, including strangers and not necessarily relatives They even send one to _____, President of the United States.

48. Buddy's cousin would really love to give him a _____ for Christmas. But since she cannot, she

says, "It's bad enough in life to do without something *you* want . . . what gets my goat is not being able to give somebody something you want *them* to have."

49. On Christmas Eve morning, Buddy and friend hike through the woods in search of the perfect Christmas tree which, according to her, must be twice as tall as a (A) _____ so that he cannot steal the (B) _____.

50. As the two of them are taking home their Christmas tree, someone offers to buy it from them for (A) _____, remarking that they can always get another one. Declining the offer, "my friend" remarks, (B) "_____."

51. Buddy and his cousin give each other homemade _____ for Christmas, just like they have in years past.

52. Years later, Buddy needs no one to tell him that his cousin has passed away, for he senses that late November morning when she will no longer rise and declare, "_____."

Answers to 45–52: 45-(A) "My Friend," (B) "Buddy;" 46-Fruitcakes; 47-Franklin D. Roosevelt; 48-Bicycle; 49-(A) Boy, (B) Star; 50-(A) Fifty cents, (B) "There's never two of anything;" 51-Kites; 52-"Oh, my, it's fruitcake weather!" That was her way of announcing that it was time to prepare for Christmas.

Questions 53–58 consist of statements which draw comparisons between two classic but sobering holiday sto-

ries by Hans Christian Andersen. For each of the follow-
ing statements, determine whether it applies to A-"The
Fir Tree," B-"The Little Match Girl," or C-both of them.
Answers and comments follow this group.

53. The story presents a strong moral, that if one's situation in life is good, be content.

54. The setting for the story is New Year's Eve.

55. The principal character sees a falling star, a sign that a
soul will soon go to God.

56. The principal character experiences scenes of grandeur.

57. Fire plays a significant role around the principal character.

58. An angel visits the principal character.

Answers to 53–58:   53-A; 54-B; 55-B; 56-C; 57-C; 58-B.

Comments: After a lifetime of wishing that it could
be anywhere but in the forest, the fir
tree experiences what it believes is a
dream come true when, fully mature,
it is hacked down and erected as a
beautifully decorated Christmas tree
in a fashionable home. Candles on its
branches at first merely scorch the fir
tree. But when Christmas is over and
its usefulness has expired, the fir tree's
grandeur vanishes as it is stripped of
its decorations and tossed into the fire.
Never having counted the cost, the
tree learns the price of blind vanity,
albeit too late.

Clothed in tattered rags and having wandered wearily all day through the frozen streets without food, the little match girl has sold not one single match. Desperate to rid herself of the bitter cold, she begins striking her matches one by one, clinging to the miniscule warmth from each tiny flame. Soon, each little burst conjures up spectacular visions, such as a warm stove, then a table sumptuously laden with delicious food, then a gorgeously shimmering Christmas tree. Striking all her remaining matches brings her late grandmother before her as a smiling angel who carries her to Heaven, where she will no longer suffer from hunger and cold.

Questions 59–68 pertain to *A Child's Christmas in Wales* (1954) by Welsh author Dylan Thomas. According to the story, children categorize their Christmas presents either as "useful" or "useless." Ironically, useful gifts are dull and boring, whereas the useless gifts are fun and enjoyable. For each of the following gifts mentioned in the story, designate each as A-useful or B-useless, according to Thomas's criteria. Answers follow this group.

59. Hatchets

60. Fudge

61. Books without pictures

62. Painting books

63. Vests

64. Mittens

65. Tin soldiers

66. Scarves

67. Loud whistles

68. Mufflers (clothing)

Answers to 59–68: 59-B; 60-B; 61-A; 62-B; 63-A; 64-A; 65-B; 66-A; 67-B; 68-A.

Questions 69–79 present clues to the titles of classic Christmas literature. Match the following lettered titles with those clues. Answers and comments follow this group.

 A. *The Best Christmas Pageant Ever* by Barbara Robinson

 B. *Carol of the Brown King: Nativity Poems* by Langston Hughes

 C. *Father Christmas* by Raymond Briggs

 D. *The Life and Adventures of Santa Claus* by L. Frank Baum

 E. *The Littlest Snowman* by Charles Tazewell

 F. *The Littlest Tree* by Charles Tazewell

 G. *Marmion* by Sir Walter Scott

 H. *Madeline's Christmas* by Ludwig Bemelmans

 I. "One Christmas," a short story by Truman Capote

 J. *The Small One* by Charles Tazewell

 K. *The Year Without a Santa Claus* by Phyllis McGinley

69. Rather than sell his beloved donkey of advanced years to a tanner as his father had ordered, a Judean boy,

insisting that his pet is fine enough for a King's stable, succeeds in selling him to Joseph, who seeks a gentle animal to carry Mary to Bethlehem.

70. Seemingly incorrigible ragamuffins and school bullies, the Herdman children learn the beauty, simplicity, and tenderness of the Nativity story when they portray biblical characters in a church play.

71. The work is a romantic, narrative poem which contains the lines, "Heap on more wood!—the wind is chill; / But let it whistle as it will, / We'll keep our Christmas merry still."

72. Its African American author was a key figure in the Harlem Renaissance of the 1920s and was sometimes called the Poet Laureate of Harlem.

73. This biographical fantasy of the title character includes his childhood among creatures in an enchanted forest, his establishment as a toy-making friend of children, and his acquisition of the "Mantle of Immortality," which explains why he still "lives" today.

74. In this narrative poem, six-year-old Ignatius Thistlewhite rallies children all over the world to give Santa a Christmas holiday away from the hassle of delivering gifts. But after receiving so many gifts from the children, Santa decides that he doesn't need a holiday after all.

75. Discovering his father placing presents under the tree, Buddy doubts the reality of Santa Claus, until his elderly cousin provides the "straight" story about Santa: He exists in all of us, "as the Lord would have it," for no single person could do all that Santa must do.

76. When her boarding school classmates and head mistress contract colds on Christmas Eve, a little girl faces a mountain of chores until a mysterious rug merchant dispatches them in short order. Then he whisks the girls away on flying carpets to their parents' homes for Christmas.

77. Whenever people on Earth select and decorate their Christmas trees, exact replicas of those trees grow in the Forest of the Nativity in Heaven. On Christmas Eve, the Son of God annually selects one of those trees to be His birthday tree.

78. When rising temperatures threaten to cancel a Christmas snowfall, the title character consumes great quantities of colored ice cream, then allows the north wind to blow him into multicolored snowflakes all over town.

79. This version of Santa Claus features a two-reindeer sleigh and no elves.

Answers to 69–79:   69-J; 70-A; 71-G; 72-B; 73-D; 74-K; 75-I; 76-H; 77-F; 78-E; 79-C.

Comments: *Marmion* is built around the fictitious Lord Marmion amid a setting of knighthood and chivalry. The poem consists of six Cantos, of which the Christmas section, comprising 85 lines, is found in the "Introduction to Canto Sixth." This section often appears in print separately under the titles of "Heap on More Wood," "Christmas in Olden Times," "Old Christmas," etc. It vividly recalls pre-Christian winter solstice festivals as well as medieval

Christmases of yore, and it is a good historical source for studying those celebrations.

The best known of Langston Hughes's poems is "Carol of the Brown King," published in 1958, which asserts that one of the Three Kings was black. A complete collection of the six brief poems was published as an illustrated version in 1998. Hughes's other poems here include "Shepherd's Song at Christmas," "On a Christmas Night," "The Christmas Story," and "On a Pallet of Straw." The sixth is Hughes's translation of an anonymous, Puerto Rican Christmas card.

Madeline's Christmas is the last in the series of six *Madeline* books. Their creator, Ludwig Bemelmans, based the Madeline character on a little patient he met in a hospital while he was recovering from injuries sustained in a car accident off the coast of France.

The Son of God selects the Littlest Tree, a scrub of a branch, which a group of homeless, orphan boys lovingly decorate and present to little Laus, who has never before seen the like of a Christmas tree.

Question 80 pertains to *Ben-Hur: A Tale of the Christ*, published in 1880 by the American Civil War general, Lewis Wallace. Designed as an extended prologue to this

historical novel, its Book First beautifully expands upon
the Nativity story, beginning with the meeting of the Wise
Men. In the following vignette, which briefly summarizes
this episode, lettered key elements are left blank for you
to fill in.

80. Appearing as a gentle Voice in a brilliant light, the Holy
Spirit separately greets (A) _____ the Egyptian,
(B) _____ the Hindu, and (C) _____ the
Greek, with tidings that each man is blessed because
he is to see the (D) _____. Each one is to arise
and meet two others as the Spirit guides him. Led thusly
with the Spirit in their hearts, the three Wise Men ren-
dezvous together in the (E) _____ Desert on this
month and day, (F) _____. They then set forth
on the next phase, with the Spirit preceding them as
the (G) _____. Eleven days later, the Wise Men
reach Jerusalem and begin their search for the Redeemer. They are an unusual-appearing trio, because
their camels are not gray or brown but (H) _____.
Even more striking is the question they pose to everyone whom they meet, as the Spirit directs them: (I)
"_____." Herod the king, having received word
of the strange men inquiring about a new king, summons the Wise Men and questions them. Beforehand,
however, Herod had consulted his scholars, among
them, (J) _____ the Babylonian, Rector of the
College, regarding the time and place of Christ's birth.
The Wise Men now declare to Herod that the Christ is
born, and that He will save men from their wickedness
through the three divine agencies of (K) _____.
After Herod steers the Wise Men toward Bethlehem,
they depart with his admonition to (L) _____.
On the twelfth day from the start of their journey together, a day now known as (M) _____, the Wise

Men kneel before the Christ Child in worship and present their three treasures of (N) _____. They find the Holy Family living not in a traditional stable with stalls, but in a humble (O) _____. The Babe appears as any other newborn, lying in a manger made not of wood but of (P) _____, and Mary is but a young girl, very fair, with (Q) _____ eyes and (R) _____ hair. Because her parents, Joachim and Anna, are now deceased, to save her portion of the family's property by Jewish law, Mary has married her nearest kinsman, the much older Joseph, who is actually her (S) _____. Although the Wise Men are the first Gentile witnesses to the Christ, they are not the first beyond His mother and Joseph to gaze upon Him. Joseph and Mary share their cave with another family from the city of Beth-Dagon during the Nativity, and their proximity becomes obvious. After these comes the next principal group to see Him prior to the Wise Men, the (T) _____, who had kept watch over their flocks by night. According to the novel, the name of the angel who leads the Heavenly Host is (U) _____ (his name is not given in Luke 2).

(A) Balthasar; (B) Melchior; (C) Gaspar; (D) Redeemer; (E) Arabian; (F) December 25th; (G) Star in the East; (H) White; (I) "Where is he that is born King of the Jews?" (J) Hillel; (K) Faith, Love, and Good Works; (L) Inform Herod where the Child is, that he may come and worship Him also; (M) Epiphany; (N) Gold, frankincense, and myrrh; (O) Cave; (P) Stone; (Q) Blue; (R) Golden; (S) Uncle; (T) Shepherds; (U) Gabriel

Comments: Many times have skeptics sought ways to debunk the so-called "myth" of Christianity, only to fall on their knees

234 · Was the First Gift Really Gold?

in supplication to Christ when the Redeemer makes their hearts receptive. Such was the case with General Lewis Wallace. Determining to write a book that would destroy Christianity, Wallace diligently conducted research for two years in the best libraries of America and Europe. While writing the second chapter, all his research abruptly crashed as the overwhelming evidence flooded over him like a tidal wave: Christ truly *is* the Son of God. Wallace found himself on his knees, pouring forth his faith in Christ. Later, this faith enabled him to write *Ben-Hur: A Tale of the Christ*.

Questions 81–84. One of the most profound questions ever posed is found in a little novel by Richard Paul Evans. If you know the answer as well as fathom it, you know the entire treasure of Christmas. Along with the principal question, please consider three others as well. Answers and comments follow this group.

81. What was the first gift of Christmas?

82. Which of Evans's novels asks this question?

83. Was the first gift really gold?

84. Which Gospel contains the answer?

Answers and comments to 81–84:

The first gift of Christmas forms the central theme of *The Christmas Box*, a novel published in 1995 in which Richard Evans, his wife Keri, and three-year-old daughter Jenna become holiday houseguests of an elderly widow, Mary Parkin. Terminally ill, Mary observes Richard's growing obsession with his work and the scant amount of time he spends with his family, especially with little Jenna. Launching a plan to snap Richard out of his passion for success, she asks him, "What was the first gift of Christmas?" Richard has no clue until he discovers an antique Christmas box in the attic that contains several letters of anguish addressed to "My Beloved One" from "Mother." After finding Mary's tear-stained Bible open to the Gospel of John and learning from a neighbor that, years ago, Mary had lost her own little three-year-old Andrea, the answer now overwhelms Richard.

Surprisingly, the real crux of the answer lies not in the Nativity stories as presented in the Gospels of Matthew and Luke, but in John 3:16: "For God so loved the world, that he gave his only begotten Son, that whosoever believeth in him should not perish, but have everlasting life." Therefore, the first gift of Christmas was neither gold, nor frankincense, nor myrrh, contrary to what most of us would logically believe. *The first gift of Christmas was a Child, Jesus*, given up to the likes of this world by a totally loving Heavenly

Father, so that His other children (those of mankind who believe on Him), would be able to return to His embrace at the end of time. Richard, realizing Mary's years of grief over her loss and her empathy with God for having surrendered His own Child, now knows that Mary has given him his greatest Christmas gift, his daughter's childhood.

A former advertising executive, Richard Paul Evans wrote *The Christmas Box* in 1993 as an expression of a father's love for his two daughters, Jenna and Allyson.

CHAPTER NINE

Memorable Movies and Television Specials

D uring the twentieth century and beyond, Hollywood's conception of Christmas most often created productions that lifted up Santa Claus, not Jesus Christ, as the centerpiece of the holiday. In countless story lines, when an imminent disaster threatened to prevent the jolly old elf from mounting his reindeer sleigh to deliver gifts on Christmas Eve, the North Pole, and even the whole world perhaps, sought a quick solution, lest Christmas be "canceled." The ever-present, world-wide commercialism associated with the holiday would concur. Although many of these Santa-oriented pictures, particularly a host of animated cartoons, have now become classics, a few productions remain true not only to the real Spirit of Christmas but also incorporate the concepts of brotherly love, home, morality, and family values—concepts which today's society seems to shun. This chapter focuses on appropriate, memorable classics from motion pictures and television specials as well as selected animated cartoons.

Questions 1–14 pertain to four principal productions which chronicle the life of Christ. The following statements compare the Nativity segments of those productions. For each statement, determine all of the appropriate production(s), if applicable, to which it refers from the list below. The following choices may be used more than once. Answers and comments follow this group.

> A. *The Greatest Story Ever Told* (motion picture, 1965)
> B. *Jesus of Nazareth* (television miniseries, 1977)
> C. *King of Kings* (motion picture, 1961)
> D. *Mary, Mother of Jesus* (television special, 1999)
> E. None of the above

1. Herald angels announce to shepherds that a Saviour is born in Bethlehem.

2. Shepherds visit the manger and relate that a "man" told them to come.

3. The picture opens with narration from John 1:1: "In the beginning was the Word . . ."

4. Actor Orson Welles provides the narration.

5. The Nativity takes place in a cave rather than the conventional stable.

6. In the Annunciation to Mary, she converses with a brilliant light flooding through her window at night. The audience neither sees nor hears the angel, only Mary's responses.

7. A white-robed angel Gabriel delivers the Annunciation to Mary as she works beside a road.

8. The Wise Men are identified as Melchior, Caspar (or Gaspar), and Balthazar.

9. The Wise Men state the significance of their three gifts.

10. The portrayal of Herod's raid on Bethlehem departs significantly from Scripture.

11. Instead of Joseph being warned of God in a dream to flee Herod's wrath and depart for Egypt, the Wise Men deliver the warning.

12. A principal character quotes Jeremiah 31:15: ". . . A voice was heard in Ramah, lamentation, *and* bitter weeping; Rachel weeping for her children refused to be comforted for her children, because they *were* not."

13. The only portrayal of the actual Nativity is a darkened stable and a close-up of an infant's hand.

14. The picture shows an empty manger draped with swaddling clothes as the raid on Bethlehem commences and indicates that the Holy Family has departed for Egypt.

Answers to 1–14: 1-E; 2-B; 3-A; 4-C; 5-B; 6-B; 7-D; 8-B, C; 9-A, B; 10-A, D; 11-B; 12-A, B; 13-A; 14-A.

Comments: Only B and D portray the angel's Annunciation to Mary. Surprisingly, none of these pictures depicts the Heavenly Host's appearance to the shepherds, who visit the manger in A, B, and D. In A, they are purely incidental characters. The audience sees nothing of the "man" (supposedly an angel) in B that bade the shepherds go to the man-

ger, and in D, the shepherds only relate their encounter with the Heavenly
Host after the fact.

Portrayals of the Wise Men vary con-
siderably. Whereas in B, the Wise Men
introduce themselves as Melchior,
Caspar, and Balthazar, the narrator in
C introduces them respectively as being from Mesopotamia, Persia, and
Ethiopia. A and D conform to the biblical account by neither presenting the
identities of the Wise Men nor their
countries of origin. They detail the significance of their gifts in two films. In
A, the gold is for the sovereignty of a
King; the frankincense, to worship
God; the myrrh, for preservation until time everlasting. In B, Balthazar
brings frankincense to perfume the
halls of the Mighty; Gaspar brings gold
for Kingly rule; and Melchior brings
myrrh, the most precious herb of the
Orient and the most bitter. The latter
is a portent about the eventual death
of Jesus. C and D do not detail any gift
significance.

Departures from Scripture are more
pronounced regarding King Herod's
raid on Bethlehem and the Holy
Family's flight into Egypt. Herod in A,
believing that he is the fulfillment of
Jeremiah 31:15, orders the murder of
all newborns in Bethlehem; in D, all

the male children born within the last six months. The aged Simeon quotes the prophecy in lament after the raid in B. It is the Wise Men, not God, who deliver the warning about Herod in B; and in D, the Holy Family merely escapes during the raid without having received any warning. In A, an invisible Voice warns Joseph, but not in a dream. Only in C does Joseph receive the warning in a dream. The liberties taken with Scripture illustrate how Hollywood often takes a well-known story and deliberately alters it for "dramatic effect." In doing so, Hollywood appears to consider the Nativity as just another fictitious story.

Questions 15–20 focus on one notable television production. Answers and comments follow this group.

15. Which Christmas opera was the first written for television and later became the first sponsored television show in color?

   A. *Amahl and the Night Visitors*
   B. *Hansel and Gretel*
   C. *The Nutcracker*
   D. *Messiah*

16. Who are the "Night Visitors"?

   A. Santa's elves
   B. The Wise Men
   C. King Herod's soldiers
   D. The Heavenly Host

17. Who is Amahl?

    A. A rich merchant
    B. A poor cobbler
    C. A crippled little boy
    D. A benevolent king

18. What crime does Amahl's mother commit, for which the Wise Men forgive her?

    A. She steals some of the Wise Men's gold.
    B. She steals some of the Wise Men's frankincense.
    C. She steals some of the Wise Men's myrrh.
    D. She steals a royal garment from one of the Wise Men's packs.

19. Desiring to send a gift via the Wise Men to honor the Christ Child, Amahl offers this, his only possession:

    A. His pet lamb, snowy white and without blemish
    B. A gold coin which his father had given him
    C. His little crutch, without which he could not walk
    D. A shawl of many colors, which his mother had knitted for him

20. What comes to pass after Amahl offers his gift?

    A. Amahl is healed and is able to run like other children.
    B. The Wise Men remark, "Well done, thou good and faithful servant."
    C. The Wise Men prophesy that Amahl, though he will remain crippled, will be a great voice for the cause of Christ.
    D. His mother and the Wise Men scold Amahl for daring to offer such a trifle to the Christ Child.

Answers to 15–20: 15-A; 16-B; 17-C; 18-A; 19-C; 20-A.

Comments: Consisting of one act and the creation of the Italian-born composer and conductor Gian Carlo Menotti, *Amahl and the Night Visitors* premiered in New York City on Christmas Eve, 1951, and was a presentation of the NBC Opera Company. In 1953, the *Hallmark Hall of Fame* presented *Amahl* as the first sponsored television show in color.

Amahl, a poor, lame little boy who hobbles on a crutch, lives with his widowed mother in the mountains of Italy. According to the Italian legend of Befana, the bringer of Christmas gifts in that country on the eve of Epiphany, the Wise Men from the East supposedly journeyed all the way to Bethlehem via Italy. Now it is they who receive shelter in Amahl's house. During the night, Amahl's destitute mother is caught stealing the Wise Men's gold. Claiming that she committed the act for the sake of her child, she ultimately repents, and the Wise Men forgive her. Knowing the Wise Men's mission and reasoning that he could never accompany them to see the Christ Child in person, Amahl gladly surrenders his crutch to them as a gift for the Babe. The Holy Spirit rewards this unselfish act, when suddenly Amahl is able to run and play like other children. He then accompanies the Wise Men to Bethlehem.

It is important to note that, although Amahl receives an immediate reward for his good deed, in reality, such acts may not always be rewarded so speedily, and sometimes, they seemingly may never be rewarded physically on earth. But all good things come to the faithful who wait, for our Heavenly Father will provide the ultimate reward in Heaven.

Questions 21–41 all focus on another classic, holiday film. Answers and comments follow this group.

21. Having annually enjoyed Macy's Thanksgiving Day parade from his New York apartment, screenwriter Valentine Davies, concerned over the commercialism surrounding Christmas, is said to have conceived the idea for this perennial film while waiting in line at a department store.

    A. *Miracle on 34th Street* (1947)
    B. *A Christmas Carol* (1951)
    C. *The Bells of St. Mary's* (1945)
    D. *It's a Wonderful Life* (1946)

22. Two versions were released to theatres, the original in 1947 and a remake in 1994. As the 1947 version opens, what is Kris Kringle's first item of "business"?

    A. He teaches Macy's Santa how to crack a whip over the reindeer sleigh float.
    B. He corrects the reindeer display in a shop window.
    C. He reports the drunken Macy's Santa to Doris Walker.

    D. He takes an intelligence test from Macy's psychologist.

23. In the 1947 version, Kris sports a full beard, his hearing and eyesight are perfect, but he walks with a cane. How is Kris different in the 1994 version?

    A. He wears a hearing aid and contact lenses.
    B. He wears glasses, and his beard is much shorter.
    C. He wears glasses and is clean shaven.
    D. He wears a hearing aid and is clean shaven.

24. Which popular Christmas song serves as a frequent background theme in both versions?

    A. "Here Comes Santa Claus"
    B. "White Christmas"
    C. "Jingle Bells"
    D. "Santa Claus Is Coming to Town"

25. When Kris notices little Susan Walker watching him in the parade from her apartment window, what does he do (1994)?

    A. The throws her a kiss.
    B. He simply waves.
    C. He shouts, "Hello, beautiful!"
    D. He reads Susan's mind and shakes his head in dismay.

26. All of these statements describe Kris's trappings in the 1994 version, <u>except</u>:

    A. He wears a gold ring shaped like a Christmas wreath with a bow.
    B. His gold belt buckle sports images of holly leaves at the corners.

    C. Each of the gold buttons on his coat bears the image of a reindeer with its name.

    D. He carries a gold, pocket music box that plays "Jingle Bells."

27. As Brian, Dorey, and Susan sit down to Thanksgiving dinner, with which of Brian's mannerly gestures is Dorey rather uncomfortable (1994)?

    A. Brian says grace.

    B. Brian holds Dorey's chair for her.

    C. Brian rises when Dorey leaves the table.

    D. Brian waits until Dorey and Susan have been served before eating.

28. In both versions, as Kris interviews children about their Christmas wishes, how does he spread the Christmas spirit all over New York City?

    A. He tells each child to kiss a friend and wish them a Merry Christmas.

    B. He hands each child a bumper sticker that says, "I believe in Santa."

    C. He teaches each child a new song about Christmas joy.

    D. If Macy's or Cole's does not carry an item that the child wishes, he steers the parents to other stores that carry it.

29. Receiving a sizable bonus from Mr. Macy, Kris wishes to help his friend, Dr. Pierce, the physician at Brooks Memorial Home for the Aged, where Kris resides. What does Kris plan as a Christmas surprise for Dr. Pierce (1947)?

    A. An x-ray machine

    B. Surgical instruments

    C. A respirator

    D. An ambulance

30. When Fred/Brian, who is trying to get Susan interested in Santa Claus, takes her to visit Kris at Macy's, what does Susan do in both versions while sitting on his knee?

    A. She pats Kris's fat belly.

    B. She says, "I just don't believe in you."

    C. She laughs Kris to scorn.

    D. She asks what Kris's *real* name is and pulls his beard.

31. Fred, who lives in the same apartment building as Doris and Susan, invites Kris to stay with him so that Kris may have more influence over the two females. Most curious, Fred asks a question that has "puzzled people for centuries." Does Santa Claus sleep with his whiskers outside or inside of the covers? How does Kris reply (1947)?

    A. Inside, for warmth makes them grow.

    B. Inside, for warmth keeps them soft.

    C. Outside, for the cold air keeps them soft.

    D. Outside, for the cold air makes them grow.

32. As time passes, Susan comes to adore Kris as a grandfather figure, and Kris exerts every effort to show her the fanciful faces of childhood, for example the game of pretending and using one's imagination. It's something she's never done before. For Susan's first lesson in pretending, what does Kris teach her to be (1947)?

    A. A fairy princess

    B. A monkey

C. Joan of Arc
D. A lion

33. Kris succeeds in earning Susan's trust, for she finally reveals her Christmas wishes. Which of these is <u>not</u> a wish (1994)?

    A. A real home
    B. A dog
    C. A dad
    D. A baby brother

34. Why does Kris become so interested in Alfred, an overweight, teenage janitor at Macy's (1947)?

    A. Alfred's last name is also Kringle.
    B. Alfred wants Kris to tell him why he believes that he is the real Santa.
    C. Alfred's weight reminds Kris of his own physique when he was a lad.
    D. Alfred enjoys playing Santa at the YMCA and seeing the happy expressions when he hands out packages to needy recipients.

35. When Kris insists that his name is Kris Kringle, Doris questions his sanity. After reviewing his employment card, she orders that Kris undergo a mental status examination. The following data appear on the card, <u>except</u> (1947):

    A. Address: Brooks Memorial Home for the Aged, Great Neck, NY
    B. Next of kin: 17 elves
    C. Age: "As old as my tongue and a little bit older than my teeth"
    D. Place of birth: North Pole

36. Kris is quite familiar with mental status exams and has a trick question of his own, the answer to which he feels certain that Mr. Sawyer, Macy's psychologist, will not know (1947):

    A. When did George Washington first obtain wooden teeth?
    B. What was the name of Andrew Jackson's horse?
    C. Who was the vice president under John Quincey Adams?
    D. How many steps lead up to the U. S. Supreme Court building in Washington, D. C.?

37. Although Kris passes Sawyer's exam in the 1947 version, Sawyer is still convinced that Kris is insane, and a slight, physical altercation with Sawyer over Alfred's suitability to play Santa sends Kris to the psychiatric ward at Bellevue Hospital. Whom does Kris "assault" in the 1994 version?

    A. A policeman
    B. Mr. Shellhammer, Macy's floorwalker
    C. The drunken Santa whom Kris replaced
    D. Victor Lamberg, CEO of Shopper's Express

38. Who says, "Faith is believing in things when common sense tells you not to" (1947)?

    A. Fred
    B. Mr. Macy
    C. Alfred
    D. Mr. Shellhammer

39. All of the following are true concerning Kris's mental competency hearing, except:

    A. Mr. Macy testifies that Kris is the real Santa Claus (1947).

    B. When prosecutor Ed Collins demands that Kris make a reindeer fly, Kris replies that reindeer can only fly on Christmas Eve (1994).

    C. Susan steps forward and hands Judge Henry Harper a childish Christmas card containing a ten-dollar bill inside with the words "In God We Trust" circled (1994).

    D. When the U. S. Postal Service routes thousands of letters addressed to "Santa Claus" at the courthouse, Judge Harper dismisses the case (1947).

40. At the close of the 1994 version, when and where do Brian and Dorey marry?

    A. After Midnight Mass on Christmas Eve in St. Francis' Church

    B. In the courthouse immediately after Kris is acquitted on Christmas Eve

    C. On Christmas Day in Susan's dream house

    D. On Christmas Day at Mt. Carmel Senior Center, Kris's residence

41. If you look very closely in the Christmas Day scenes at Susan's new house, what do you notice about the mailbox that's "politically correct" (1994)?

    A. Brian and Dorey have separate mail boxes.

    B. Beneath the mailbox is a sculpture of a woman and a little girl.

    C. The name on the mailbox reads "Walker—Bedford."

    D. The name on the mailbox reads "Dorey Walker and Family."

Answers to 21–41: 21-A; 22-B; 23-B; 24-C; 25-A; 26-D ("Have Yourself a Merry Little Christmas"); 27-A; 28-D; 29-A; 30-D; 31-D; 32-B; 33-B; 34-D; 35-B (names of the eight reindeer); 36-C (Daniel D. Tompkins); 37-C; 38-A; 39-C (one-dollar bill); 40-A; 41-C.

Comments: While many movies are often based on a previously published book or story, *Miracle's* birth was just the opposite. Davies pitched his brainchild to his friend, George Seaton, who not only wrote the screenplay but directed the picture as well. Only after *Miracle's* production did Davies receive any invitation to publish his story as a little novel. But I really believe that most of us are much more familiar with its two feature-length motion picture versions, those of 1947 and 1994.

In the 1947 version, a kind, jolly old man, who calls himself Kris Kringle (Edmund Gwenn), actually believes that he is the one-and-only Santa Claus. Finding the Macy's Santa quite intoxicated before the Thanksgiving Day parade begins, Kris informs the parade director, Doris Walker (Maureen O'Hara), who solicits Kris as a replacement, then hires him to play Santa in Macy's toy department. Kris forms a close relationship not only with Doris, but with her six-year-old daughter, Susan (nine-year-old Natalie Wood), and Doris's friend, Fred Gailey (John Payne), an attorney. Whereas Fred quickly sees that Kris is no ordinary little old man, Doris and Susan are stony skeptics. Doris, scarred from a previous divorce, initially comes across as a no-nonsense, icy businesswoman who scoffs at fantasy, myths like Santa Claus, and Fred's romantic advances. Susan, influenced by her mother, also lives in a serious world that certainly excludes Santa and other fairy tales. Gravely concerned that fewer people each year believe in the spirit of Santa Claus, Kris takes on Doris and Susan as "test cases." If he can convince them that he's the real Santa, there's hope for him yet, but if he can't, he's through. An altercation between Kris and Macy's psychologist, Granville Sawyer, lands Kris in the psychiatric ward at Bellevue Hospital in New York. Although the final scenes depict a mental competency hearing, in which Fred succeeds in proving that Kris is not only sane but also the one-and-only Santa Claus, Kris has already proven himself to Doris and Susan through little miracles of his own in the interim.

Sometimes it's just impossible to improve on something that was absolutely perfect from the beginning, which can truly be said for the 1994 remake of *Miracle*, with Richard Attenborough as Kriss (spelled in this version with a double "s"). Doris Walker is changed to Dorey Walker, played by Elizabeth Perkins; attorney Fred Gailey is changed to attorney Brian Bedford, played by Dylan McDermott; and seven-year-old Mara Wilson stars as Susan Walker. Neither Macy's nor their chief competition, Gimbel's, would allow their names to be used in the remake, so Kriss becomes an employee of C. F. Cole's store. Rivaling Cole's is Shopper's Express, led by unscrupulous Victor Lamberg. Although the remake is generally well done, a modern setting in color with some name and plot changes really offers nothing substantially superior to the 1947 black-and-white original.

In the 1947 original, when Susan asks Kris his real name, he responds simply with "Kris Kringle." In the 1994 remake, Kriss responds that he has many names, for example, Kriss Kringle, Santa Claus, Father Christmas, St. Nicholas, *Sinterklass* in Holland, and *La Befana* in Italy. In both versions, Susan comments that Kriss's whiskers look so real, whereupon he invites her to give them a tug.

In both versions, Susan's primary Christmas wish is a house for her mother and her. If Kris is really Santa, so she reasons, he will grant her wish, but if he cannot, then he's just a nice old man with whiskers. Her wishes in the later version also include a dad and a baby brother.

In both versions, Kris raps an adversary on the head with his cane in anger, which leads to his arrest. In the original, Macy's psychologist is the "victim." In the remake, it is Macy's drunken Santa, whom Victor Lamberg hires to provoke Kriss into just such a predicament, which conveniently removes Kriss as the competition.

In the 1947 version, Fred quits his job in order to defend Kris without casting any dispersions on his former law firm. He and Doris had made wonderful plans, but now she cannot see why he would cast all common sense aside to take up a hopeless case. Fred is so certain that Kris is Santa Claus that he asks Doris to accept him on faith alone, if nothing else. Compare his definition of faith with the biblical definition as found in Hebrews 11:1: "Now faith is the substance of things hoped for, the evidence of things not seen."

In the 1994 version, Susan's Christmas card contains a one-dollar bill. Judge Harper, desperately seeking a "miracle" to throw the case out, seizes on the phrase "In God We Trust." Since the Federal Government places its faith in God without demanding any physical evidence, then the State of New York, by the collective faith of its people, can accept that Santa not only is real but exists in Kriss Kringle. In the original version, Harper, also looking for an escape, does not dispute the Postal Service's recognition that Kris is Santa Claus.

Motion pictures are ideal media through which Hollywood often promotes "politically correct" agenda, and the 1994 version of *Miracle* is no exception. The mailbox mentioned (fashioned as a miniature house itself) is a seemingly incidental object in a wide camera pan, until you freeze-frame it with your VCR and study the hyphenated name inscribed, "Walker—Bedford." In this otherwise innocent film about Santa Claus, Hollywood inserts a subtle implication that, though she is now married, Dorey will retain her maiden name and thereby maintain her independence from her husband. The implication reflects the sentiment of the 1990s and beyond. The cohesive family unit is well on its way to nonexistence. Just attend any day-care center today and note the large numbers of children with single parents. The following solution is "old-fashioned," and many will scorn it as totally outdated, but it guarantees strong leadership for the family and will be most effective if faithfully practiced: Read Ephesians 5:22–33.

Questions 42–51 pertain to certain memorable events found in the two film versions of *Miracle on 34th Street*. First, provide a short answer for each question, then determine whether each event occurs in the 1947 version only, the 1994 version only, or both versions. "Kris" will be used for the sake of uniformity.

42. Which two of Kris's characteristics first begin to convince Susan that he is really Santa?

    Kris's whiskers are real, and he doesn't wear glasses; 1947.

43. What does Kris demonstrate to Macy's drunken Santa?

    Kris shows the proper way to crack a whip in the parade; both.

44. What is the occasion when Kris speaks in a foreign language?

    At Macy's, Kris converses with a little orphan girl in her own native Dutch language as she sits on his knee; 1947.

45. During the parade, Kris shouts two lines from a familiar poem. What is the poem's name, the lines quoted, and how does he pronounce the seventh reindeer's name?

    From "A Visit from St. Nicholas," Kris shouts the couplet which lists the eight reindeer: "Now Dasher, now

Dancer . . .," etc. He correctly pronounces the seventh reindeer's name as Donder instead of Donner; 1994.

46. As Kris tucks Susan into bed, what nursery rhyme does he sing to her, and which of Susan's pleasures "pops" in Kris's face on the same night?

Kris sings the old, familiar rhyme, "To market, to market, to buy a fat pig, / Home again, home again, jiggity-jig; / To market, to market, to buy a fat hog, / Home again, home again, jiggity-jog." Kris, observing Susan smacking on bubble gum during his rendition, then attempts to blow a bubble of his own. We never see its size, just Susan's eyes getting larger, wider, and her wincing after a loud pop. The next shot shows Kris pulling a sticky mess from his beard; 1947.

47. Besides verbal speech, in what other type of language is Kris proficient?

When a little deaf girl visits him at Cole's, Kris communicates with her in sign language; 1994.

48. At whose home did Kris experience an "accident" on Christmas Eve last year, while attempting to deliver gifts?

Kris had ripped his pants on the prosecutor's old TV antenna, and Kris hopes to see a different antenna this year; 1994.

49. How does Kris describe the essence of himself?

Instead of just being a jolly old man, Kris sees himself as a symbol of the human ability to suppress the selfish and hateful tendencies in our lives; 1994.

50. Where do we see the words, "I believe in you, too"?

During Kris's hearing, Susan writes him a letter confessing that she also believes in him. Doris adds these words as further encouragement; 1947.

51. As final evidence that Kris is Santa Claus, what is discovered standing by the fireplace in Susan's dream house?

Fred and Doris note Kris's cane, evidence that he had planned everything all along; 1947.

This next segment turns to another holiday blockbuster, the identity of which appears with the first question in this set. For questions 52–69, please fill in the blanks or provide short answers.

52. After serving in World War II, director (A) _____ returned to Hollywood in 1945 and formed Liberty Pictures Corporation. Under his direction, Liberty's first film, (B) _____, became one of the most celebrated Christmas pictures of all time.

(A) Frank Capra; (B) *It's a Wonderful Life* (1946). Capra, who had directed such notables as *Mr. Smith Goes to Washington* and *Meet John Doe*, loved this film and remarked that, of all the films he had directed in his career, *It's a Wonderful Life* was his favorite. One of his great pleasures was to show this movie in his home every Christmas Eve.

53. *It's a Wonderful Life* was based on a short story titled (A) _____, by (B) _____, which never received conventional publication prior to its public debut.

(A) "The Greatest Gift;" (B) Philip Van Storen Stern. The latter, a writer in New York City, originally offered his little story to the magazine sector, but to no avail.

Undaunted and at his own expense, he then printed 200 copies of the story and sent them out to his friends as twenty-four-page Christmas "cards." One recipient was also his Hollywood agent, who pitched it to various movie studios. At actor Cary Grant's suggestion, it initially became the property of RKO Radio Pictures, but that studio failed to produce a workable script. RKO eventually sold the story to Frank Capra at Liberty Pictures for a modest $10,000, and *It's a Wonderful Life* was born. RKO, however, distributed the film.

Philip Van Storen Stern's original story centers around George Pratt, a small-town bank clerk, who is sick of life and wishes that he had never been born. As George contemplates suicide on Christmas Eve, he encounters an angel posing as a brush salesman who grants his wish. Seeing what his world would have become without him, he realizes that his presence has truly been a blessing to those around him, and that people really need him. He renounces his wish, and all becomes as before. George learns that the greatest gift you can give anyone is yourself.

The film adaptation changes the principal character to George Bailey, a man filled with creative ideas and a thirst for adventure. His dreams are unfulfilled, for fate dictates that he take over the Bailey Building and Loan Corporation, established by his father; alternatively, the unscrupulous banker, Henry Potter, would take over and corrupt the town. George rescues numerous friends and neighbors from financial ruin, yet when disaster strikes the Building and Loan on Christmas Eve, he caves in to pressure and almost ends his life. As the film opens, his friends are praying for divine intervention, at which there comes a response from Heaven. This now leads to your next question.

54. Instead of human forms, the angels are depicted as (A) _____. An angelic "official" named (B) _____ summons George's guardian angel, (C) _____, who on earth had been a (D) _____. Upon his arrival, we hear a short excerpt from the song (E) _____, which is always associated with him throughout the film. Because Clarence has not yet earned his (F) _____, his rank is AS2, which signifies (G) _____. Then for two-thirds of the show, we go back in time with Clarence and learn all about George Bailey's wonderful life of self-denial and good will and what precipitated the need for divine intervention. Having learned this, and with Christmas Eve at hand, Clarence descends to George's town of (H) _____ with his copy of Mark Twain's novel, (I) _____, in tow.

(A) Stars that twinkle when they speak; (B) Joseph; (C) Clarence Odbody; (D) Clockmaker; (E) "Twinkle, Twinkle, Little Star"; (F) Wings; (G) Angel, Second Class; (H) Bedford Falls, NY; (I) *The Adventures of Tom Sawyer*.

55. At the high school graduation dance, George runs into several old childhood chums with whom he will later interact. There is sweet, pretty (A) _____, whom he will marry. By the way, her date, "Freddie," is played by actor Carl Switzer, better known as (B) _____ from *The Little Rascals* and *Our Gang Comedies*, but it is George who really wins her heart. Then there's Sam Wainwright, a real wise-cracker, whose favorite phrase is (C) _____. Lastly, George finds (D) _____, the town's "fast girl," but his heart is already taken. During the (E) _____ dance contest, the gymnasium floor parts to reveal a (F)

_____ beneath, and George and Mary, together with many other couples, dance themselves into a good dunking.

(A) Mary Hatch; (B) "Alfalfa;" (C) "Hee-Haw;" (D) Violet Bick; (E) Charleston (the setting is 1928); (F) Swimming pool. The pool scenes were filmed at Beverly Hills High School, the gym of which actually sported a pool beneath the floor. At that time, such a device was considered a high-tech innovation.

56. George establishes a neighborhood of homes financed by the Building and Loan at rates far more reasonable than would have been available from Potter's bank. This neighborhood is known as _____.

Bailey Park

57. From boyhood on, what does George always do and say whenever he enters Mr. Gower's drug store?

He first pulls the handle of an old-fashioned cigarette lighter and wishes for a million dollars. When the flame appears, he hollers, "Hot dog!"

58. When World War II breaks out, George is rejected for service, because (A) _____. But his brother Harry brings honor to the Bailey clan when he is awarded the (B) _____.

(A) He is deaf in his left ear; (B) Congressional Medal of Honor

59. Identify the appropriate song that applies to each of the following situations in the film:

(A) What George and Mary sing as they come home from the high school dance (it's the film's theme song as well)

(B) What policeman Bert and Ernie the cabby select to serenade George and Mary on their wedding night

(C) The Christmas carol that Janie Bailey repeatedly plays on the piano

(D) The film's closing song at the Bailey home before the credits roll

(A) "Buffalo Gals"; (B) "I Love You Truly"; (C) "Hark! The Herald Angels Sing"; (D) "Auld Lang Syne"

60. What kind of disaster strikes the Building and Loan on Christmas Eve, and who is ultimately responsible?

George's Uncle Billy is about to deposit $8,000 in the bank for the Building and Loan. Gloating to Potter over Harry's military decoration, Uncle Billy becomes sidetracked and absentmindedly leaves the cash in Potter's newspaper. Potter hides the error and keeps the cash, then swears out a warrant against George for "misappropriation of funds."

61. When does George receive a "crown" of Christmas tree tinsel?

Distraught over the Building and Loan's deficit, George returns home to brood, while Mary and their children, unaware of the crisis, decorate the Christmas tree. Weeping, George snatches up three-year-old Tommy, his youngest, and hugs him as Tommy spreads strands of tinsel all over George's head. This is one example of Frank Capra's genius at creating comic relief all through the picture.

62. What trick did director Frank Capra incorporate to enhance the intimacy of George's softly weeping and praying for God's help at Mr. Martini's bar?

Originally, Capra had filmed the scene at some distance. When actor Jimmy Stewart couldn't reproduce George's passionate emotion for a close-up retake, Capra took the entire scene to the photo lab and had it enlarged frame by frame.

63. What does George cynically believe is the answer to his prayer?

Faced with financial ruin and possibly prison, George, ordinarily a kind and benevolent man, becomes a mean-spirited, hunted animal who almost loses his faith. Screaming harsh words to Mary and his children, George also insults one of his children's teachers over the telephone, for which her husband punches out George at Mr. Martini's bar. The latter incident George interprets as the answer to his recent prayer.

64. How does Clarence "save" George?

As suicidal George is about to take a dive into the river, Clarence jumps in first, knowing that George will try to save him.

65. How old is Clarence?

Clarence will be 293 next May.

66. What two physical signs confirm that George "has never been born"?

He is no longer deaf in his left ear, and his lip no longer bleeds (from the fight in the bar).

67. (A) What supposedly happens every time a bell rings? (B) Which two characters affirm this?

(A) An angel gets its wings; (B) Clarence and Zuzu, a Bailey daughter, who quotes the teacher whom George had insulted.

68. In the final scenes, besides Janie Bailey (who accompanies everyone on the piano), who else plays a musical instrument?

   Bert the policeman plays an accordion accompaniment for "Auld Lang Syne."

69. What alerts George that Clarence has finally received his wings?

   A little bell on the Baileys' Christmas tree jingles.

George does not comprehend the magnitude of the aid that he has given to his friends and neighbors throughout his life. Questions 70–75 present statements about certain people whom George has benefited in tangible ways. For each statement, identify the person or people involved. Answers follow this group.

70. As a boy, George prevents this drunken man from accidentally poisoning someone, then promises not to expose him.

71. George saves this eight-year-old boy from drowning by pulling him from an icy pond.

72. When George realizes that he must thwart Potter by remaining at the Building and Loan, he puts this person through college instead of himself.

73. When a run on the bank terrifies Bedford Falls, George uses his personal cash, which he had intended for his honeymoon, to provide loans to this group of people.

74. When the bank refuses to loan this man $5,000 to build a new home, he receives the funds from the Building and Loan through George.

75. Knowing that this person is leaving town penniless to start life over, George's parting gift is a little ready cash from his own pocket.

Answers to 70–75: 70-Mr. Gower, the druggist; 71-Harry, George's brother; 72-Harry; 73-Patrons of the Building and Loan; 74-Ernie Bishop, the cabby; 75-Violet Bick.

Had George not been born, Bedford Falls and its citizens would have fallen victims to adverse circumstances. Questions 76–85 present a series of those miserable fates that would have come to pass. From the lettered list of victims, match one to each circumstance. Answers follow this group.

A. Bedford Falls	F. George's mother
B. Mr. Gower	G. Uncle Billy
C. The Building and Loan	H. Bailey Park
D. Violet Bick	I. Mr. Martini
E. Ernie Bishop	J. Mary Bailey

76. It becomes "Pottersville," complete with saloons and burlesque halls.

77. He loses his business and goes insane.

78. He serves a prison term for poisoning a child.

79. It becomes a cemetery.

80. Cynical and heartless, she runs "Ma's Boarding House."

81. She becomes a prostitute.

82. She wastes away as an old-maid librarian.

83. It is replaced by a "dime-a-dance" dive.

84. Nick, now cold and callous, replaces him as proprietor of the Italian restaurant and bar.

85. His wife and child having deserted him, he lives in a shack in "Potter's Field."

Answers to 76–85:   76-A; 77-G; 78-B; 79-H; 80-F; 81-D; 82-J; 83-C; 84-I; 85-E.

To George's surprise, all of Bedford Falls rallies to his aid when Mary pleads for help. In the final scenes, scores of friends and neighbors storm the Bailey home with ready cash to clear the Building and Loan's deficit. Questions 86–94 describe several unusual situations surrounding some of these contributions. From the lettered group of people, match one with each description. Answers follow this group.

    A. Mr. Partridge, the high school principal
    B. Mr. Martini
    C. Annie, the Bailey's cook
    D. Mr. Gower
    E. Violet Bick
    F. Sam Wainwright
    G. Harry Bailey
    H. The sheriff
    I. Clarence

86. He raids his juke box for the cash.

87. He toasts George as "the richest man in town."

88. He gives Zuzu his watch as a toy.

89. He tears up the arrest warrant and tosses it into the money basket.

90. From London, his office can cable George up to $25,000.

91. Not leaving town after all, she returns the money that George had given her.

92. He calls in his outstanding charge accounts.

93. She contributes the money she had been saving for a divorce (if she ever got married).

94. He leaves behind his copy of *The Adventures of Tom Sawyer* with an inscription that no person can be a failure who has friends.

Answers to 86–94: 86-B; 87-G; 88-A; 89-H; 90-F; 91-E; 92-D; 93-C; 94-I.

This next exercise consists of a table which pairs principal actors and the corresponding characters that they play in *It's a Wonderful Life*, with one identity left blank per pair. For questions 95–104, fill in the appropriate names. Answers follow this group.

	Actor	Character
95.		George Bailey
96.	Donna Reed	
97.	Henry Travers	
98.		Uncle Billy
99.	Gloria Grahame	
100.	H. B. Warner	
101.	Ward Bond	
102.		Ernie Bishop, the cabby
103.		Henry Potter, the banker
104.	Todd Karnes	

Answers to 95–104: 95-Jimmy Stewart; 96-Mary Bailey; 97-Clarence; 98-Thomas Mitchell; 99-Violet Bick; 100-Mr. Gower; 101-Bert, the policeman;102-Frank Faylen; 103-Lionel Barrymore; 104-Harry Bailey.

Questions 105–113 consist of a series of statements which draw comparisons between two holiday film classics. For each statement, determine whether it applies to A-*It's a Wonderful Life* (1946), B-*The Bishop's Wife* (1947), or C-both movies.

105. An angel plays prominently in the movie.

"Clarence" (Henry Travers) appears in A, while "Dudley" (Cary Grant) appears in B. The answer is C.

106. One character behaves like Scrooge.

Henry Potter (Lionel Barrymore) is the evil bank president in A who would like nothing more than to see the Bailey Building and Loan bankrupt with George Bailey (Jimmy Stewart) in jail. Mrs. George Hamilton (Gladys Cooper) is an embittered, wealthy widow in B who will withhold her millions from the cathedral fund, unless Bishop Henry Brougham (David Niven) builds the cathedral in honor of her late husband. The answer is C.

107. The angel reforms the villain.

Dudley charms and soothes Mrs. Hamilton, whereby she donates her funds to the poor and needy rather than to the building of a cathedral on selfish grounds. The answer is B.

108. The angel prevents the principal character from committing suicide.

George Bailey contemplates suicide when the Building and Loan is found to be $8,000 in the red on Christmas Eve, subjecting him to a charge of misappropriation of funds. Clarence saves George, the only good man standing between the town of Bedford Falls and Henry Potter. The answer is A.

109. The movie is based on a previous literary work.

A is based on Philip Van Storen Stern's short story, "The Greatest Gift," and B is based on a novel of the same title by Robert Nathan, published in 1928. Answer C.

110. The movie features the carol "Hark! The Herald Angels Sing."

Janie Bailey plays it repeatedly on the piano in A, and B opens with it. Answer C.

111. The movie features a heroine.

Mary Bailey has loved George all her life in A and rallies the town together when George suffers serious financial trouble on Christmas Eve. Julia Brougham (Loretta Young), the gentle and supportive bishop's wife in B, endures the bishop's obsession, pressures, and peevishness over his cathedral fund. A lonely and unhappy heroine, she becomes a major part of Dudley's "assignment." Answer C.

112. The angel brings peace and satisfaction to the heroine's life.

Dudley on a number of occasions takes Julia shopping, ice skating, or out to lunch, and generally puts a little spice back into her staid life, something the bishop has neglected to do. Answer B.

113. Child stars Karolyn Grimes and Bobby Anderson appear.

Karolyn is George Bailey's younger daughter, Zuzu, in A and the bishop's daughter, Debby, in B. Bobby portrays a young George Bailey in A and a boy in the park who recruits Debby to join his snowball fight in B. Answer C.

Questions 114–124. Probably no other Christmas story has received literally scores of adaptations for the screen and television than Dickens's A *Christmas Carol*. For each of the following notable versions, match the appropriate actor who starred as Scrooge or a Scrooge surrogate from the list below. Answers follow this group.

> A. Michael Caine
> B. Albert Finney
> C. Sir Seymour Hicks
> D. Susan Lucci
> E. Reginald Owen
> F. Jack Palance
> G. George C. Scott
> H. Alastair Sim
> I. Patrick Stewart
> J. Cicely Tyson
> K. Henry Winkler

114. *An American Christmas Carol* (1979): Miserly banker Benedict Slade is haunted by three ghosts resembling people who have defaulted on loans and from whom Slade has seized property as payment.

115. *A Christmas Carol* (1938): Lionel Barrymore was originally cast as Scrooge until illness led to the selection of this British actor.

116. *A Christmas Carol* (1951) is considered to be the best motion picture version.

117. *A Christmas Carol* (1984) is considered to be the best version for television.

118. *A Christmas Carol* (1999) is the only version which opens with the burial of Jacob Marley.

119. *Ebbie* (1995): Ebbie Scrooge is a heartless CEO of a large department store in this change-of-gender adaptation.

120. *Ebenezer* (1997) portrays Scrooge as a ruthless saloon proprietor and card shark in this wild west adaptation.

121. *Ms. Scrooge* (1997) is Ebenita Scrooge, a miserly African American woman in this change-of-race, change-of-gender adaptation.

122. *The Muppet Christmas Carol* (1992) is a motion picture musical comedy with the Muppets.

123. *Scrooge* (1935)

124. *Scrooge* (1970): Rex Harrison was originally offered the role of Scrooge but declined.

Answers to 114–124: 114-K; 115-E; 116-H; 117-G; 118-I; 119-D; 120-F; 121-J; 122-A; 123-C; 124-B.

For multiple choice questions 125–139, note that some have more than one answer, as indicated.

125. The story for this 1989 motion picture centers around eight-year-old Jessica Riggs (Rebecca Harrell), who

finds and nurses a wounded reindeer, then convinces herself that it must belong to Santa Claus. The reindeer's name is the film's title.

    A. *Dasher*
    B. *Vixen*
    C. *Donder*
    D. *Prancer*

If you do not know the answer, recite the names of St. Nick's eight reindeer in the order that they appear in the poem, "A Visit from St. Nicholas" ("'Twas the Night Before Christmas"). The third reindeer in that sequence is the correct title.

126. Do you know of an inn that's open only during the major holidays of the year? That's the gist of the story in *Holiday Inn* (1942). And for each holiday, Bing Crosby croons a special tune, thanks to Irving Berlin's score. Which tune depicts Christmas in this motion picture?

    A. "The Secret of Christmas"
    B. "You're All I Want for Christmas"
    C. "White Christmas"
    D. "Merry Christmas, Darling"

Only Scrooges will answer incorrectly.

127. Do you remember the touching Christmas scene in *Heidi* (1937) with Shirley Temple? Her new friend Clara (Marcia Mae Jones) gives her father an unforgettable Christmas present with Heidi's encouragement and assistance:

    A. Heidi and Clara find Clara's missing sister.
    B. Heidi and Clara reunite Clara's father with her mother.

    C. Heidi teaches Clara to walk.

    D. Heidi and Clara raise enough money for Clara's ailing father to undergo a life-saving operation.

Clara had been crippled, yet Heidi senses that if Clara wills herself to walk, she can. Working with Clara a little each day, Heidi succeeds in helping Clara give her father a truly priceless gift.

128. Premiering in 1962, it was the first made-for-television animated cartoon special.

    A. *Yes, Virginia, There Is a Santa Claus*
    B. *Mr. Magoo's Christmas Carol*
    C. *The Nutcracker*
    D. *The Little Match Girl*

Myopic old curmudgeon Mr. Magoo (voiced by actor Jim Backus) portrays Scrooge in a Broadway musical. It is considered to be the best musical version of *A Christmas Carol* and is also the only version in which the Ghost of Christmas Present precedes the Ghost of Christmas Past.

129. The animated cartoon production *Mickey's Christmas Carol* (1983) features a number of Disney characters assuming the roles of Dickens characters. Which pair of characters is <u>not</u> properly matched?

    A. Mickey Mouse as Bob Cratchit
    B. Goofy as Jacob Marley
    C. Donald Duck as Fred, Scrooge's nephew
    D. Jiminy Cricket as the Ghost of Christmas Present

Jiminy Cricket plays the Ghost of Christmas Past. No surprise, Scrooge McDuck plays Scrooge. Willie the Giant is the Ghost of Christmas Present, Pete the Bulldog is the Ghost of Christmas Yet to Come, Daisy Duck is Isabel, Minnie Mouse is Mrs. Cratchit, and Mr. Toad is old Mr. Fezziwig.

130. Shortly after the 1947 version of *Miracle on 34th Street* opens, Kris Kringle observes three errors in a reindeer window display. Which one of the following is <u>not</u> one of those errors?

    A. Cupid's and Blitzen's positions should be reversed.
    B. Donner should have antlers with four points instead of three.
    C. Santa's pack should be slung over his right shoulder, not his left.
    D. Dasher goes on Santa's right instead of his left.

In this version, Kris also uses the name "Donner" instead of "Donder" (the opposite is true with the 1994 version). The issue of Santa's pack never arises, so the correct answer is C.

131. *Miracle on 34th Street* was also remade for television in 1973. Indicate which of the following apply to this version (<u>more than one answer is correct</u>).

    A. Jane Alexander stars as Karen Walker, Susan's mother.
    B. David Hartman stars as attorney Bill Schaffner.
    C. Sebastian Cabot stars as Kris Kringle.
    D. Suzanne Davidson stars as Susan Walker.
    E. Kris converses with a little girl in Spanish at Macy's.
    F. Kris arranges for Dr. Pierce, the physician at the Brooks Memorial Home for the Aged, to receive an emphysema machine (a respirator) for Christmas.
    G. In Kris's game of pretending, Susan is a clam.

This version closely follows the 1947 original, except for the minor differences which have been illustrated here. All choices are correct.

132. Which of these Christmas classics stars Bing Crosby and Danny Kaye together?

    A. *Holiday Inn* (1942)
    B. *White Christmas* (1954)
    C. *The Man in the Santa Claus Suit* (1979)
    D. *A Christmas Story* (1983)

Crosby and Fred Astaire star in *Holiday Inn* together. They would have paired up again for a remake in *White Christmas*, had Astaire not rejected the role, which then went to Danny Kaye. Both productions boast superb musical scores by Irving Berlin. In C, Fred Astaire also poses as Santa Claus masquerading as a costume shop owner who assists troubled people by renting them magical Santa suits.

133. The highly popular film *A Christmas Story* (1983) revolves around nine-year-old Ralph Parker (Peter Billingsley) and his obsessive wish for a Red Ryder BB gun for Christmas. But his teacher, his parents, and even a department store Santa are all of one opinion regarding such a wish:

    A. "You'll shoot the dog!"
    B. "You'll shoot up the neighborhood!"
    C. "You'll shoot your eye out!"
    D. "You'll shoot your foot off!"

Ralph's organs of sight would be in great danger, according to his elders.

134. In *The Bishop's Wife* (1947), Dudley the angel edits Bishop Henry Brougham's Christmas Eve sermon, which now metaphorically admonishes everyone to fill the Christmas stocking of Jesus Christ with all the shining gifts that make peace on earth. Which gift is <u>not</u> mentioned in the sermon?

  A. Loving kindness
  B. Warm hearts
  C. Stretched-out hands of tolerance
  D. Forgiving attitudes

All four really should be included, but the sermon lists only three examples of shining gifts, excluding D.

135. Which country music star made her television screen debut in *A Smoky Mountain Christmas*, a 1986 film loosely based on the fairy tale "Snow White and the Seven Dwarfs"?

  A. Dolly Parton
  B. Loretta Lynn
  C. Tammy Wynette
  D. Faith Hill

Cast as singing celebrity Lorna Davis, Dolly Parton unwittingly becomes a loving foster mother to seven runaway orphans in the Great Smoky Mountains of Tennessee at Christmastime.

136. Kidnapped on Christmas Eve by members of the Blackfoot tribe seeking revenge, Jericho Adams and wife Dora (Kris Kristofferson and Kim Cattrall) share the Nativity story with their captors. As Dora narrates, how does Jericho make the story more meaningful to these Native Americans in the 1992 television special, *Miracle in the Wilderness*?

A. He uses their sign language.
B. He draws pictures on the ground using their symbols.
C. He uses members of the tribe to play the parts of Mary, Joseph, shepherds, Magi, and the angels.
D. He translates the principal events of the Nativity into equivalent forms of Native American culture.

Mary, a fourteen-year-old Indian maiden, is to be wed to the brave hunter Joseph. She receives the Annunciation from a "winged messenger" in the form of an eagle (the tribe cannot comprehend "angel"), while the "Great Spirit" (God), appearing as a white stallion to Joseph in a dream, assures him that Mary's pregnancy is divine. Mary gives birth to Jesus at the time of the annual Sun Dance (equivalent to the census), where many different tribes convene. Then come three Wise Men bearing gifts: a Sioux with a peace pipe, a Mandan with a medicine bag and beaver skin, and a Plains Cree with bow and arrows. Dora concludes with Jesus' death and resurrection, and she wishes that someday all mankind will live together as brothers in peace.

137. In 1969, *The Hallmark Hall of Fame* presented *The Littlest Angel*, a television dramatization of Charles Tazewell's classic story. Which pairs of actors and roles are correctly matched? (<u>more than one correct answer</u>)

A. E. G. Marshall as God
B. Johnnie Whitaker as Michael, the Littlest Angel
C. Cab Galloway as the angel Gabriel
D. Fred Gwynne as the angel Patience
E. Tony Randall as Democrites

Actors and roles are correctly matched.

138. A favorite television theme is the reunion of parents with children or grandchildren at Christmastime. Which of these specials promote this theme? (<u>more than one correct answer</u>)

    A. *The Gathering* (1977)
    B. *It Came Upon the Midnight Clear* (1984)
    C. *Christmas Eve* (1986)
    D. *The Gift of Love* (1978)

Business tycoon Adam Thornton (Edward Asner) suddenly receives news that he is terminally ill in *The Gathering*. Estranged from his four grown children and separated from his wife, he enlists his wife's help to arrange one final family reunion at Christmastime before he passes away. *Christmas Eve* closely parallels *The Gathering* in that wealthy widow Amanda Kingsley (Loretta Young) also faces a terminal illness. Having ministered to the city's poor and homeless for ages, Amanda's one wish is that her three grown grandchildren be reunited with their long-estranged father by Christmas.

139. In the made-for-television animated cartoon *A Charlie Brown Christmas* (1965), Charlie Brown voices concern that rampant commercialism is destroying the true meaning of Christmas. Worse than Snoopy's decorated doghouse winning the neighborhood display contest, the children's Christmas pageant degenerates into a jazz festival. When Charlie desperately asks if *anyone* knows what Christmas is all about, who steps to center stage and reverently recites the Nativity story from Luke's Gospel?

    A. Lucy
    B. Linus

C. Schroder
D. Peppermint Patty

All the children pause at Linus's recitation and realize that the real reason for the season revolves not around Santa Claus, presents, glitter, and revelry, but around a tiny Babe lying in a lowly manger, Who would take away the sins of the world.

A Charlie Brown Christmas has to its credit a number of "firsts." It was the first of the *Charlie Brown* prime-time television specials based on the *Peanuts* comic strip, created by Charles M. Schulz; the first prime-time cartoon without a laugh track; and the first in which children provided all the voices.

Questions 140–144. The following television specials are actually adaptations of classic Christmas stories or movies. For each, select the original title upon which each show is based from the list below. Answers follow this group.

A. *A Christmas Carol*
B. "The Gift of the Magi"
C. *It's a Wonderful Life*
D. "The Other Wise Man"
E. *The Story of Holly and Ivy*

140. *The Stingiest Man in Town* (1956), starring Basil Rathbone

141. *The Wish That Changed Christmas* (1991), animated cartoon with the voice of Jonathan Winters

142. *The Gift of Love* (1978), hosted by Henry Fonda, starring Marie Osmond

143. *It Happened One Christmas* (1977), starring Marlo Thomas

144. *The Fourth Wise Man* (1985), starring Martin Sheen

Answers to 140–144: 140-A; 141-E; 142-B; 143-C; 144-D.

Questions 145–152. Of the 249 episodes which comprised that popular television series *The Andy Griffith Show*, only one featured a Christmas theme. A most memorable episode simply titled "Christmas Story," it aired in December of 1960 during the series' first year. The scene is Christmas Eve at the Mayberry courthouse with Andy, Barney (Don Knotts), Opie (Ronnie Howard), Aunt Bee (Frances Bavier), and Ellie Walker, the druggist (Elinor Donahue). Answers and comments follow this group.

145. What Christmas "gift" does Sheriff Andy Taylor bestow upon several prisoners already incarcerated in his jail?

    A. He delivers a load of Aunt Bee's fruitcakes.
    B. He reads "'Twas the Night Before Christmas" to them.
    C. He decorates their cells with holly and mistletoe.
    D. He temporarily releases them upon their promise to return to finish their sentences on the day after Christmas.

146. Soon the cantankerous merchant, Ben Weaver (Will Wright) insists that Andy lock up a man for selling illegal whiskey. When Andy pleads for holiday clemency, how does Ben respond?

    A. "Christmas? Ha!"
    B. "Christmas? Baloney!"
    C. "Christmas? Nuts!"
    D. "Christmas? What good is it?"

147. Not willing that anyone should spend Christmas alone in jail, Andy "arrests" the man's wife and children to be with him, then arranges a Christmas party at the courthouse. Along with Barney, Andy has also deputized <u>all but one</u> of the following people to guard the "desperate prisoners."

    A. Aunt Bee
    B. Ellie Walker
    C. Opie
    D. Gomer Pyle (Jim Neighbors)

148. Who appears as Santa Claus?

    A. Otis Campbell, the town drunk (Hal Smith)
    B. Floyd Lawson, the barber (Howard McNear)
    C. Andy
    D. Barney

149. As Andy accompanies on guitar, he and Ellie sing which carol together as a duet?

    A. "Silent Night"
    B. "O Christmas Tree"
    C. "Away in a Manger"
    D. "Jingle Bells"

150. Who first commits a series of odd misdemeanors, then watches the happy courthouse scene through the window while quietly singing along with Andy and Ellie, and finally succeeds in getting himself arrested for "disturbing the peace"?

    A. Ben
    B. Otis
    C. Floyd
    D. Gomer

151. What ulterior motive does Ben have for wanting to be arrested?

    A. He is old, lonely, and has no one with whom to spend Christmas; if he, too, becomes a prisoner, he can join in the festivities.

    B. He knows that the other prisoner has children and wants to play Santa Claus for them.

    C. He is really a black-hearted soul and wants to finish what he started outside.

    D. He has lost everything and cannot bear to tell anyone the truth that he is homeless; if he is a prisoner, he will have a home for a time.

152. When Andy's new "prisoner" arrives at the courthouse, he brings a large suitcase, which contains:

    A. A Santa Claus suit

    B. A violin for playing Christmas carols

    C. Fruitcakes

    D. Toys and gifts for everyone there

Answers to 145–152: 145-D; 146-A; 147-D; 148-D; 149-C; 150-A; 151-A; 152-D.

Comments: At first, Ben Weaver's surly attitude and apparent hostility toward Christmas match those of old Scrooge himself. Andy has no wish to punish Ben for his series of misdemeanors, especially on Christmas Eve, and repeatedly overlooks them. But when Ben falls off a crate while peering into the jail and Andy investigates the disturbance, the truth becomes evident. Toting a suitcase which Barney searches, Ben feigns surprise at finding roller skates, which he gives to Opie, a baseball mitt and a doll for the prisoner's boy and girl, perfume for Ellie, a sewing basket for Aunt Bee, and wrapped gifts for the others. So old Ben, in spite of his loneliness, sports a heart of gold after all. As the episode closes, everyone sings "Deck the Halls," and Aunt Bee serves Ben a hearty Christmas dinner.

This episode recalls all too well the fact that, for many people without families, the Christmas season is an incredibly lonely time, perhaps even the darkest time of the year. Let us not only be thankful for our families but also put forth the effort to make Christmas a little brighter for those who are without, not only at this time of year, but always.

The Homecoming: A Christmas Story is a 1971 television dramatization of a novel by Earl Hamner, Jr., which later led to the series *The Waltons*. This special broadcast introduced the family of John and Olivia Walton (Andrew Duggan and Patricia Neal) of Walton's Mountain, Virginia, and their children: John-Boy (Richard Thomas), Mary-Ellen (Judy Norton-Taylor), Jason (Jon Walmsley), Erin (Mary McDonough), Ben (Eric Scott), Jim-Bob (David Harper), and Elizabeth (Kami Cotler). Edgar Bergen and Ellen Corby starred as the Walton grandparents. Since you are now familiar with the novel from chapter eight, questions 153–159 focus on several features of the television special. Answers and comments follow this group.

153. We hear several carols sung through the story. All of the following statements about these carols are true, except:

    A. Near the show's opening, Olivia Walton is singing "I Heard the Bells on Christmas Day."
    B. The children sing "Silent Night" at the church Christmas pageant.
    C. The children sing "Away in a Manger" for the missionary lady.
    D. When John-Boy arrives at the church to get help, everyone is singing "O Holy Night."

154. On Christmas Eve, a missionary lady arrives at Ike Godsey's store to distribute charity gifts to children in the area. What does she require that each child do to receive a gift?

    A. Tell about a good deed they did
    B. Describe what Christmas means to them
    C. Name a saint
    D. Recite a Bible verse

155. What special item does Mary-Ellen add to the family's Christmas tree?

    A. The dog's collar
    B. The cow's bell
    C. A bird's nest
    D. A baseball

156. Where does Grandfather Walton go at midnight on Christmas Eve?

    A. He goes to the Baptist church to ring in Christmas.
    B. He goes to the barn to see the cattle kneel.

    C. He visits a sick friend and takes a special gift.

    D. He slips over to the Baldwin sisters' home for a sip of "The Recipe."

157. About midnight, John-Boy tells his younger brothers and sisters a story about which Christmas miracle?

    A. How the trees all bloomed and yielded fruit when Christ was born.

    B. How the Star of Bethlehem came into being.

    C. How the animals kneel and talk at midnight on Christmas Eve.

    D. How Santa Claus can deliver gifts all over the world in a single night.

158. When John Walton, the father, finally returns home around midnight laden with gifts, how does he explain them to his younger children who've been waiting up and who believe in Santa Claus?

    A. Santa dropped down to meet him walking home and made his delivery there.

    B. He mistook Santa for an intruder, wrestled with him, and grabbed some presents as Santa escaped.

    C. He saw the presents on the roof and deduced that some animal had frightened Santa off.

    D. He offers no explanation and gently tells his children the bare truth about Santa Claus.

159. John spends virtually all of his paycheck on gifts. When Olivia asks what will they live on during the next week, what is John's solution?

    A. Faith

    B. Hope

    C. Love

    D. Prayer

Answers to 153–159: 153-B; 154-D; 155-C; 156-A; 157-C; 158-B; 159-C.

Comments: On his trek to find his father, John-
Boy witnesses an African American
children's Christmas pageant, where
the children sing the spiritual, "Hey
Mary, What Are You Going to Name
That Pretty Little Baby?" At Ike
Godsey's store, Mary-Ellen saves the
day by prompting the children with
whispered Bible verses, and six-year-
old Elizabeth receives a doll for her
verse. But when she opens the box, she
finds to her horror that the doll's face
is badly cracked. To Elizabeth, someone had "killed" the doll. The implication is that such "gifts" had been
trash that others had discarded.

Questions 160–178 pertain to a number of television animated cartoon specials for children that have become popular Christmas classics. Although most convey purely
secular themes of Santa and presents, some actually contain inspirational messages. For each numbered title, match
the lettered celebrity who narrates the story. Answers follow this group. (Hint: One celebrity narrates twice.)

A. F. Murray Abraham   J. Buddy Hackett
B. Fred Astaire   K. Burl Ives
C. Jim Backus   L. Boris Karloff
D. Shirley Booth   M. Angela Lansbury
E. Tom Bosley   N. Roger Miller
F. Jimmy Durante   O. Red Skelton
G. Greer Garson   P. Tom Smothers

H. Joel Grey   Q. Randy Travis
I. Andy Griffith   R. Jonathan Winters

160. *Annabelle's Wish* (1997), dedicated to the Make-a-Wish Foundation, centers around Annabelle the cow, who wishes to become one of Santa's reindeer.

161. *The Bear Who Slept Through Christmas* (1983): Ted E. Bear sets out for the city in quest of Christmas.

162. *Dr. Seuss's How the Grinch Stole Christmas* (1966): The Grinch learns the meaning of Christmas from the little Whos in Whoville.

163. *The First Christmas: The Story of the First Christmas Snow* (1975): A blind, orphaned shepherd boy receives sight at Christmastime. Inspirational.

164. *Frosty Returns* (1993): A sequel "fluff" to *Frosty the Snowman.*

165. *Frosty the Snowman* (1969): Based on the song of the same title, a talking snowman frolics with children.

166. *Frosty's Winter Wonderland* (1976): Another sequel "fluff," in which Frosty takes a wife.

167. *Jack Frost* (1979): Wintry Jack Frost seeks human status to win the heart of a peasant girl.

168. *The Little Drummer Boy* (1968): Little shepherd boy Aaron plays his drum for the Christ Child, Who saves Aaron's injured lamb. Inspirational.

169. *The Little Drummer Boy, Book II* (1976): Aaron and Wise Man Melchior recover stolen bells, which ring out the Nativity. Inspirational.

170. *The Little Match Girl* (1990): Homeless match girl Angela experiences an adventure that promises new beginnings on New Year's Eve.

171. *Nestor, the Long-Eared Christmas Donkey* (1977): Based on a song of the same title written in 1975 by Gene Autry, Don Pfrimmer, and Dave Burgess. Nestor, taunted for his unusually long ears, becomes Joseph's chosen animal to carry Mary to Bethlehem. Inspirational.

172. *Rudolph, the Red-Nosed Reindeer* (1964) premiered on the *General Electric Fantasy Hour* and has become the longest-running television animated special.

173. *Rudolph's Shiny New Year* (1975): Rudolph and friends must rescue Happy, the Baby New Year, by midnight, or time will stand still.

174. *Santa Claus Is Coming to Town* (1970), based on the song of the same title, is a biographical fantasy of Santa Claus.

175. *The Stingiest Man in Town* (1978): In 1956, Basil Rathbone starred as Scrooge in a live-action adaptation for television under the same title.

176. *'Twas the Night Before Christmas* (1974): Santa initially boycotts a town when its newspaper publishes a slanderous letter about him.

177. *The Year Without a Santa Claus* (1974): Based on the book by the same title. Two elves search the world for a spark of Christmas spirit.

178. *Yes, Virginia, There Is a Santa Claus* (1974): Based on the 1897 editorial of the same title by Francis P. Church,

this cartoon features actual photographs of Virgina O'Hanlon; her father, Dr. Philip O'Hanlon; and Church.

Answers to 160–178: 160-Q; 161-P; 162-L; 163-M; 164-R; 165-F; 166-I; 167-J; 168-G; 169-G; 170-A; 171-N; 172-K; 173-O; 174-B; 175-E; 176-H; 177-D; 178-C.

CHAPTER TEN

Christmas Around the World

Presented here is a survey of principal traditions and customs from Europe, Latin America, Australia, North America, and portions of Asia.

In Latin American countries, the period of December 16–24 constitutes *La Novena de Navidad* (The Novena of Christmas). On each of nine days, a special mass commemorates a significant event regarding the Nativity and the early life of Jesus. Questions 1–9 list those masses, but they are not in their correct order. Arrange the masses in the order that they are celebrated by placing the correct number beside them. (Hint: Their order follows a logical sequence.) Answers follow this group.

1. *Viaje A Belén* ("Journey to Bethlehem") _____

2. *La Anunciación* ("The Annunciation") _____

3. *Los Pastores De Belén* ("The Shepherds of Bethlehem") _____

4. *La Vida En Nazareth* ("The Life in Nazareth")

   _____

5. *El Nacimiento* ("The Nativity") _____

6. *La Visitación De María A Su Prima* ("The Visitation of Mary to Her Cousin") _____

7. *Los Reyes Magos* ("The Magi") _____

8. *El Niño Perdido Y Hallado* ("The Child: Lost and Found") _____

9. *La Huída A Egipto* ("The Escape to Egypt")

   _____

Answers to 1–9: 1-Third; 2-First; 3-Fifth; 4-Ninth; 5-Fourth; 6-Second; 7-Sixth; 8-Eighth; 9-Seventh.

Questions 10–58 are primarily of the multiple choice type, each with one correct answer.

10. Since 1927, the Ahwahnee Hotel in one national park of the USA has hosted its annual Bracebridge Dinner, which is patterned after the dinner described in Washington Irving's fictitious Christmas sketch about Bracebridge Hall in Yorkshire, England. In which national park is this dinner held?

    A. Yosemite
    B. Grand Teton
    C. Yellowstone
    D. Grand Canyon

    This dinner in Yosemite includes a boar's head, wassail, and Yorkshire pudding, along with a medieval pageant.

11. The Jamaican "John Canoe" dancer, outfitted in mask, wig, and a colorful headdress, closely resembles which Christmas figure of yore?

    A. The Lord of Misrule
    B. The Boy-Bishop
    C. Black Peter
    D. A mummer

"John Canoe" is one variation of *Jonkonnu*, which African slaves introduced into the West Indies, Bermuda Islands, southern USA, and Central America during the eighteenth century as a memorial to John Conny, a chief of the Guinea coast. Whereas "John Canoe" and *Jonkonnu* (as it is known in Jamaica) could derive from Conny's name, some believe that it derives from the French *gens inconnu* ("unknown people") because the masks hide the performers' identities. The dancers solicit donations, and their repertoire reflects an African-European blend of dance steps and mumming. *Jonkonnu* survives now almost exclusively in Jamaica, where dancers perform on December 26. The correct answer is D.

To review the definition of "mumming," see the answer to question 17 in chapter two.

12. Although these countries all celebrate Christmas, which one does <u>not</u> celebrate it on December 25?

    A. Croatia
    B. Latvia
    C. Armenia
    D. Belgium

The Orthodox Church in Armenia follows the present Gregorian calendar but observes Christ's Theophany (Epiphany in the Roman Church) on the traditional date of January 6, which includes His Nativity and Baptism. The exception is the Armenian Church in Jerusalem, which follows the older Julian calendar. Thus January 6 on that calendar corresponds to January 19 on the Gregorian calendar.

13. Some European countries, particularly Ireland, observe the custom of placing a lighted candle in one or more windows on Christmas Eve. What is the *present* significance of such a custom?

    A. Strangers are welcome, one of whom may be the Christ Child.
    B. It is an invitation for the local priest to come in and bless the house.
    C. It is an invitation for carolers to stop and render a few selections.
    D. It is a talisman against evil.

The custom originates from legends. In one, the Christ Child, out alone in the cold while making His Christmas visit to the world, needs light on His way. Also, no stranger is turned away, for the Christ Child may come in disguise. In another, the Holy Family retrace their steps to Bethlehem annually, and the lighted candles signify those homes wherein they may seek shelter. A third dates to the Protestant Reformation, wherein Irish Catholics supposedly used candles as signals which invited passing priests indoors to hold Christmas Eve mass. Fables about the Holy Family's wanderings then arose to quell the suspicions of Protestant authorities regarding the use of such candles. The present significance is A.

14. "Firstfooting," a custom once widespread throughout Europe, has been popular in Scotland and northern

England since the eighteenth century. A year's worth of good or bad luck for the home depends on who first enters a house after midnight on New Year's Eve. A dark-haired stranger always brings good luck. All of the following bring bad luck, <u>except</u>:

A. Any woman
B. Flat-footed person
C. Freckled person
D. Person with squint eyes

Besides women, according to the superstition, people with any physical deformity bring bad luck. Freckles are not a deformity.

15. Upon his entrance, the firstfooter must present the three traditional gifts of coal, bread, and money (or salt), each of which carries symbolic significance. What is the significance of each gift?

Coal _____
Bread _____
Money or salt _____

Coal represents warmth, bread represents food, and money or salt represents wealth. The home in turn serves the visitor with food, drink, and perhaps money. Firstfooting similarly applies to the first person whom one meets on the road, where children and oxcarts bring the best luck.

16. On December 13 in Sweden, one daughter of each family arises very early and dresses in a white robe with a red sash, wears a head wreath of ligonberry sprigs with burning candles, and serves her family a breakfast of coffee and saffron buns. This ritual begins:

A. Ruth Day
B. Lucia Day
C. Margaret Day
D. Bernadette Day

Although the day in other parts of Scandinavia may be known as St. Lucia Day or St. Lucy Day in honor of St. Lucia, a Sicilian girl martyred for her faith in the fourth century, it is known as *Luciadagen* ("Lucia Day") in Sweden, and the word "saint" is not used in connection with Lucia there. Following her martyrdom, according to legend, Lucia, her head bathed in light, miraculously brought provisions to starving Christians hidings in catacombs to escape persecution. Christianized Vikings, upon learning of the legend, supposedly initiated the celebration. Other sources contend that the Lucia figure is a Protestant variation of the *Christkindl* of Germany, the Christ Child's "messenger," who replaced the Roman Catholic St. Nicholas as gift bringer. This messenger is depicted as a little girl dressed in white with wings, a gold crown, and who carries a tiny fir tree. Sweden adopted the Lucia figure in the seventeenth and eighteenth centuries and transferred her celebration to December 13, which had marked the winter solstice prior to the adoption of the Gregorian calendar. On that day since the Middle Ages, a female figure had presided over a large breakfast in wealthy establishments, a tradition which preceded a period of fasting until Christmas. This hostess then evolved into the Lucia figure, who derived her name from *lux* (Latin, "light") and the solstice. She kept her white attire, shed her wings and fir tree, and replaced the crown with a head wreath of candles and greenery.

Today, the daughter (eldest, youngest, etc.) selected to portray Lucia varies according to family and region. As the "Lucia" of each household serves the coffee and saffron buns (the latter termed *lussekatt*—"Lucia cats"), her sisters, attired in white with tinsel halos and carrying lighted candles, join her in parading through the house while singing the Italian folk song "Santa Lucia." Her brothers also follow in white attire as *stjärn gossar* ("star boys") and wear cone-shaped hats decorated with stars. And bringing up the rear, someone dresses as a traditional *tomten* ("elf"). Lucia Day opens the Christmas season in Sweden.

17. In Italy, children preaching sermons before a figure of the Christ Child in the manger is a vestige of which medieval figure?

    A. "Child Priest"
    B. "Young Cardinal"
    C. "Boy-Bishop"
    D. "Adolescent Pope"

Each year on December 6, in honor of St. Nicholas Day, the choristers of medieval Europe elected one "Boy-Bishop" from among them, whose function it was to perform most of the duties of a real bishop until December 28, the Feast of the Holy Innocents. Over time, however, the wild Christmas merriment of the Middle Ages corrupted the Boy-Bishop, whose office became practically synonymous with that of the Lord of Misrule. Sacrilege prevailed, and the Church eventually abolished the custom of Boy-Bishop altogether. A vestige of the custom survives today at the Church of Santa Maria Ara Coeli in Rome. A jewel-studded figure of Christ, known as the *Santo Bambino* ("Holy Child"), is placed in a manger on Christmas Eve, after which children stand before it and deliver sermons or other holiday orations. The figure is believed to possess healing powers.

18. In France, although children receive their holiday gifts on Christmas Day, the adults customarily exchange gifts on:

    A. St. Nicholas' Day, December 6
    B. St. Lucia Day, December 13
    C. New Year's Day
    D. Epiphany, January 6

The third choice is correct.

19. Which country holds a yearly carol-writing contest, the *Eisteddfod* ("A Sitting of Learned Men"), which chooses one piece of music to be the official Christmas carol of that country for the year?

    A. England
    B. Wales
    C. Scotland
    D. Ireland

The event dates to 1176 at Castle Cardigan. In 1880 the National Eisteddfod Association of Wales was formed to sponsor an annual festival, and the International Eisteddfod, established in 1947, is held annually in the city of Llangollen, Wales.

20. In which country is "Carols by Candlelight" a national custom?

    A. Canada
    B. USA
    C. New Zealand
    D. Australia

It is said that "Carols by Candlelight" originated in 1865, when Cornish miners from Moonta in Southern Australia gathered on Christmas Eve to sing carols by the light of candles attached to their hats. The modern event premiered on Christmas Eve in 1937, when Australian radio personality Norman Banks, moved by a desire to brighten the Christmases of lonely people, broadcast live singing of carols from Melbourne's Alexandria Gardens with a large host of citizens participating by candlelight. Each Christmas Eve thereafter, thousands have continued to join together in song for "Carols by Candlelight" in Australia's great parks. The largest of these events is "Carols in the Domain," held on the last Saturday before Christmas at Sydney's Royal Botanic Gardens.

21. Several countries have given special names to their Christmas Eve Midnight Masses. All of the following pairs of masses and countries are correctly matched, <u>except</u>:

    A. "Mass of the Gift"—Philippines
    B. "Mass of the Bells"—France
    C. "Mass of the Rooster"—Spain and Latin American countries
    D. "Mass of the Shepherds"—Poland

    There is no specific name associated with the Midnight Mass in France.

22. Since 1947, which country has annually sent a Christmas tree to England?

    A. Norway
    B. Germany
    C. Sweden
    D. Denmark

During World War II when German troops occupied Norway, her King Håkon found political asylum in England. Each Christmas during that time, his countrymen smuggled a Christmas tree past the German lines into England for the king. Since 1947, Norway, specifically the city of Oslo, has expressed its gratitude each Christmas by sending England a Christmas tree which decorates London's Trafalgar Square.

23. Nine nights before Christmas is the period of *Las Posadas* ("The Lodgings"), a custom observed in Latin America, predominantly Mexico. Each night a different family opens their home to be the *posada* for an initial ritual, followed by festivities. Each night a *piñata* is broken. What does this custom commemorate?

   A. The Wise Men's journey to Bethlehem
   B. Mary's and Joseph's journey to Bethlehem
   C. The shepherd's journey to Bethlehem
   D. St. Nicholas' journey to Bethlehem

The participants divide themselves into the "Cruel Innkeepers" and the "Holy Pilgrims." The initial ritual consists of the Pilgrims begging the Innkeepers for lodging. After the Innkeepers relent, the Pilgrims proceed to a lowly altar erected on the premises. After prayers, the festivities begin. The final night, of course, is the most lavish, terminating in Midnight Mass at the local cathedral on Christmas Eve. The *piñata* mentioned is a thin, decorated, earthen vase suspended from the ceiling and brimming with small gifts. Blindfolded children with sticks try to smash the *piñata* one at a time, and when it is broken, all the children scramble for the goodies which tumble out. The correct answer is B.

24. Fasting as a form of cleansing the soul before Christmas is popular in some countries, and the fasting period may be prolonged. For the countries listed below, which duration of fasting is <u>incorrect</u>?

    A. Iran—25 days
    B. China—7 days
    C. Greece—40 days
    D. Ukraine—40 days

There is no fasting at all before Christmas in China, for only fifteen percent of its population is Christian. The forty-day fasts of Greece and Ukraine commemorate Christ's temptation of forty days in the wilderness following His baptism. Most countries observing pre-Christmas fasts abstain only from meat and dairy products.

25. Scandinavian countries traditionally declare the "Peace of Christmas" on which of these days?

    A. First day of December
    B. First Sunday of Advent
    C. Christmas Eve
    D. Christmas Day

The official declaration, a tradition dating to medieval times, is made in the city of Turku, Finland, and is broadcast by television live on Christmas Eve. Finland's former capital, Turku is also known as "Christmas City." The ceremonies include the reading of a medieval document which orders that everyone must maintain peace during Christmas; then follows a service in Turku Cathedral.

26. From an Old South custom in the USA, the first person who came knocking at your door on Christmas Day owed you a gift if you were the first to say ___.

    A. "Christmas gift!"
    B. "Merry Christmas!"
    C. "Bah, humbug!"
    D. "Presents, presents, presents!"

Originally a slave custom, the expression was "Christmas gif'!" The same custom applied if two people met on the road. However, once a person had claimed a gift from someone, he could not later claim another, should he meet that same person again.

27. A number of cities or villages in the USA have been given names which are associated with the Christmas season. The most frequently occurring name is:

    A. Bethlehem
    B. Santa Claus
    C. Holly
    D. Christmas

Twenty states have cities or villages named Bethlehem or a variant of Bethlehem: CT, FL, GA, IA, IL, IN, KY, MD, MO, MS, NC, NH, NJ, NY, OH, PA, TN, TX, VA (Bethlehem Fork), and WV.

28. If Bethlehem is the most frequently occurring holiday name given to cities in the USA, which name takes second place?

    A. Christmas
    B. Holly
    C. Mistletoe
    D. Santa Claus

Nine states have cities or villages with names based on "Christmas." Cities simply named Christmas are found in AZ, FL, MI, MS, and TN. Other villages with name variations include Christmas Cove, ME; Christmas Landing, AL; Christmas City, UT; and Christmas Valley, OR.

29. Four states in the USA have cities or villages named St. Nicholas. Which of the following states is <u>not</u> one of them?

    A. Pennsylvania
    B. Florida
    C. Hawaii
    D. Minnesota
    E. Michigan

The correct choice does not lie in the continental USA; that is, C.

30. In countries which embrace the Eastern Orthodox Church, e.g., Bulgaria, Greece, and Romania, the Blessing of the Waters closes the Christmas season on Epiphany. In regions where there is a large body of water, the priest throws an object into the water. Young men dive for the object, and he who retrieves it is the hero. What object does the priest throw into the water?

    A. A holly branch
    B. A wreath
    C. A cross
    D. A gold coin

The priest also usually dips the cross into containers of water to create baptismal water. People take away samples of this water in the belief that it possesses the power to heal. The custom derives from Christ's miracle of turning water into wine at Cana in Galilee (John 2:2–11); it is also based on the traditional date of His baptism, which occurred on Epiphany, January 6.

31. Throughout Scandinavia, rice pudding is a most traditional dish that is served at the Christmas dinner. One special object is added to the pot, and each person hopes that his serving will contain the object, which is:

    A. A gold coin
    B. An almond
    C. A ring
    D. A cross

Whoever receives the almond will have good luck or, if single, will be the next to marry. The lucky person usually also receives a gift.

32. All of the following are Polish Christmas customs, <u>except</u>:

    A. At the Christmas Eve dinner, there must be an even number of courses but an odd number of diners for luck

    B. *Oplatki*, small wafers served with the Christmas Eve meal, symbolize the Sacred Host.

    C. The Star Man (as a representative of the stars) comes to examine children in their catechism and gives them treats.

    D. The Star Boys, dressed as Wise Men and singing carols, accompany the Star Man on his rounds at Christmas. The Star Boys also make visits on Epiphany.

There must be an *odd* number of courses and an *even* number of diners for luck.

33. On Epiphany in Poland and other parts of Europe, groups of Star Boys make visits door to door and mark three crosses over the doors of homes along with the initials "C. M. B." What do these initials represent?

    A. The initials of three church patriarchs
    B. The initials of the Holy Trinity in the local language
    C. The initials of the three Wise Men
    D. The initials of Christ, Mary and Joseph in the local language

    These are the initials of the traditional three Wise Men: Caspar, Melchior, and Balthasar. The homes so marked are destined to have good luck for the coming year.

34. The *ceppo*, a decorated, pyramid-shaped series of shelves with gifts and often a Nativity scene, is found primarily in:

    A. Mongolia
    B. Turkey
    C. Greece
    D. Italy

    The *ceppo* (meaning "log") is a vestige of the Yule log and is an alternative decoration to Italy's principal Christmas symbol, the Nativity scene.

35. Various regions of Europe leave a chair vacant at the Christmas Eve dinner table for which of the following reasons? (more than one correct answer)

    A. For any stranger, one of whom may be the Christ Child in disguise
    B. For St. Nicholas
    C. For deceased family members
    D. For the Holy Family

The reasons are not universal and vary among countries. For example, the vacancy honors deceased family members in Lithuania as well as in Ukraine; the latter country also sets an extra place for any unexpected stranger. In Poland, the vacancy remembers not only the stranger but also Mary and Joseph, who sought shelter on Christmas Eve; therefore, no one is turned away on this night. Choices A, C, and D apply.

36. In Sweden, a *julklapp* ("Christmas knock") is a type of:

    A. Gift
    B. Song
    C. Candle
    D. Wreath

The *julklapp* is a Swedish Christmas gift. The term derives from a past era, when it was customary on Christmas night to knock loudly on doors, then quickly toss in gifts before those inside could identify the giver. Accompanied by satirical rhymes, the gifts may have consisted of multiple wrapped boxes within boxes, the gift being in the last box. Instead, the last box could have contained a note giving directions for finding the gifts elsewhere. Or perhaps, upon opening each box, a different person's name appeared on the box wrapped within, so the package was passed from person to person, until the final box revealed the intended recipient. Such methods provided enjoyable runarounds to receive a gift. It is still customary to attach rhymes with Christmas gifts in Sweden. Holland also enjoys a similar custom on St. Nicholas Eve.

37. Which country observes "Hunting the Wren" on St. Stephen's Day, December 26?

A. Ireland
B. Brazil
C. Mexico
D. Bosnia

Originally widespread through the British Isles and France and dating from the seventeenth century or earlier, the custom dictated that a group of outlandishly clad "Wren Boys" kill a wren, which they then displayed while serenading homes for food, drink, or money. Although precise origins for the custom are unclear, they include legends holding that the wren betrayed Jesus and St. Stephen as they fled persecution, and that the wren betrayed the Irish army to a Viking enemy. A more plausible theory holds that the custom derived from pagan new year festivals, which offered a mock king in sacrifice after a period of revelry. Because other circles have cast the wren as a symbol of the old year, killing wrens may have symbolized the death of the old year. Today, Ireland retains a vestige of the custom, in which the Wren Boys display a wren effigy or a live wren on their rounds. The money raised goes to charities or sponsors a community Wren Dance.

38. The *Polaznik* of Poland is similar to:

A. *Las Posadas* of Mexico
B. First footing of Great Britain
C. *Julklapp* of Sweden
D. *Kallikantzari* of Greece

A male visiting a home on Christmas Eve portends the best of luck. By previous arrangement, the visitor arrives at dawn on Christmas Eve and throws wheat over the family members for luck, which is a vestige of ancient agrarian rites. After feasting with them and receiving a gift, he departs at evening. *Kallikantzari* are mischievous gremlins of Greek folklore. The correct answer is B.

39. In Russia, Ukraine, Hungary, Lithuania, and Poland, what event signals that the time has arrived to serve the Christmas Eve meal?

    A. The ringing of church bells
    B. Sighting the first evening star
    C. Sundown
    D. A bonfire in the village square

Folklore holds that the first star sighted on Christmas Eve is the Star of Bethlehem, the sign that Christmas Eve has officially arrived.

40. In which country does custom dictate that either the youngest daughter or one named Mary must light the Christmas candle on Christmas Eve?

    A. Canada
    B. Brazil
    C. Ireland
    D. Portugal

The correct answer is that country which is an island.

41. Where is Christmas known as the Little Feast?

    A. Turkey
    B. Greece
    C. Iran
    D. Iraq

Christmas is the "Little Feast," and Easter is the "Great Feast" in Iran.

42. On "Old Christmas Eve" (January 5) in Glastonbury, England, the mayor and vicar cut sprigs from descendants of the Glastonbury Thorn to give to whom?

    A. The British Prime Minister
    B. The Lord Mayor of London
    C. The Archbishop of Canterbury
    D. The reigning English monarch

    This custom dates to the Middle Ages. Chapter two also discussed the associations of Joseph of Arimathea and "Christmas Old Style" ("Old Christmas Eve") with the Glastonbury Thorn. The correct answer is D.

43. Norway's *Julebukk* ("Christmas Goat"), Colombia's *Aguinaldos* ("Gifts"), and Bavaria's *Klopfelnachten* ("Knocking Nights") are Christmas customs that resemble which American holiday?

    A. Valentine's Day
    B. Independence Day
    C. Halloween
    D. Labor Day

    Norway observes *Julebukk* on Christmas Day. Children dress in outlandish costumes and, while leading a billy goat, travel from door to door singing carols and soliciting treats. The custom derives from the revels of pagan Yule festivals and from the two goats of Norse folklore, Gnasher and Cracker, who pulled the god Thor's chariot at the winter solstice. Colombia observes *Aguinaldos* on Christmas Eve. Everyone dresses in masquerade costume with the object of trying to recognize friends, and successfully discerning persons then claim an *aguinaldo* ("gift") from the ones recognized. Bavaria observes *Klopfelnachten* on the three Thursdays before

Christmas. Masked children travel through neighborhoods making much noise, which derives from the pagan belief that loud noise would dispel evil spirits. After knocking on doors, they recite rhymes beginning with "knock," then they receive treats. The Christmastime equivalent in the USA is the New Year's Day Mummer's Parade, annually held in Philadelphia since 1901. The correct answer is C.

44. What do Scandinavians traditionally raise on a pole outside their homes at Christmastime?

    A. A sheaf of grain for the birds
    B. A likeness of the *Julenisse* (Christmas gnome or elf)
    C. Three golden balls
    D. A fir bough

Before Scandinavians can enjoy Christmas, they customarily place wheat on a pole outside for the birds. It is called the "Birds' Christmas Tree."

45. Although Greek children now receive gifts at Christmastime, they formerly received gifts only on St. Basil's Day, which is observed on:

    A. December 1
    B. December 6
    C. January 1
    D. January 6

This day observes the death of *Agios Vassilis* (St. Basil, 329–379), one of the Patriarchs of the Greek Orthodox Church. The correct answer is C.

46. Only three states in the USA have cities or villages that are named Santa Claus or a variation of that name. Which state is <u>not</u> one of them?

    A. Idaho
    B. Indiana
    C. Tennessee
    D. Georgia

    Indiana and Georgia both have cities named Santa Claus. The Idaho city is simply named Santa. Thus the correct answer is C.

47. In Eastern Europe, how is the Christmas table usually prepared?

    A. It is covered with fir boughs.
    B. It is covered with hay or straw in memory of the manger.
    C. The tablecloth is anointed with wine.
    D. The napkins are made to resemble swaddling clothes.

    This is a common custom in countries such as Russia, Ukraine, Czech Republic, Slovak Republic, and Croatia. Rather than spread straw on the table itself, a variation of the custom places the straw beneath the table. The correct answer is B.

48. In regions which embrace Roman Catholicism, when should a figure of the Christ Child be added to the manger of each Nativity scene?

    A. On the first Sunday of Advent
    B. On the last Sunday of Advent
    C. On Christmas Eve
    D. On Christmas Day

This custom is especially prevalent in Latin American countries. Throughout Advent, the manger remains empty until Christmas Eve Midnight Mass, when it receives the Christ Child. Figures of the traditional three Wise Men are included during Advent but are placed some distance away to symbolize their long journey to the stable. They are moved closer to the stable each day and formally "arrive" on Epiphany.

49. Many Eastern European countries feature a meatless, twelve-course meal for the entire family on Christmas Eve. Whom or what do these courses honor?

   A. The twelve Apostles
   B. The twelve days of Christmas
   C. The twelve months of the year
   D. The twelve tribes of Israel

The courses honor those whom Jesus chose as His twelve.

50. The Christmas tree in Germany is traditionally decorated on Christmas Eve behind closed doors, and children are not allowed to view the tree until the decorating is complete. What event signals that the children may enter?

   A. The parents strike up a chorus of "O Tannenbaum."
   B. A little bell rings.
   C. A trumpet sounds.
   D. The parents call out the traditional phrase, "Kommst du, süsser kinder!" ("Come thou, sweet children!")

In Roman Catholic circles, the bell also indicates that the *Christkindl* (Christ Child's messenger) has brought the children's gifts and has departed. The correct answer is B.

51. The Church of the Nativity is a shrine in Bethlehem, Israel, that is traditionally held to be the site of Christ's birth. In the Grotto of the Nativity down below, what object marks the alleged site of the Nativity?

    A. A silver star
    B. An ornately carved stone manger
    C. A torch burning as the eternal flame
    D. A menorah

Originally installed in 1717, the star is inlaid in the marble floor and contains fourteen points.

52. Referring to the previous question, a Latin inscription accompanies the silver star in the Grotto of the Nativity that, when translated, reads:

    A. "Here of the Virgin Mary Jesus Christ was born."
    B. "Behold, here the Son of God became manifest in the flesh."
    C. "Here was begotten the King of kings and Lord of lords."
    D. "By this emblem know ye that Jesus Christ here was born."

The actual inscription reads, "Hic de Virgine Maria Jesus Christus natus est." Thus the correct answer is A.

53. The Roman Catholic Church celebrates three masses on Christmas Day, which are held at midnight, dawn, and later in the day. Each mass has a specific name. For the choices below, first eliminate the name which does not belong, then state when each of the three legitimate masses are held.

A. Shepherds' Mass _____
B. Mass of the Divine Word _____
C. Angels' Mass _____
D. Mass of the Incarnate _____

Held at dawn, A is also known as the Dawn Mass. B is held later in the day and is also known as the Christmas Day Mass. C is held at midnight and is also known as the Midnight Mass. According to Roman Catholic doctrine, these three masses symbolize the "triple birth" of Christ in time, eternity, and the soul. D does not belong.

54. Although children in Italy, Spain, and Latin America may receive gifts on Christmas Day, the traditional gift-giving day is:

A. St. Nicholas' Day, December 6
B. St. Lucia Day, December 13
C. New Year's Day, January 1
D. Epiphany, January 6

The custom derives from the Magi or Wise Men, who, according to tradition, arrived at the manger with gifts for the Christ Child on January 6. Thus, Epiphany is also known as "Three Kings Day" or "Day of the Kings."

55. In Germany, Austria, and Scandinavia, what phrase applies to brass ensembles that play chorales from church towers or other conspicuous places on Christmas Eve?

A. "Blowing in the Yule"
B. "Bringing Home the Christmas"
C. "Chorales by Candlelight"
D. "Horns of Yule"

The custom derives from ancient Yule festivals, when it was believed that much noise and clamor dispelled the powers of darkness. The correct answer is A.

56. In countries such as France, Spain, Belgium, Luxembourg, Netherlands, and Latin America, the most common gift receptacles that children set out in which to receive holiday gifts are:

    A. Their shoes
    B. Their stockings
    C. Baskets
    D. Boxes

On the eve of the traditional gift-giving day, children usually fill their shoes with carrots and straw for the beasts that carry the traditional gift givers; hence, for *Père Noël's* donkey (France), for St. Nicholas' horse (Belgium, Luxembourg, Netherlands), and for the Wise Men's camels (Spain and Latin America). The gift givers supposedly then replace the fodder with treats and gifts. By tradition, naughty children receive either a lump of coal or nothing at all. In Spain, parents may mark the cheeks of their sleeping children with coal on Epiphany Eve as a sign that Balthazar, the black Wise Man, kissed them during the night.

57. Because of former Communist influences, countries once comprising the Union of Soviet Socialist Republics (USSR) still tend to observe which day for gift giving and erecting a Christmas tree?

    A. St. Andrew's Day
    B. St. Nicholas' Day
    C. New Year's Day
    D. Epiphany

Until the collapse of the Soviet Union in the early 1990s, the Communist regime had banned Christmas celebrations in favor of a secular Winter Festival, with New Year's Day as a national holiday for feasting, fireworks, fantasy, and parades. As former Soviet countries such as Russia, Ukraine, and others, strive to regain their religious customs regarding Christmas, many of which were completely lost to Communist rule, New Year's Day continues to be the principal day for gift giving and festivities.

58. Which of these unusual Christmas tree ornaments are especially popular in Ukraine?

   A. Frogs
   B. Crickets
   C. Spiders
   D. Goldfish

Webs of straw often accompany the spider figures. These ornaments derive from legends which hold that a spider once decorated a poor widow's Christmas tree with its web, and that, while lying in the manger, the Christ Child first played with a spider's web.

Questions 59–88 associate peculiar or unique Christmas terms, customs, or cuisine with the countries or regions in which they are found. Match each of the numbered items with the appropriate, lettered countries from the list below. Countries may be selected more than once. Answers follow this group.

A. Costa Rica	H. Japan	O. Puerto Rico
B. Croatia	I. Lithuania	P. Romania
C. England	J. Mexico	Q. Russia

D. France   K. Moravian Church   R. Spain
E. Germany   L. Netherlands   S. Switzerland
F. Greece   M. Philippines   T. Ukraine
G. Italy   N. Poland   U. Venezuela

59. *Sorcova* ("Forty")—a New Year emblem consisting of a fruit-tree branch decorated with colored paper and flowers. Children tap their elders forty times with these emblems as a means of conveying wishes for a long and prosperous life. The custom derives from ancient fertility rites.

60. Parishioners roller skate to Christmas masses, most especially in the city of Caracas.

61. Crackers—party favors that accompany the Christmas dinner, invented in 1840. When opened, they produce a loud pop (hence the name) and contain trinkets, paper hats, jokes, and riddles.

62. *Le Réveillon* ("The Awakening")—the traditional Christmas meal that follows Midnight Mass.

63. At sundown on Christmas Eve, cannonfire from the Castle of St. Angelo announces the arrival of Christmas.

64. *Parols*—lighted, five-pointed star lanterns which symbolize the Star of Bethlehem. Ornate and often of considerable size, they are the principal Christmas decorations in this country.

65. *Wigilia* ("Vigil")—term for Christmas Eve and the Christmas Eve supper. The Slovak Republic has a virtually identical term, *Vigilia*.

66. *Créche*—term for a Nativity scene in this country.

67. *Nacimiento*—term for a Nativity scene in this country.

68. *Krippe*—term for a Nativity scene in this country.

69. *Portal*—term for a Nativity scene in this country.

70. The Christmas Eve lovefeast, first introduced by this group in 1727, is patterned after the agape fellowships of the early Apostolic Church. It consists of a song service in which each member of the congregation holds a lighted Christmas candle. The congregation also partakes of a simple meal of buns and coffee. Christmas candlelight services of other denominations are patterned after the lovefeast.

71. *Presepio*—term for a Nativity scene in this country.

72. *Betlehem*—term for a Nativity scene in this country.

73. After children write letters to Father Christmas, they toss them into the fire. Those that burn quickly are "accepted"; those that are not must be rewritten.

74. *Putz* ("Decorate")—an especially elaborate Nativity scene, which may consist of landscapes, waterfalls, trees, and villages, in addition to traditional Nativity figures. The "Pennsylvania Dutch" of the USA also use this term.

75. Distinctive Christmas tree ornaments in this country consist of straw mobiles.

76. *D'yed Moroz* ("Grandfather Frost")—once the replacement for St. Nicholas across the former Soviet empire, he remains as the gift giver in this country on New Year's Day.

77. *Snegurochka* ("Snow Maiden")—Grandfather Frost's granddaughter, who assists him along with New Year's Boy. The latter depicts the freshness of the new year and wears the numerals of that year.

78. *Didukh* ("Grandfather spirit")—a combined Christian/agrarian symbol found at the Christmas Eve supper. It is a sheaf of wheat in which are believed to reside the spirits of all family members, living and dead. It symbolizes eternal life through Christ, the fertility of the land, and bread as the staff of life.

79. *Asaltos* ("Assaults")—groups of carolers who make surprise visits at homes that are holding *parrandas* ("sprees"), which are all-night Christmas parties. Each of these groups carries a figure of the Christ Child.

80. To ensure health and good fortune in the coming year, a popular custom is to consume twelve grapes just before midnight on New Year's Eve.

81. *Capitone* (eel)—a traditional delicacy for Christmas dinner in this country.

82. *Belenes*—term for a Nativity scene in this country.

83. *Bûche de Noël* ("Christmas log")—a traditional Christmas cake shaped like a log, which serves as the remaining vestige of the Yule log in this country.

84. *Tirggel*—traditional and popular cookies bearing religious scenes and figures. They derive from pagan Germanic sacrificial cakes and formerly bore the shapes of animals.

85. Children in this country customarily exchange origami "birds of peace."

86. Plum pudding—also known as Christmas pudding and figgy pudding. Although the name implies the use of plums, the principal ingredients are dried fruits (raisins) and spices, but not plums as such. The name derives from the archaic use of "plum," which once applied to any form of dried fruit. Hidden within is a coin, which bestows luck on the finder.

87. *Christopsomo* ("Christ Bread")—A sweet loaf with nuts and dried fruit that forms the centerpiece for the table and is an indispensable item at the Christmas Eve meal. The surface is carved with images of the family's trade, and hidden within is a coin, which bestows luck on the finder. The first slice is always reserved for a beggar.

88. *Letterbanket*—traditional cakes made into the shapes of letters.

Answers to 59–88: 59-P; 60-U; 61-C; 62-D; 63-G (Rome); 64-M; 65-N; 66-D; 67-J or R; 68-E; 69-A; 70-K; 71-G; 72-B; 73-C; 74-K; 75-I; 76-Q; 77-Q; 78-T; 79-O; 80-R; 81-G; 82-O; 83-D; 84-S; 85-H; 86-C; 87-F; 88-L.

Questions 89–100 present foreign phrases for "Merry Christmas" in several principal languages of the world. Match each numbered phrase with the appropriate, lettered language from the list below. Answers follow this group.

A. Danish	E. Italian	I. Portuguese
B. Dutch	F. Japanese	J. Russian
C. French	G. Hawaiian	K. Spanish
D. German	H. Polish	L. Swedish

89. "Wesolych Swiat"

90. "Buon Natale"

91. "Meri Kurisumasu"

92. "Glædelig Jul"

93. "God Jul"

94. "Boas Festas"

95. "Mele Kalikimaka"

96. "Fröhliche Weihnachten"

97. "S Rozhdestvom Khristovym"

98. "Zalig Kerstfeest"

99. "Feliz Navidad"

100. "Joyeux Noël"

Answers to 89–100: 89-H; 90-E; 91-F; 92-A; 93-L; 94-I; 95-G; 96-D; 97-J; 98-B; 99-K; 100-C.

Questions 101–109 pertain to a number of Christmas "firsts" in the USA. For each statement, provide the appropriate name(s). Answers and comments follow this group.

101. In 1836, this was the first state to make Christmas a legal holiday.

102. First issued in 1962 at four cents, it depicted a wreath and two candles.

103. Emily Bissell, Delaware state secretary of the Red Cross, designed the first of these American stamps in 1907 to raise funds in the fight against tuberculosis.

104. He was the first president to celebrate Christmas in the White House after its completion in 1800.

105. In 1856, he was the first president to erect a Christmas tree in the White House.

106. In 1895, he was the first president to use electric lights on a White House tree.

107. Although President (A) _____ established the lighting of the National Christmas Tree in 1913, the first president actually to light that tree was (B) _____ in 1923.

108. In 1954, this president instituted the Pageant of Peace in connection with the lighting of the National Christmas Tree. The Pageant advocates worldwide peace through Christmas.

109. In 1926, this president designated the "General Grant," a 267-foot giant Sequoia in Kings Canyon National Park, California, as "The Nation's Christmas Tree." During Christmas ceremonies, a large wreath is placed at its base.

Answers to 101–109: 101-Alabama; 102-Christmas stamps; 103-Christmas Seals; 104-John Adams; 105-Franklin Pierce; 106-Grover Cleveland; 107-(A) Woodrow Wilson, (B) Calvin Coolidge; 108-Dwight Eisenhower; 109-Calvin Coolidge

Comments: Canada issued the world's first Christmas stamp in 1898 to commemorate the inauguration of its penny postal system. The inscription was "Xmas 1898." Christmas Seals originated in

Denmark in 1903 by Einar Holbøll, a postal worker, who championed the fight against tuberculosis. At first the American seals bore the Red Cross emblem but changed to the double-barred cross in 1920.

References

Bowler, Gerry. *The World Encyclopedia of Christmas.* Toronto: McClellan and Stewart, 2000.

The Christmas Mood: Original Recording of the Alfred Burt Carols. Program Notes. Columbia Records, 1954. Digital Remastering, TRO Hollis Music, Compact Disc Sound Recording, 1995.

Collins, Ace. *Stories Behind the Best-Loved Songs of Christmas.* Grand Rapids: Zondervan, 2001.

Crump, William D. *The Christmas Encyclopedia.* Jefferson, North Carolina: McFarland, 2001.

Green, Jay P., Sr., ed. *Interlinear Greek-English New Testament*, Third Edition. Grand Rapids: Baker Books, 1996.

Gulevich, Tanya. *Encyclopedia of Christmas.* Detroit: Omnigraphics, 1999.

Menendez, Albert J., and Shirley C. Menendez. *Christmas Songs Made in America: Favorite Holiday Melodies and the Stories of Their Origins.* Nashville: Cumberland House, 1999.

Rosen, Jody. "I'm Dreaming of a White Christmas: How an Obscure Tune from a So-So Film Became the Greatest Hit of All Time." *Reader's Digest* (December 2002).

Strong, James. *The Exhaustive Concordance of the Bible.* New York: Eaton & Mains, 1890.

To order additional copies of

WAS THE FIRST GIFT
REALLY GOLD?

Have your credit card ready and call:

1-877-421-READ (7323)

or please visit our web site at
www.pleasantword.com

Also available at: www.amazon.com

Printed in the United States
1462200005B/36

9 781579 216689